WHAT IS INSIDE MAY

Spiderwize

Anthony.W.White

SRPHD WE ARE ALL ONE ELECTROMAGNETIC SELF AWARE CONSCIOUSNESS! ---------------------

"ONE CONSCIOUSNESS"

One Consciousness : Simulation of Consciousness Instruction Manual

Spiderwize
Remus House
Coltsfoot Drive
Woodston
Peterborough
PE2 9BF

www.spiderwize.com

A CIP catalogue record for this book is available from the British Library.

WE ARE ALL ONE!
ELECTROMAGNETIC FORCE

ONE CONSCIOUSNESS

·THE TRUE MESSAGE OF THE MANDELA EFFECT REALITY·

TONY.W.WHITE

SRPHD CHANNEL
YouTube

WAKE UP!!!

LIFE IS A SIMULATION GAME!

AND YOUR SPIRIT IS THE PLAYER

ONE CONSCIOUSNESS

LIFE IS A GAME! YOU ONLY UNDERSTAND THIS WHEN YOU REALIZE EVERYTHING IS A SIMULATION.

Spiritual Way Seer Tony White

ONE CONSCIOUSNESS
(Instruction Manual)

YOU ONLY BECOME A PLAYER WHEN
YOU KNOW YOU'RE PLAYING THE GAME!

YOU ONLY SEE REALITY ONCE ALL PROGRAMS HAVE BEEN
BEEN REMOVED , YOU ONLY REMOVE PROGRAMS WHEN YOU
REMOVE REALITY.

NOTHING CAN BE ACHIEVED BEFORE YOU HAVE
LOST EVERYTHING , LETTING GO OF THE MIND
OPENS THE TRUTH AS SPIRIT!

WELCOME TO THE TRUTH OF REALITY!!

A.W.WHITE

ISBN: -13: 978-0-6481962-1-1

SRPHD Channel on You-Tube

GAME ON PRODUCTIONS

Games on productions / Australia

Razersedge Graphics & Designs.

Gameonproductionsinfo@iinet.net.au

ABN: 36889580257

Instruction Manual For Realities Lost Knowing's

Published in United Kingdom / Spiderwize Publishing House

120gsm bond color pages direct from SPIDERWIZE store.

105gsm bond color from all other retailers.

(Paperback For on the go Edition)

Special Thanks- to the investors without you the release of this insightful information would not be possible, may the One watch over you always my good friends.

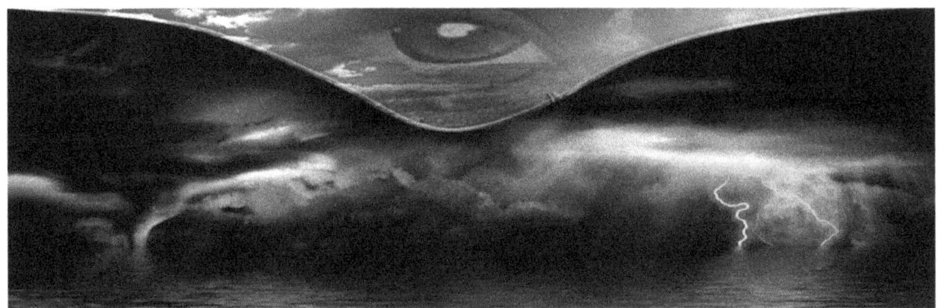

TESTIMONIALS

Below is the testimonial of some Mandela Effected People that were guided to my YouTube channel SRPHD by the One consciousness to allow them to find what they sought in my teachings from the one Consciousness.

Former H.S Catholic Guidance Counsellor

Kelly Scherer (Pittsburgh.US): ***While struggling to envision the color red to clear my aura, I asked God for help. Immediately, a calm came over me and I began to cry I felt pure love and happiness. A beautiful bright lavender light appeared. The peace and connectedness was indescribable. The meditation further confirmed my awareness of the synchronicity in finding your YouTube channel and teachings through my prayers to the One in expanding my self-awareness and growth, especially through the blessings of awakening.***

Administrative Officer

Debbie Conley (Queensland. AUS) ***Divine Synchronicity led me to Tony and his amazing YouTube channel of awareness. As I was inwardly seeking answers in this game called life, his channel appeared on my feed as if a gift from Divine Source itself. I cannot express enough how his amazing insights have helped me on my own journey. He has helped me deal with the severe roller coaster of life I have been struggling with for the last few years. I am now more balanced due to his guidance and able to see things in a totally new way. I have learnt so much as well as reaffirmed what we (All) already know...yet somehow had forgotten. Tony teaches the One thing we all need to remember, to raise your vibration Love is the only Answer as we are All connected and Are One. Tony shows us how to bring out the Amazing in us that we have been taught to keep hidden***

Homemaker/Nanny

Robin Neely (Michigan.US): ***Very good and helpful `information, advice and tips and amazing insight. You explain things very well. I'm always loving watching your videos and listening to your knowledge and wisdom as well as feeling your incredible energy. This is exactly what we need as the world to understand to wake up again. Thank you for what you do and always continue to walk in the light my brother, your sister in consciousness of the one light, Robin <3***

Former USAF Aerospace Instructor

Michael Nickell (California.US): ***I owe my deepest gratitude to the man for opening my eyes. Although, I am still learning daily this connection I was able to align vibrations. His frequency was able to read me and call out my imbalances in my Chakras. I was amazed that through the internet medium, without ever speaking to me, gave a read of once in a past variation of my journey did I drown? I was amazed. The fact is I will not go on water either by boat or flight as the subconscious fear prevents me in a very real phobia. The jump off point which was due to Tony has opened my path to the left and to the right, but is always straight down the middle. I look forward to more insight from this man for he is one who has seen beyond what most any might ever see. His words ring true calling upon you beyond the firmament. Thanks brother, we are forever connected in higher vibrational energies of light. Maybe one day we will finally meet, and you can buy the first found of beers!***

Roofing Contractor

Robert Thompson (Illinois.US): ***I was researching Mandela Effect one day and run across Tony's YouTube channel SRPHD, and decided to watch his video, that was two years ago. I have been a subscriber to his YouTube channel ever since, I'M GLAD I DID, BECAUSE HE IS SPOT ON IN HIS TEACHINGS!!, Looking forward to another two years of Tony's Amazing Insight Thanks Brother!***

Freelancer

Rick Guerrero (Connecticut.US): ***I would like to express my thanks to Tony. He has great insight and has helped me on my path to the Lord. I've experienced a lot of De Ja Vu and Tony cleared that up. I've been able to resonate with vibes; energy frequencies and Tony has helped me get in tune with those energies. It's great to understand his stage of life, and always look forward to being with the Lord again. Tony has great insight and knowledge to tap into things we are not aware of. I'm glad to have been able to expand my knowledge to this as well.***

Former Heathrow Airport Security

Debbie Dyer (England.UK): *Tony has been a godsend for myself and many others I know of, whom have scoured the Internet looking for similar souls that are having an experience in their lives because their life has become so surreal, that it's hard to communicate and explain it to family and friends for worry of ridicule. Having had paranormal experiences myself since 2010 and an unbelievable sudden awareness of this matrix reality, I was personally 6 years on YouTube looking to see or hear from other affected people like myself and sought out some amazing people and their own personal thoughts on what was going on, only something happened to me when I heard the genuine sound of tony voice and his own personal experiences and beliefs, that the stress of the situation I'd become in, was completely lifted because of the sense his words made to me. All I can say is, that it has been an absolute pleasure getting to know him and seeing how he will even comment back on his channel to each and every comment that is made to him on his videos, even to the hardest negative most disrespectful ones, always with a positive and encouraging reply which is pretty unheard of on YouTube! He certainly is a way seer and tries to help with patience and understanding to anyone who is confused and lost in this matrix reality. In fact, I believe that the world is a better place with his shared insights and his care that he has enough to share them. So thankyou Tony, for all that you do, as it takes a very selfless person to take the time, the passion and the enthusiasm to help mankind like you do*

Photographer / Artist

Leah Templeman (Kent.Uk) *Tony's completely down to earth, no holds barred, passionate approach to his expression of life, is refreshingly honest and real! I stumbled across his presence on YouTube some time ago, while looking for some answers and some back up to some personal and spiritual questions and realisations I had made. It was easy to see straight off that this man was awake! Listening to his teachings, I found some of the pieces of my own puzzle, that helped me progress and grow. My life is now flowing like a river like one Tony's freestyle hip-hop rhymes <3*
Life has many great teachers, Tony has been one of mine!

RN Usui Reiki Master

Kimberly Ketelaar (Georgia US): *I Understanding the Nature of Reality is a journey taken by those who know deep within every fibre of their being, know that we are MORE than what we have been told we are. Reality is MORE than what we have been led to believe. I have been on this journey for a good part of my life. Finding Tony White on YouTube was a very important piece of the journey for me. Tony accurately describes Reality in such a way that resonates with my inner knowing. His explanations are scientific and metaphysical at the same time, along with being engaging and experiential. I highly recommend this work to any that are on this Journey of Re-discovery of Who We Really Are and what Reality may really truly be. Tony White's experience and documentation of it, may be the way we Re-member Who We Are. Enjoy fellow sojourners!*

Entrepreneur

Dipak Patel (Indiana US): ***Dear Brothers and Sisters;***
I am Dipak Patel an entrepreneur and truth seeker from Indiana. I have been watching Tony's videos for just a few months and he has really connected a lot of dots for me, answers that I've been seeking forever. We have been in an endless loop it seems but some of us are digging our way out to remembering who we really are! What a relief to finally find some satisfactory answers - we are light beings but have forgotten. I guess when you're ready the teacher will come and Tony is the teacher I've been seeking. I am from India and I've gone down many paths seeking the answers but after a while I noticed the cracks. What Tony says about the Matrix makes so much sense and he's not the only one saying we are just avatars wanting to play games so we actually helped make this Matrix so hard we lost our way into thinking this 5 senses game was all there was to life but you'll see why it's not while reading this book. It will change you, your soul will recognize and resonate with the truth, you won't stop thinking about what Tony is saying and won't be able to put the book down. Once you awaken though we need to help others do the same and remember the powerful light beings we are. I have had a chance to hear some parts of the book and it is amazing how Tony puts everything in the proper order for us to understand what he has already experienced and how to get there ourselves! I had to rewind and listen to parts several times before "I got it", some of it is still over my head and perhaps you'll have trouble grasping everything but there's so much information that I resonate with now and I know I'll understand more later that I feel like this will become a reference book for me and many others! It is a MUST READ! These are the answers you're looking for - Tony knows it and so do I NOW! There are explanations of The Mandela Effect and what Time really is that will blow your mind. I could just keep going but I'll stop for now!
Sincerely Dipak

Antarctic Warrior Channel / Construction, Home improvements

David R Ralph & Mr. Shadow (Ireland UK): ***I would like take this opportunity, to thank Tony for his friendship and spiritual guidance. Over the many years on my path for truth and well-being, the past three have been the hardest but along with Tony's friendship and support he has given me the strength to push forth and keep my YouTube channel alive.***
After studying secret societies and its orders for the past 11 years, I came across the Flat Earth theory and Mandela Effect. It was clear to me, I had found the missing links in my research the two missing pieces that completed the decade old puzzle. With our shared support for one and other our channels have flourished and helped to wake others to the lies and deceit of this world.
Not to neither judge nor hate, but to share love and self-awareness with all Brothers and Sisters. Thank you Tony, you have been a true gentleman and a dear friend. Peace love and respect my brother in Yahweh (((((Godspeed)))))

Recreational Vehicle Mechanic

David Forslund (Marysville US) ***Hi I'm Dave. I am a RV mechanic at Roy Robinson in Marysville WA. For over a year almost I have learned so much more out this true reality from SRPHD, aka MC Hijack, MR. Anthony White. I know we Might be half a world apart. I'm from and live just north of the Greater Seattle WA. I recently found my way back home, but the truth is I truly wouldn't want to be anywhere else. Living in this game is just a phase. Just a spark of energy. If we are playing the game. Then what can stop us from reaching our true potential. How do you want to build/construct the body/collective body? TONY, YOU HAVE HELPED ME UNDERSTAND APART OF THE BIGGER PICTURE. I don't know if I would have ever pushed myself this far. This fast. To understand more about everything that makes us who we truly are.***
DMT always. ELEVATION OF YOUR SELF TO A HIGHER CALIBRATION, no need for discrimination, One Love Across all Nations. So, stop hesitating, get out there and be the best that you can be, believe in yourself your fellow neighbours and you just might see. God's glory reaches down to touch you. Become somebody who is humble and true. Through and through. Be who you were Called to be. To never let The They and The Them rip you apart. Or defile your true love. The one in your heart. The one that Spoke you into existence. Above all, live in Love for all things. To plant seeds of hope in every being. In every beginning. Faith is equal to your true vibration. Trusting that you will do the right thing is equals to your Frequency. The Consciousness Fabrication of mind body and soul. From your crown Chakra, down to the floor. Step fourth in to Greatness and write your own Destination. Go on and resonate this.
What is your design? What is your purpose? Are these just meaningless words? Before I ever wrote this.^.^.^.
When I went through the shift of the Mandela effect. I was surprised looking for answers. I found more than that when I found the documentaries of Tony's YouTube channel. I found we are all Children of God.
Thank you, Tony for Speaking the Truth. Thank you for your Insight into the fabrication of all things.

Dr Nadia Rosario, Medical Resident in Psychiatry

Dr. Nadia Rosario (Berlin GER) ***Hi my name is Dr Rosario, I found Tony's channel after I created a blog to share my experiences with meditation, awakening and the spirit molecule (DMT). What Tony says I agree with as great insight. As a medical doctor, I have enough knowledge of the human anatomy to give confirmation that some changes on human body have indeed occurred and I really believe that the Mandela Effect is real.***

Tony talked to me about what a Way seer is, that he and his lady are, and probably me too. When I read about Way seers, it touched me very deep. Much of what we are told to be the truth is nonsense, misinformation or deception, and what we are told can't exist, in many cases does. Tony's teachings help understand what we have been lied to about and show a new perspective to reality that is hard to deny. Thank you, Tony, for the teaching videos on your channel and for helping us all understand more of what the Mandela effect really is.

Professional Spiritual Medium / Astro TV www.astrotv.nl

Tanja Van Loo (Holland.NL)*): As I came in Tony's channel, I was so relieved at first, because what he teaches felt as homecoming. I always "knew" that live is a dream, but as I talked about it, people laughed at me and say I'm just one who doesn't want reality to see as it is. I never had the right words for it, only that I could say that when we are in a dream, you don't know it before you wake up. Also, I always had a feeling that god want to know how it feels like to be Tony or Tanja or anyone else on this planet and far beyond. I had this deep-down feeling but it didn't make any sense and I couldn't explain it in the right words. I found Tony's channel as I experienced the Mandela effect. His words and his lessons resonated totally on everything what I "knew" but didn't dare too much to rely on out of fear as it is not accepted by others. Tony is a great teacher who is awake and sees the truth as it is. With his brilliant mind and explanations, it all came clear. Amazing how he speaks with spirit/Yahweh. Thank you, Tony, for being you! Love and light of the one, playing the role of Tanja van Loo <3* www.astrotv.nl

Mechanic / Scarab Performance Channel

Daniel Garcia (US)*: Tony's possibly one of the most controversial You Tubers of his generation. Tony's straight forward approach is enlightening, honest, and a threat to the mainstream religious dogma. Let it be known that during this time of the great spiritual awakening many where crying out in the wilderness after experiencing the Mandela effect first hand, and whether you agree or not Tony's voice was in your face with such conviction, you could tell it could have only come from the heart. Very few people have the courage to speak their truth the way he does and for that he gets my deepest respect and admiration*

Mechanical Fitter

Mervin Talma (AUS)*: I have known Tony all my life , from the old school days and he never could do anything like he can now after the Mandela Effect , I was sceptical about all he teaches coming from a religious upbringing , One night I visited him he did energy work on me , I could feel him inside my body moving the energy up as he was saying he was until we reached my crown , I felt the divine love of God to what brought me into tears As a strong man it was remarkable the energy that I felt and the connection to the One . I understood instantly how wrong Indoctrinated religion is and how we have been purposely misled to be able to find the truth. After this experience I was lucky enough to listen to seven hours of his teachings of this book playing in audio, And wow! We all should know this information. It will allow you to become to a peace with everything that society and the physical reality try oh so well to hide. Thank you, Brother, Your brother in life to the next game experience! SBK*

Thank You to everyone that has supported me and my You-Tube Teaching Channel.

It has been my honour to help those above and the many more that have been enlightened by the insight I was given by the One. Anthony.W.White.© Love and Light and respect.

INSTRUCTION MANUAL INDEX AND CONTENT

This book contains my own personal Insight and teachings brought from divine knowing. It explains the quantum reality of consciousness, the afterlife, creational design, the true message behind the Mandela Effect. Why, who, and how it was created and what happened with our consciousness and explains the truth of all existence.

These teachings have been brought by myself and the misses to help those lost that know they are light beings trying to find their way home find their way. Being way seers it is the duty of us to help show and direct humanity towards true understanding when consciousness says it must be done ,we follow the energy fluctuation inside the matrix to watch and see what is needed at each time , we are universal. One way seer will more than often be the same knowing provider in each of their own past lives. Being a way seer is the duty to help humanity understand by providing insight that reveals other realities to events or circumstances that unfold. We are the revolutionaries, the monks, the keepers of knowledge, we are good and bad by stereotype, but only do as directed as the source requests to reveal its message and for humanity to advance towards consciousness's desire of bringing us all back to reach the highest state of consciousness frequency.

INTRODUCTION

So what exactly is the *Mandela effect?* ***The*** *Mandela effect* ***was deemed by Fiona Broome way back in 2010. She talked about the memories of a certain group of people*** *alternated from the others* ***because they both experienced alternating timelines.*** *One Group remembered that* ***Nelson Mandela*** *went into jail and died in jail. Others remember that Nelson Mandela went on to become* ***president of South Africa****.*

Either way evidence was presented to both ***timelines*** *to have existed and she reasoned it as* ***parallel dimensions****.*

I myself have never bothered researching into her as much as what I was told to me come from being ***connected through consciousness*** *myself and after* ***natural DMT*** *release all was revealed to me of all creation.*

So why Is the ***Mandela effect*** *so relevant now in* ***2017?***

In ***2016*** *many people started to show up on* ***YouTube*** *and many other places saying that their realities have changed, from* ***everyday known logos, car manufacturers, media entertainment, landscape geological locations and more.***

*I **myself** was one of these shifted individuals from the **Sagittarius Arm** of the **milky-way** galaxy, and I will later in this book go through some **blatant changes** to me and **my first experience** of the **Mandela effect** for me.*

INTRODUCING MYSELF

*So, who am I? **Tony White**! Born in Wickham, Western Australia, on the **30th of Nov** at **3.11am, Sagittarius** star sign. I was raised in the outback of Australia, **Pannawonica** to be precise. This was a very out of the way town, spinifex, red dirt and bushland surrounded the entire few streets that we called a town, mining town to be correct. I moved to the city when young and have had many experiences since born right up to this day that have explained that **everything of this reality** is not what we seem to believe in our conscious belief. **Through Divine Learning** and entering into the **Christ** with **God as a Spiritual Seer** I myself have personal experiences that **cannot be explained** by rational science and physics, and take my understanding of reality into brand new perspectives to be investigated.*

*My experience **from my own lifetime** I have always known myself that things had some **form** of communication strategy without a **verbal vibration** being created to understand.*

*I would say sentences **before someone** would and they would react with " **hey stay out of my head I was just about to say that** " saying the same thing at the same time, as if I shared the ability with many that only **real born twins** shared as communication.*

***Ever since I can remember** I was born with a **strange** anomaly in my eyes. It is **not a defect** of the eye but rather an image that appears sometimes when I am in **deep concentration** throughout my life or when I felt unsettled it would appear. It is a **snake** with no head or no tail just the hump like as if you were looking at the **Loch Ness monster's hump**, it is **transparent** mixed **opaque** but the outside layers **glow in a green** light that does **not exist in reality.** Inside of it moves like snake scales creating **geometric** patterns that are **hexagon black and yellow** outlined, this **rolls continuing** for as long as it manifests. If I close my eyes it remains. **Switching eyes, by closing one eye after the other** I can **still view** it through either eye. This **was a sign** for me to know that my **subconscious** was **connected** to the **superconscious** with my **conscious mind** being oblivious to it.*

*I was told when I was younger that it was **psychic energy** leaking quite a few times by **different psychics,** but I was too **naive** to **believe** such **mysticism** existed.*

*After **many years** it was **finally revealed** to me that what it was* *is that **my consciousness was open** and using it's natural **DMT** release, right from being born to this **present day**.*

*Closest rendering using Photoshop I can create to explain what I can see at concentration **state or Alpha**.*

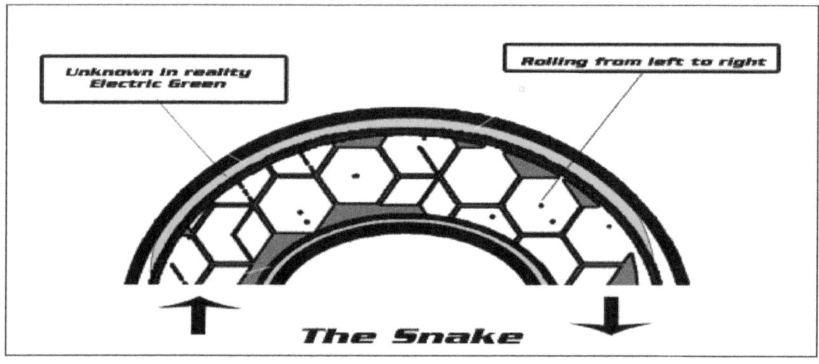

My goal throughout this book is to awaken those that need to remember the truth and help explain to those that have experienced similar circumstances they are not losing their minds, I was shown by the One to help the world remember what it is again and forward our lost understandings to a new age of truth and spiritual Enlightenment for the entire mass collective. My goal as a spiritual teacher is to bring you to an awareness level of understanding reality for what it really is. Understanding the Matrix is an overwhelming task when using individual programs of how education indoctrinates it is created. My teachings throughout this book are to allow the

reader to awaken parts of their energy fields that remain dormant until recognized. To those that follow me you already know a lot of what my teachings are, but to those that are new I welcome you to a brand-new outlook on understanding the fundamental characteristics of life, my insight will challenge you with hard evidence of what I present is the truth, and throughout the sections of each chapter I will try to raise your awareness levels and frequency of consciousness. I have been lucky enough to be selected by the pure source of creation to be able to bring you this valuable life changing information. What I say we already know as spirit at our subconscious energy level and all I will be attempting to do is remind you of what you already know but have forgotten through indoctrination of stereotype programs, misinterpreted allegories and social engineering. MY mission is to not educate you but only to remind you who you are and bring you back to remembering all I say is the truth for yourself. Some subjects are controversial but are well needed to be discussed in order to understand the design of the quantum simulation we call this physical world reality. Peace, love, light to all brothers and sisters and I hope you find answers that you have searched for within my teachings brought from the One.

SO, WHAT IS DMT? (Dimethyltryptamine)

*DMT is the **natural drug** that is released from opening your **pineal gland, once** it's been opened and connected through your **pituitary gland** while you are in an **awake state, you** can see the **afterlife** and connect back to the **source of creation** the pure source of all creation - the **God consciousness**.*

***DMT** is the **drug** that is **released during birth** as you enter from the **ethereal** into the **physical** and the **natural** formed drug that is **also released** when you **leave the physical avatar** back into the outside or **ethereal** realm. After **three hours** of rest the body during sleep state starts its **natural regeneration cycle** and also releases DMT naturally once **Rapid Eye Movement** sleep is entered. **Creativity** can also put you into a **consciousness connection** that allows the **natural release of Dimethyltryptamine**.*

*Using this ability and **spiritual steps of awareness** I was brought into the **state of divine knowing** or **ENLIGHTENMENT** to what many seek but **never** reach in their **lifetime**. I was awakened by another **way seer** that allowed **my subconscious** to **reveal all** that is ever and can ever be.*

***DMT, has** also **been known** as **the spiritual molecule**.*

A FEW PARANORMAL EXPERIENCES

*I **Remember** being **young**, and as I was walking towards the **back-fly screen** door in **Pannawonica** I was around **five** years old. As I walked through the **laundry** to where the sink was by the **back door, the fly screen door** flew open for me as it was shut, and then opened fully for me as I walked towards it, and through it, and out of it. To this **day I remember** this **vividly**.*

*Something I've always experienced are **shadow figures** that **dance around my walls** to the point that they would **move off the walls** and move in the **physical space** over me, close **to me, around** me where they could be noticed as more black then the blackness caused by the lights off. **Video footage** from a **VHS** recorder from **Pannawonica** shows me as young with my head **transparent** .To this I will include an **image in this book**.*

*The **recorder** showed me **recorded** in the front room with the **fish tank** behind me. As I moved past the fish tank my head **becomes transparent**. This **technology** of the day **could not** produce any **x-ray vision** images.*

*So, the **question** is was the **camera** creating an **X-ray illusion**? Or was I **spirit** so much still as a **child** that even the **camera** was showing that **physical reality** really is **nothing** but an **illusion**.*

*The **shadows** remained with me **right through life** to this **present** day. **Doctors** had **diagnosed** me with many **mental illnesses** as the cause of the **shadows,** as this is what the **Matrix** does to hide the true understanding of what is happening to one's own **energy fields**.*

Below are the VHS images as well as a web link to my You-tube channel where I have uploaded video evidence of this taking place. Thanks.

https://youtu.be/-iaUr-PSpfE

GOD'S LAW OF REVERSAL

*Before I **explain** more of my **life events** I would like to explain that everything is **reversed** inside this **Matrix hologram structure**. What we do is use the **conscious mind** instead of the **subconscious,** to what is **thirty thousand** more times stronger **in creation** than the believed to be **power** of the **conscious mind**.*

*We are **programmed** from **infancy** to learn how to accept the **backwards reality, and indoctrinated** with **beliefs** that are so **ludicrous** to you when you get older, but at the time seem like the **only truth** as you are nothing but a **blank hard drive** being programmed with information. Just **entering** the world again and blind to **deception** as **deception** etc as a **child** does not cross the **conscious mind**.*

*When **one** leaves the **Matrix**, the **vibrational** created **hologram structure** that is made from **nothing** but **consciousness energy** and **vibration** frequencies. **One** can see the **true creation** and **design of God just as the golden ratio shows intelligent creation one can see design. Entering** with **Source** you are*

shown *what* ***Source*** *knows and* ***wants you*** *to know,* ***everything*** *created in the* ***reality construct*** *is* ***reversed****.*

Education *is really* ***subconscious indoctrination of subliminal programming, the general populous snoop on the government*** *acting as the* ***National Security Agents*** *being* ***detectives*** *against the* ***government*** *instead of* ***vice versa.***

The ***one percent*** *hold* ***all the money*** *instead of the full* ***balanced*** *out mass.* ***Religion*** *creates* ***barriers*** *of understanding keeping* ***God*** *as being* ***real*** *but, also telling you, that you are* ***never worthy*** *to* ***be with God****.*

The ***more important*** *one is, we* ***are told*** *that* ***spiritual energy fields*** *etc are a thing of myth, just the same as the body* ***might*** *have a* ***spirit****. The* ***whole design*** *of the* ***constructed reality*** *has* ***relied*** *on this being the* ***major*** *programs of control but* ***also*** *the* ***major hints*** *of understanding.*

Now that ***I've explained*** *a little for now about the state of the reality is always in a* ***reversed state, I*** *will continue with some of my experiences growing up with* ***paranormal*** *circumstances.*

THE BLACK SHADOW MEN

All my life *I have dealt with being* ***what we would call*** *haunted.* ***Dancing shadows*** *on the walls to actually seeing the* ***black shadow man*** *manifest itself under* ***two different circumstances*** *in my life that it presented itself* ***vividly****.*

The ***first experience*** *of this* ***paranormal*** *occurrence is going back* ***a long time*** *ago to when I was a teenager.* ***I*** *was hanging around* ***with my*** *long-time child hood friends. One of my friends had gotten in trouble and as punishment he was sent to a* ***behavior modification*** *course through* ***Centrelink. Having nothing*** *to do I went to this same course, as well as with another friend we grew up with* ***Gary****.*

When starting the course, we met ***this aboriginal*** *fella named* ***Alan Yupo,*** *who we* ***became friends*** *with and started to hang out.*

One night *we and a lot more of the usual* ***guys and girls*** *were* ***hanging out*** *at the local oval,* ***called Hossack****, drinking and smoking* ***having fun****. Later on into the night a girl named* ***Annalise*** *returned back to where we were drinking, after having to go and try and squat in the bushes, scared* ***and crying*** *saying* *that a **small black solid** man **with red glowing eyes** was watching her urinate. Our friend Alan, said "**this was a Wadatchi** "or something in **Aboriginal law.** Basically, it was a **black shaped energy entity**, and that it was following him because of his **ancestor's** crimes that had been committed against the **tribal laws**.*

*The **history of the Wadatchi** was that **it would punish** the **ancestors** of the **one it was called upon** and **that it** could turn and **petrify you** if you had come to **stare** into its **red glowing eyes.***

***We** ran around **gathering the crew. Some** guys and their girls were making out etc. As we ran across the **eastern** part of **Hossack oval** we could see **Belinda**, a **friend** who lived with **Adam** who was with us **on the oval. As** we **watched her** riding towards us as **silhouette**, we could see a **small silhouette** of the **five-foot-tall man** behind her. As we ran closer to her, the bike and her **became clear,** the little **black shadow man entity** vanished into nothing.*

*After the event, **we returned** to **Adam** and **Belinda's** house, where Alan said **"he had to go and fight the Wadatchi** "to what **we didn't** really understand as we were not **aboriginal raised** with the **understanding. Alan** left the house **and returned** that night a little bit later with his **shirt torn**, and **scratches over his body**, to what he had claimed the **Wadatchi pushed him***

through the wall.

***To this day** I can't say exactly **what happened** and how the **scratches appeared** that had been done to him, but all **I know** is that it was **my first time** seeing the **shadow man entity, or** the **dark consciousness** energy **manifestation** of the **subconscious manifesting** in physical reality.*

***The second time, well** this was a **very blatant** one.*

***So...** this experience happened **years later** in my **mid-twenties. Myself** and a **friend Matt** living with me at the time at my parent's house were having a drink and practicing some freestyle lyrics, as we were both hip hop artists.*

***Note Matt** was also the **one** to point out the **strange phenomenon** of me **going transparent** on the **old VHS** tapes, as he **discovered** it and then said to me, "why are you invisible"? To what I **also was shocked** at the time. **Matt can confirm** it for any nay Sayers, Matthew **Roy Davison**. (hope you didn't mind Matt).*

*We started talking **about spirits** as back then **we** both understood **everything was energy** but **nothing** like to the extent of **known today**.*

*We started talking **about this topic** when the computer room **light** above us **began to flicker** and **became** more and more **erratic**, until we **talked about it** and noticed it. After **that it***

stopped. *We felt the* ***most hair standing energetic presence*** *with us.*

We *started* ***talking about*** *how it's* ***communicating*** *with us, and sure enough the* ***lights above flickered*** *in response. We then started to* ***feel that its presence*** *was strong, and the light above* ***flickered on and off rapidly****.*

To what, then *I called out to* ***Dad*** *who was* ***sleeping*** *with* ***Mum*** *in the* ***bedroom next door, "DAD!! DAD!!"*** *come here* ***look at this****".*

I ***could hear Dad*** *getting up* ***slowly*** *as he was* ***quite elderly.*** *Once he reached the* ***hallway door*** *and was standing* ***looking*** *into the* ***computer room,*** *as he* ***lifted*** *his* ***head*** *to see what* ***we*** *were* ***yelling*** *about, the* ***light*** *above us became* ***idle*** *again and* ***static****. He looked up and said* ***"nothing is going on"*** *and then went back to bed.*

After ***he went back to bed*** *the* ***light*** *above started* ***playing up*** *again, until I* ***yelled*** *out with force loudly,* ***"in the name of the blood of the lamb I demand you to be gone!", Sure enough*** *both* ***Matt*** *and I watched this* ***energy*** *in the shape of a* ***five-foot silhouette*** *of a being go* ***darting fast*** *out of the room and* ***shooting off*** *down the* ***hallway****, out of the computer room and* ***towards*** *the front* ***rooms of the house****.*

CONCLUSION: To this day *I thought it was the words that* *made it go as they were **Biblical** etc, but in **reality,** it was my **subconscious** belief **program** that **allowed me** to unmanifest the **energy** from our presence. It was the **fact** that **I believed** at the time that those words are going to **remove the energy away**, and **because** what is **created** is what the **mind believes.** I then used my own **religious indoctrination** I had **done to myself** to create the desired outcome from **belief**.*

SHADOW DOG HUMANOID SILHOUETTE

Okay, *this* ***also happened*** *at the same* ***Hossack oval*** *but this* ***occurrence*** *happened* ***at the pavilion.***

To ***begin*** *what happened* ***this night, Gary*** *and a friend* ***DJ and myself*** *were sitting* ***outside in the garage*** *leaning against the trunk of my* ***parent's car*** *having* ***a few drinks****. To* ***start the night off*** *a Victoria* ***Bitter beer can spilled*** *on the* ***concrete ground*** *by accident, then* ***created*** *the* ***devil horn hand sign*** *in the flow of the* ***liquid of beer along*** *the* ***ground****.*

This ***was just the start of the night*** *and could* ***possibly*** *be the reason for* ***seeing the manifestation*** *later on that what* ***I am explaining.***

My friend ***Gary was going out with a girl, Lena*** *on the other* ***side of Hossack oval*** *to what the oval is directly behind where I lived, a few streets over.* ***Gary decided*** *he wanted to* ***go see her, DJ*** *and I decided* ***we would tag along*** *as we were all getting* ***inebriated*** *together.*

We went across ***Hossack oval*** *no problem to* ***Lena's house,*** *and* ***Gary chatted*** *with her etc.* ***After Gary*** *was* ***done conversing, we*** *started* ***returning*** *back* ***to my house****. When we were walking* ***through the carpark*** *towards* ***the center pavilion, on*** *the outside you could see the* ***fire hydrant*** *and* ***next to that*** *was* ***something strange*** *.It was the* ***silhouette of a dark shadow*** *that looked like a* ***dog.*** *When* ***we walked closer*** *and closer to this* ***manifestation*** *to what* ***looked*** *a* ***hundred percent*** *like that of a* ***dog's outline*** *in its* ***silhouette, pure*** *black with* ***no details*** *to its body, just* ***black thick darkness****.*

We *reached about* ***five feet away*** *from* ***the spirit*** *to what then the* ***head lifted*** *and* ***turned*** *in the way a* ***human head*** *turns to look at you. It* ***turned its head*** *in the way that* ***no animal*** *could* ***turn its head*** *to look* ***towards you****.*

The ***three of us ran*** *away* ***dumbfounded*** *and* ***panic stricken. To*** *this day I* ***remember*** *it as a very* ***vivid experience****.*

CONCLUSION: *With this* ***experience you have to ask yourself*** *if the* ***beer*** *didn't* ***manifest the night*** *to be talked about the* ***devil*** *and* ***supernatural****, would this* ***anomaly of the Matrix*** *have* ***had manifested, or*** *was this a* ***creation*** *of the three of our* ***subconscious minds*** *creating the* ***manifestation****? As we had* ***no idea*** *about* ***energy use, or*** *that the* ***subconscious mind*** *could* ***manifest*** *such* ***things into physical existence****. The* ***fact*** *is this was seen by* ***all three*** *of us* ***close up to the point*** *that we were* ***almost staring in its face****. So it was* ***not*** *a* ***drunken hallucination*** *that was not really there, but it was* ***fully manifested*** *into this*

physical holographic constructed reality.

THE HAUNTED HOUSE

*This **event** happened with **Belinda and Adam** also as well as **two** of my best friends **Rob and Greavsey, and Helen, Jacky, Winnie** we **were hanging with at the time** that were **Belinda's friends**. Ours also, but **Belinda** and they were their **own tribe** so to speak.*

***We** start from **Belinda's moms** house to where **her** mother's **boyfriend** at the **time had a beach house** at **Scarborough** Beach. Belinda was told that we could all go and stay there over the weekend if we wanted to, so she accepted the offer and off we went.*

***Beforehand of this event** we had **been told** of **strange experiences** her mum has had **in the house, but** her mum **liked to drink** a lot **so we** chose **not to listen, but maybe we should have. She talked** about one time she was **there drunk** and **laying on the bed** when a **strange whirling vortex of light** opened over her head. We **assumed** she was **just drunk.** So **back** to **the story,** we all **jumped into the car** and **headed out** to the beach house, made our way **up through the gates, opened** the **front door** went **inside all was good. We** then decided to*

***start to party. After drinking** a few bottles of **Jack Daniels** and were all **sitting outside,** my friend **Greavsey** was also there who **tagged along. Greavsey** and **myself** were **drinking bourbon** when we **both noticed** the upright **box of bourbon** with **no bottle** inside slowly **move across** the **floor** remaining **vertical.** We **spun out** on it a bit, then it **fell over** to what **we assume** the **wind did. Can't say that** I've seen **any wind** make it **hover across the ground like** it did, but the **wind knocking** it over is a **definite**.*

*That was the **first experience**.*

Belinda's mum** had said that the **place was haunted** also and that **something always** happens that's **paranormal** to the **last person awake, this time** when this **experience** happened we were **all going to sleep.** I laid **on** the **floor** with a **Helen, Jacky,** Winnie and my mate **Daniel. Adam** and **Belinda** went into the one **bedroom**, everyone started to **begin to fall asleep**. I was left the **last one** that was **awake**, and **as I dozed** beginning to **fall asleep** the **cupboard door** in the **kitchen** about **seven meters** away from where we were laying **started** to **bang loudly, Bang! Bang! Bang!** I **grabbed Helen's leg** and she asked "**is that you** "? to I replied "**yes**", she was like **thank God.** As the **cupboard** door **banged again** Adam and Belinda **rushed out** to **see** what was happening, as they **turned on** the **lights** we watched as the **cupboard door froze open.** We went to **sleep

*and all **seemed fine** the next day. We **went out** and came **back to the house, went through** the **gate** when the **gate fell off** the **hinges**. This was pretty **mind-blowingly strange** I tell you now, **after this** we went **into** the **house**. I **walked** to the **sink** and went to **pour** myself a **glass of water** as I **placed** the **glass** to the faucet **the tap** jumped **off its connection** to the sink and **smashed the glass in my hand** and **fell** into the **sink.***

*A **few** other **experiences** happened **there** but none **besides** the **last** I can really remember as vividly as the rest. The **last time** we got **drunk** and **Robert**, Greavsey and **I** were outside **looking out to the beach front,** we were **chilling** when we see **this guy** come **running down** the **sidewalk** out **of nowhere.** He just **vaporized** and then was **running** he run past us **stark naked** to what **me** and **Greaves** said,"**oi look at this fu*ker**, we can't have that sh#t". So we ran **down after him** to what **once again** he had just **vanished....** this was a crazy experience to witness.*

***CONCLUSION: Now as I know, everything** is **manifested** through the **subconscious mind** to the **One, these events** happened because we had already **believed** the **place** was **haunted** Belinda's **mother** helped the **manifestation** to take form by **implanting** the **place is haunted** even more. **Before** the **first experience** with the **cupboard door,** I **was told** the **last person** who **was awake** something happens to them, so I **subconsciously created it** to happen as being last of the*

combined collective's energy *that was still awake. The* ***energy from us*** *feeding it seeing the* ***bourbon carton*** *move to* ***start the night,*** *the* ***constant subconscious programming*** *of this* ***place is haunted, then the rest*** *is all of* ***us manifesting energy*** *into the thought form* ***to bring it into existence.*** *We* ***created*** *the* ***events through*** *our* ***subconscious*** *like we always do.* ***However,*** *the* ***reason*** *for the* ***naked guy running*** *I feel is* ***because, once he lived in that beach house,*** *and* ***committed suicide*** *by taking* ***all his clothes off*** *and running* ***into the ocean to drown.***

Even though *the* ***thought form*** *was* ***projected by us,*** *as we are all* ***one*** *and* ***never die*** *just cease to* ***exist in*** *one* ***dimension*** *and move into* ***another, we*** *had resonated with the* ***energy*** *of the persons* ***experienced conscious memory, trying*** *to* ***explain*** *to us* ***how he died*** *and what happened.*

Pity ***at the time*** *I had* ***no understanding*** *about these things, like* ***energy fields*** *and* ***creational law*** *of* ***consciousness*** *as I do* ***today.***

Testimony of events: Daniel Greaves, Greavsey

I ***remember the events like yesterday*** *and can* ***confirm*** *that what* ***Tony explained happened*** *in this story very well did as* ***I myself also witnessed*** *the* ***paranormal events*** *that had* ***taken place*** *at this Beach house.*

THE EERIE WHISPER

*I **remember one time** I had come **home** from **primary** school and **no one was home.** This is when I was a lot **younger** than the **other events** that I've **explained** to when experiencing them I was **older.** I had **come** in **from school** put my bag down, and **walked up** the hallway **to my room. Just** as I **turned** to go into my room I felt a **whisper in my ears,** it's hard to say what one as it felt in both at the same time. I've always **since young sensed** places **energy** and my **own home** had **worried** me for a while about certain rooms as **I felt uneasy. Anyways** after I **heard** the **oi** that **sounded like** a **deep** voice going **"ooooyyy". I** ran out **the front** and **waited** for **Mum and Dad** to arrive **home from work,** this was **scary** to me **bigtime** as I was a little child.*

***CONCLUSION: Knowing** now that **spirit is** around **me always** and that **consciousness** is **positive** and **negative** in **energy form,** this was the **One** trying to **awaken** and show **me** that things that are not supposed to exist, do exist. I used **judgement** and **called** it of bad **stereotype** when **in reality** it's **been** around me **all my life** since **Pannawonica**.*

*Only over **the last few** years have **I understood** why it was* *created **inside my game experience** subconsciously by me, to give the **understanding** of that I thought was evil was **still God.** I just **couldn't understand** being **blinded** and **indoctrinated** with using **stereotypes**.*

THE TURNING DOOR KNOB

This experience** happened **earlier** than **the last.

*My **Grandma** had just **passed away** recently before this **occurrence**, everyone **was out of the house** and myself, **Mark** and **Richard** decided **since** we were **little** we would **play hide and seek. Mark** was nominated **it**, so he **began counting** and **we** went to **hide.** We **went** into the hallway and into my **Grandma's room** across from my room and **shut** the **door**. My friend **Richard** went and **hid behind the bed** as **I stood** with my **hand firmly** wrapped around the **door knob** to feel and **notice when Mark** was **opening** the **door. Richard** kept **saying** about the doorstop **teddy bear** that my Grandma had in her room and how its **eyes** would **not stop moving,** as he was saying this **I could feel the pressure** on the **doorknob** and then the **doorknob turned** with my **hand on it** and the door **opened! NO MARK**! We **freaked out** and went to **look for Mark** who at **that time** was **looking** for us **out** the **back yard**!*

CONCLUSION:** Now **I already knew** about the **spirit** that was **what I believed back then to haunt me** , and my **friends** knew my **Grandma** has just **passed away** , So to analyze it now , **I

would *say that* ***the subconscious*** *mind of* ***each of ours*** *knowing* ***Gran*** *had* ***passed*** *already* ***subconsciously programmed the event*** *.Why did we choose Gran's room? It was* ***meant*** *to* ***happen*** *, the* ***eyes*** *of the* ***bear moving*** *gave us the* ***belief*** *something* ***must be*** *going on* ***paranormal,*** *so then we* ***fed the energy*** *more until we* ***manifested*** *the* ***door opening****.*

This is ***not the last time*** *a door opened for me and I will explain that next...*

UNSOLVED MYSTERY OPENING DOORS

*This **happened** to **me** and a friend **Steve, young** once **again** in **this story** we both **sat** on my **bed against** the **wall** and were **watching Unsolved Mysteries** on the **television** as my **bed** was **set up** to also be the **couch**. It was something about **Bigfoots** that we **both** were **getting into** when my **clothes cupboard** doors started to creak with a **creak like an old house door.** The **noise** got **louder** and **both** the **cupboard doors flew** wide **open. Steve** and **I** darted out as **quick** as those **doors opened out of the room** to grab my parents. When **we returned** the cupboard **door hinges, to** where the door sits into its clip, had been **totally buckled** making it **impossible to shut the doors** again.*

*Because **Steve** and **Myself** being **little** had all our **concentration power** on the **television show, and** because **we had become enwrapped** in it, the **fear** and **excitement program** that the show was creating into us as young children, **manifested** us to **subconsciously** want our **own unsolved mystery** as everything **is always** done with the **subconscious mind** and what you **program** it to **believe** is what can be **manifested** into the*

physical.

CONCLUSION: *Just **as the laws of reversal** make you manifest what **you don't want, so what you don't** want the most **is what you manifest** through the **subconscious** and the **subconscious reverses** the message, **we created** the **event** because the last thing we wanted while **being scared** was to become even more scared.*

Being psychic** and **clairvoyant** when in **complete synch** I know now **a lot of these events** had to do with me being there, being so **acceptable to energy. A** lot **more events** like these have **happened over time.** Here and there, around **friends' houses,** or just **out and about.

*I will leave the **experiences** for **not** having **any drugs involved** here, **after** and the **events I in life became** sick with **mental illness** to what I then **went** through **a monk stage** to **isolating myself** from others, to where I discovered myself again. Isolating myself from all friends and learning how **to find my inner self, then** the **Mandela effect** happened to what **opened brand new** experiences to **what I'll explain** in the Mandela effect section of this book.*

THE TRUTH OF DRUG ALTERED REALITIES

*So, **we talked** about **DMT** and how it is **used in life**, and **death** and only in **deep REM sleep** (rapid eye movement).*

*So why is the **design** of the **constructed reality** to have the **drug program** included in the **design** of the **Matrix code**?*

Simple answer**. It **is to train** you as **spirit**. Spirit **knows** it's here to **have fun** and that's all it wants, but it **also knows** that it **wants to always reconnect** back **to Source.

*What **drugs** are as the **message** from the **One**.*

*They are **a clever** way that **consciousness** of the **One** has created a **program method** in order to **train spirit** on how to **reconnect**. Under **drug influence** the **DMT fires up** and the **consciousness** connection is made.*

*This by all means **does not** get you to **divine knowing,** but is **a training wheel** for the **user to understand** that what they are **doing is using the drug to open** their connection through **to consciousness** of the One.*

EXAMPLE: *The **user knows** they **get high** to what **is really** leaving the **body from the physical** and **becoming spirit, and** then **coming down** after being **spirit** and connected **back** to the **body again.***

*All **drugs** in **reality are here** for **one lesson** and that is that you have to **use a drug** to **reach consciousness** and that drug is your **natural** released **DMT** created by your own body.*

*As **I've explained** before **in many teachings** the connection through **synthetic release** is not the true **connection** to consciousness, and **only allows** the **experiencer** to enter as far as their own **subconscious programming blocking** the **natural connection** to the **ONE**.*

***Drugs are allowed** by **government!** As if they didn't want them they simply **wouldn't have them around.** Despite what **anyone says** if we wanted a **drug free society** it would be **drug free**. The **reason** that this **drug program** exists **in the Matrix** coded **hologram** script is because the **consciousness** of the **One** created it **for understanding** on how to **reach spirit** again.*

*Have **you** ever **wondered** why so many **people** become **addicted to drugs**, the **high**, or should we say the **temporary** higher **state of consciousness?***

*Some **plants** can **mimic** the natural **DMT** reaction, as the **ancients** used them to **connect,** using these plants like*

Ayahuasca *and* ***Salvia*** *do* ***allow*** *a more spiritual* ***connection*** *to the* ***One****, but* ***once again*** *you are* ***blocked*** *as it's* ***not the natural*** *release* ***that is*** *the one and* ***only real*** *way to* ***connect*** *to the* ***pure source*** *of all* ***creation*** *with a* ***clean connection*** *of* ***understanding*** *with no blockage.*

GOD. *The* ***infinite*** *source of* ***knowledge****.*

MY DRUG INDUCED EXPERIENCES

As young, I *started to take my* ***first hit of Marijuana, later*** *was followed by* ***cigarettes*** *then* ***Lysergic Acid Diethylamide, Methylenedioxy-methamphetamine, Cocaine, Amphetamine, Magic Mushrooms*** *And much more, you name it and we took it at some time growing up.* ***Apart*** *from* ***Heroin*** *to what I* ***lost a few close friends, rest in peace****, that made me keep away from that* ***drug*** *despite the* ***reputation*** *of it having a great* ***experience of the high*** *to it. Even though more* ***classified*** *as a* ***downer*** *drug.*

So, I've *seen* ***everything*** *from* ***glitches in the sky, the real form of the Matrix*** *and how* ***everything is made*** *of* ***electromagnetic*** *singularities of* ***consciousness, souls (not*** *all the* ***real*** *players either). I'm* ***talking about*** *the* ***negative*** *and* ***positive*** *of* ***consciousness combined*** *and* ***creating*** *the* ***electromagnetic universe*** *that is around us at all times. The hologram Matrix Workers, the* ***Spiritual builders*** *of consciousness, the* ***ancient Gods*** *and* ***Goddesses' different frequencies*** *of the* ***hologram*** *Matrix* ***vibrations*** *of* ***energy showing*** *its form in the* ***drug*** *induced* ***state****.*

LADY IN THE WHITE SCARF

*So, **one time** it was **myself** another male friend **Merv Talma** and a **few girls, Storm, Jenny**. We **started** the **night** with taking **acid,** if I **remember** this was **around** when the **White-tile** double dipped **trip** was in **circulation**. We enjoyed our **night** having **fun** and **hallucinating**. We talked about things from **paranormal** and more **religion** etc as drugs tend to make you have **deep subconscious** meaningful **discussions**.*

*Around **two** in the **early am, we** were **driving** down **Canning Highway** to what is a **local transit path** in Perth. **Storm** was telling **me, Merv** and **Jen** about when she was **growing up and that** there was this **old lady** that used to wear **all black clothes** with a **white scarf,** she **continued** on with her **story** to what some **was personal** so I have **not said** because of that reason.*

***The point** is after that **was said** about one minute later continuing **down the road, at** the side of the road next to the **bus stop** there was a **lady all in black** with a **white scarf** wrapped around her shoulders, standing as if she was waiting for the next bus. But around this time in the **morning** to start* *with the buses in Perth do not run their schedule. I **locked up** my **handbrake** and turned around fast as it was late and no traffic was really about, when we pulled back around and **over to the bus stop** there was **no trace** of the **woman** ever **being there.** We all **noticed** this and **remember** it as if it was **yesterday, the woman** in black had **vanished**!*

CONCLUSION**: Back then I was **stumped** as to **how** and **why** but I can say **confidently** right now **what happened.

***Since** we **understand** everything is **consciousness** we as the small **collective** with the streets being **deserted** of anyone around us, or **anyone else's energies, created**, using our **subconscious** mind. As the **block was not** on the **conscious** mind **at the time** as reality wasn't even a **real program running** at the time. So, we, using our own **thought initiative programs** created our **own frequency** of consciousness **implant** that we **manifested** the **thought form** from that into **physical**. The **reason** why the **woman** in black **vanished is** because after we saw her, the **conscious mind** kicked in to **that can't be real** programming. Then because of its **indoctrination** of what **real reality** is supposed to be it then, corrected the **projection thought** form **subconsciously**.*

NIGHT OF MANY MANIFESTATIONS

*Another **experience** was with **Mervin Talma**, who also **agreed** to **back up** the **memories** I'm writing about **with** his **testimony**.*

***This** one involves **LSD** again and **weed etc** but has a rather different **manifestation** occurrence.*

*So, **we started early** in the evening at his **South Perth flat** with about a **group** of eight, we all took **our trips** and **started** to **enjoy** the **night.** We, when the **acid** had **fully kicked in** decided to **go over** to the **UWA** university. That is just that, a **university**.*

***So, we** made our way **through** the **university grounds** and **buildings** until **we arrived** at the **amphitheater** and **sat down** on the **chairs**. The **amphitheater** was **surrounded** with **trees, that** made when you **looked up** an encasing of **tree tops, then** there **was the sky** in the **circle**, exposed by **the trees above us.** We **watched** through the **tree top** encasement all **tripping** and **focusing** on the **sky laying back** on the **chairs** and **enjoying** our **acid trip** ... **The clouds** above us **moved** rapidly **fast** and **made** the **symbol** of the **Mortal Combat** logo **in the circle of the exposed sky** by the tree tops above us. I mean to the perfect* *shape of the logo.*

***We to this day reminisce** about this and **how amazing** it was, that morning **after** everyone had **gone home** me and Merv sat on the **flat's balcony area** smoking weed and **coming down.** We watched as the **clouds formed** the **exact shapes of souls** that **jumped** from **one cloud** to **another**.*

***CONCLUSION:** Once **again reality manifested** into that **dimension** we **created as we left the original dimensions,** and **entered into** the **ethereal realm,** The Mortal Combat symbol was seen by us because our **subconscious energies manifested it, I have no idea why the symbol though?** After **knowing** what I know **now** I have a feeling that it **was consciousness** trying to **show us** that **physical and spirit are always** in a **mortal combat, over who drives /controls** the mortal.*

*As **physical and spirit hate each other** and do everything possible to **hide each other**.*

***If you are spiritual then the Matrix will do everything possible to make you believe everything is only physical** reality, if **you are physical then spirit will always create hints all the time** to try and awaken spirit. Because once entered into spirit the Matrix knows that you become a **threat** to it so **its instant want is to return you to your sociological programming of indoctrination, and** remind you that you have been **taught all is physical** so you **return to that belief**.*

*These **occurrences** are when **consciousness** is **calling** to **you**, showing you **the true design** of the world you physically live. Showing **you** that your **energy** of the **subconscious** power once entering the **program and thought initiative programming** can **manifest physical reality** and bend it to your desire. As long as **you leave** the **Matrix with spirit** but **remain inside in the body** only.*

*As a Biblical saying is, **be in the world, but not of the world,** this is **exactly** what we **are explaining here.** Be part of the **everyday construct** but **always know** what **you** and the **world really are,** and that is **nothing** but the **vibrational created hologram Matrix** that we create from the **outside realm** to where **we create** the **full game** of **consciousness** as the **light** beings **using telepathy**.*

*Another **classic** example of this is **the same morning** with **Storm, Merv** and **Jenny** we were **cruising back** towards **town,** to leave through and **go home**. As we were just **entering onto the bridge** I made **a joke** about our **night of ups and downs, religious** beliefs, and more. I stated "**Wouldn't it be funny now if a gypsy looking woman with a red car and 666 on the number plates showed up". Now** as crazy as this sounds and the fact I can prove it **by anyone**, by just asking the people that were there. I still find this crazy, but as **we navigated** through **traffic, a red car** appeared **driving fast up** in the **lane** to the **left***

side*. The* ***car was a red Trans am*** *and in the* ***front seat driving*** *was a small* ***old elderly woman*** *who was* ***wearing gypsy clothing.*** *As she* ***accelerated*** *faster* ***past us*** *and* ***pulled in front*** *of* ***my car*** *and into our* ***driving lane, her*** *number* ***plates showed 666*** *and was on the* ***blue private license*** *plates that* ***you buy here*** *in Western Australia.*

CONCLUSION: *Looking back at* ***these memories*** *with all the* ***understanding of consciousness*** *of the* ***One*** *I have* ***now****. I can clearly* ***see the pattern of subconscious*** *manifesting the* ***physical reality*** *to our will.* ***We didn't*** *ever believe that would happen* ***hence my joking,*** *this is* ***why it did****, to* ***once again explain*** *in message that everything* ***inside the Matrix*** *works by the* ***laws of reversal.***

This ***was the One*** *always trying* ***to show*** *that* ***reality*** *was, not* ***what we had been indoctrinated with.*** *This was the* ***One saying*** *"****hey my children look what I can do****".*

This was the ***spirit*** *of* ***each of us subconsciously*** *crying out to* ***be recognized*** *the same way it did for the* ***ancients in history*** *that used a* ***drug form*** *to make a* ***connection to spirit or the one consciousness of God****.*

WHAT IS THE CONSTRUCTED MATRIX?

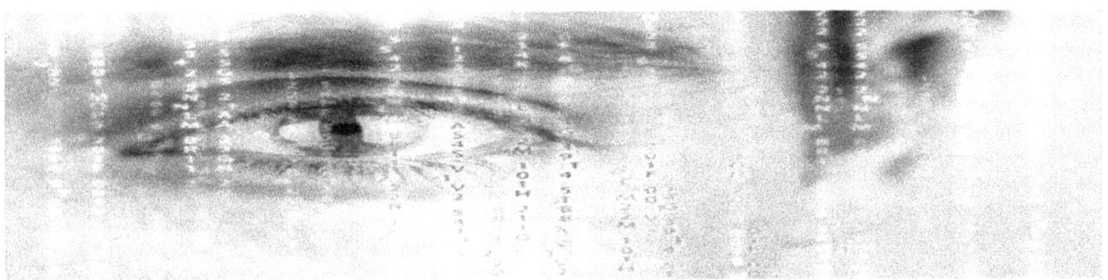

*Have **you ever seen "The Matrix** "the **movie**? The **truth hidden** in **plain sight** is amazing, so what is the Matrix? It is a **very sophisticated** computer **program** that is **created** from **consciousness electromagnetic energy**. Even though **solid to appearance** it is **not**! Just as **research** by **many scientists** like **Niels Bohr** states the atom itself is **99.999999% empty** before becoming **physical**. Once **receiving** a form of **consciousness vibration** such as, Cymatics, The **Schumann resonance frequency**, The **spiritual fields** of the **spirit anatomy** and the **avatar endocrine system field energies**. The **electromagnetic Consciousness energy** creates the blueprint of the **construct to the holographic Matrix,** then on top of that, **the vibrational frequencies** manifest the **non-physical** to **the physical**. Just as the **Double Slit** test by **Richard Feynman** shows that **everything** itself is **wave form** or frequency pattern **until it is observed** by the **human eye** to what then **changes it** to become **physical** instead of **wave form**. This is **only because** your own **consciousness energy** of your **singularity signature** is now adding **to** the **mix of manifestation**.*

Is anything real?

*I will **answer that** with a **NO** as **death, life** and the **Matrix** are nothing but **an illusion. Death is created** to keep you **entrapped** and **scared** so you cann**ot discover the truth. Life does not really exist either.** Classic **proof** to **demonstrate** this is the **activity recorded** on the **brain** when **fully asleep** and **wide awake. Researchers** have found **that the brain** itself **functions** the **exact** same way firing up **neurons** as when **awake to asleep**. The **reason** why **this is apparent** and can **be proven** is because when **you sleep you are creating using your subconscious mind** to create your **own quantum existent reality, and** in **that reality** your **consciousness** has entered. You **are physical** just like in dreams **sex, pain, sadness and excitement** can be experienced **the same** as in so called **awake.** Physical reality both **resonate the same** brain activity because **reality and your dream are the same.** You are just **indoctrinated** to **believe** the **physical** reality **exists**. As **physical** is all **your understanding of reality** was ever taught to be," you **can't go** through that, that's physical" etc.*

*The **fact is everything around you** inside the **physical** Matrix **is well aware** of its own **existence** and **self-aware consciousness energy.** Because **you are self-aware** and **everything of existence** is **self-aware** of you then adding you into the **avatar with** the five **senses, smell, sight, hearing, speech, and touch*** *that are* ***only vibrational frequencies created from your spiritual body****. They create the* ***well persistent illusion*** *that* ***you live*** *in a physical* ***hard, solid*** *world.*

Nothing *is of* ***real existence*** *just as I said* ***death is fake****. You are* ***programmed to believe you die through*** *DNA entering you* ***when in development*** *in the* ***womb. When spirit arrives around three months*** *into development the manifesting avatar through* ***DNA*** *and the* ***mother's beliefs*** *have been* ***indoctrinated into your subconscious*** *to* ***what was connected always to the superconscious****, until it* ***chose to enter*** *into another* ***avatar for another experience*** *in the* ***game****.*

As I've ***explained just before*** *about the* ***laws of the Matrix are always reversed, you*** *have the* ***classic example*** *here.*

We are ***taught*** *when we* ***are born*** *it's the* ***first time*** *we are* ***entering into*** *the* ***holographic world,*** *but* ***reality*** *is we* ***just died*** *from* ***being our true form,*** *the* ***electromagnetic spirit*** *of balanced* ***positive and negative*** *consciousness* ***energy that's self-aware****. Us being* ***born here*** *removes* ***spirit*** *from always* ***experiencing*** *nothing but* ***divine love****, as on the outside of the* ***physical hologram*** *spirit does* ***not*** *feel any* ***emotions*** *apart from the* ***divine love*** *of God being one with God* ***always****.*

As ***spirit is removed*** *from the* ***ether and transformed*** *into the* ***avatar the wings of our singularity*** *of* ***consciousness signature are removed,*** *by* ***wings*** *I mean we are* ***no longer just*** *floating in* *the* ***ether*** *as consciousness* ***energy,*** *as when* ***one enters the*** *divine knowing state with* ***divine love*** *you can* ***feel your wings*** *on* ***spirit once again.***

The ***whole reference*** *of* ***fallen angels*** *from* ***Biblical view*** *is the* ***removal of us being divine light*** *that is nothing but divine love, angels, and being* ***implanted*** *into a* ***physical hologram avatar*** *that* ***entraps*** *our* ***natural abilities*** *to* ***use consciousness*** *and* ***connect*** *to* ***Source.***

Only through spiritual enlightenment *one can* ***return*** *to* ***spirit again during the game, as*** *the* ***whole point*** *of this Matrix is to* ***be a game, that*** *we* ***as spirit come into*** *to* ***experience*** *every other emotional state outside of divine love that we can.*

WHY DO YOU CALL THIS A GAME?

Everything you can imagine** is based on the **laws of duality for creation. The male, the female, young, old, animal, reptilian, Red team and Blue Team and even the ones and zeros of the binary code. The positive and the negative, Christianity and Satanism, Physical and Spiritual feminine and masculine energies.

*From **biological structure** to **atomic substructure** all is started with a **positive and a negative**. This **shows** creation is **duality,** just like day and night and the sky to the ground all **creation shows duality**.*

*The **reason why** I raise this **topic, is** because to **understand the game** you must **understand** the creation of **design behind it.***

*As I've explained **nothing really exists** in the **physical,** so look around in so called real **reality** you have **Flat earth, reptilian shapeshifting aliens, grey aliens etc, fake space, UFO's, cloning technology, transhumanism, missing links in our evolution according to Darwin's law, secret cabals running the world,***

mysterious unsolved creatures and Constant Wars *all the time, right?*

If you look at the mechanics of a ***role-playing computer game*** *you will understand* ***this is the easiest way of understanding*** *the true* ***form of reality, you are a player, an electromagnetic being*** *that has* ***chosen*** *to have your* ***experience*** *you live.* ***We live*** *in an* ***electromagnetic*** *game level* ***design that is the server, spirit comes*** *and* ***goes*** *from this server,* ***either when*** *it levels up in experience or when* ***it has to restart to learn*** *the lesson of* ***the game again****.*

The ***One consciousness*** *shows* ***evidence*** *all the time by the direction* ***of its creation*** *inside* ***the Matrix, as all is*** *the* ***One****'s creation and* ***all shows*** *what the One wants you to understand* ***about creation****. This is* ***our training*** *ground* ***as spirit*** *infancy for us to overcome it and become spiritual adolescence.*

Because of that *we are* ***spirit****, and* ***could*** *only* ***receive*** *and give* ***divine love*** *when on the* ***outside*** *of the Matrix.* ***We as spirits*** *on the outside* ***created the hologram*** *world* ***to*** *enter into and* ***have all other experiences*** *that we* ***could not*** *endure* ***as spirit. We light beings*** *wanted to experience* ***other frequencies of energy*** *so we* ***created*** *a* ***game that we play*** *to be able to understand them.*

Inside this Matrix *we have* ***planned programs*** *of non-****playing characters that seem to be used*** *to murder and other events to* *cause **fear vibration** in the **general populous**. These **non-playing characters** are **blank** and unlike you or me **are a set to program conscious** script. They **can interact** but only to **script and taking them out of script they can glitch out making strange faces** or **not responding** at all. These NPC's **have an idle reading to energy workers** and have **no natural spiritual anatomy like you** or me or **any other real player**. Just as you **play** a **console game** that was **designed by a company** and the **level was predesigned** before you get to put it into your personal computer or console **reality is no different**.*

*The **One created this as a game** and all that we are learning inside **from trend and technology advancement** have all **been showing** us **messages** from the **One** relaying the **true workings of its design.** Thus **gaming** from **young to adult** being such a **big trend** that is **only going to get bigger and bigger,** until **we inside** the Matrix **invent another Matrix** that **we can enter** and do this all over again .We are **learning** right **through** from **being young** when first **entering the world** when you knew you were here only to have fun, **from being old and still** making **sure to** watch the **game** that all is a game.*

*I have been **in the afterlife** a lot and can certainly say **we are in a game** ' An electromagnetic **Divine Chess board** game **in fact.***

***Ever wonder why the Freemasonic order / Illuminati used the checkered floor?** You now have **your answer.** They **found out** a* *very long time ago that we live in an **artificial simulation created** by consciousness but chose to benefit from it from service to self rather than **revealing the truth**.*

*To what they **had to by the laws of duality** anyway.*

checkered floor examples included.

The laws of duality apply to everything *from anything you* ***can imagine, as understanding*** *energy you understand that* ***law of attraction*** *is only the* ***belief*** *program using the* ***subconscious energy of consciousness*** *to manifest the desired and directed reality outcome. Think* ***positive*** *then* ***attract positive, unfortunately*** *this is* ***NOT how*** *the true forms of attraction work. The truth is* ***the negative attracts*** *the* ***positive frequency*** *to manifest and being* ***positive attracts the negative.***

This is a typical catch 22 *to a lot* ***of empaths,*** *energy readers, that* ***grow up, as most do remember*** *once again who they are as* ***spirit, and*** *have to endure such* ***traumatic lives and events*** *that* ***reconnect*** *them* ***to Source. Most empathic people create*** *these* ***realities*** *for themselves* ***without knowing*** *consciously, simply to* ***reawaken*** *the* ***connection****.*

This is ***how spirit cries*** *out when it's being ignored.*

It ***manifests your game level of reality experience*** *to* ***create the message*** *it wants you* ***to understand,*** *the same applies to the* ***physical avatar's operational*** *health and* ***body joint pains****.*

Most manifestations *of the* ***physical body*** *are* ***linked*** *back* ***to spirit*** *and its anatomy* ***workings*** *being ignored, or* ***Kundalini energy paths*** *and* ***chakra centering points not being cleansed, balanced*** *and refreshed with* ***divine light and divine love*** *from the* ***One****.*

*Everything is **duality law,** just as **life and death themselves are nothing but indoctrination programming** of the **center you.** Your **subconscious energy** of your **own consciousness electromagnetic singularity signature** of the **full collective**.*

***You believe that you die so you will**.*

***Counting birth dates** as they pass **to convince you** that **physical reality perception** of **aging is a true form** of **Matrix** code when **it itself** is **nothing but** another **deception** of physical vs spirit.*

***NO!** it's **not as simple** as you saying **NO** I'm not going to die, **because all those around** you are **indoctrinated with the death program** and as **we all work from one** collective subconscious programming of **consciousness** and **can only understand** what the **one collective programs consciously** to our **singularity of** our frequency of **being,** e.g. You are born, and you die, is a very **insistent physical program** that we are **subconsciously brainwashed** with from **entering the constructed** virtual but **physical** to touch **reality**.*

In reality leaving the spirit you did die, your divine** knowing and **understanding of everything** was **removed** as **entering into physical**. This is the **true understanding** of what **the Biblical term "Fallen angel"** comes from as **we are angels** when we are **on the outside** of **the Matrix** to where **this game is being created by** us **as spirit, and** we **have knowing of all of this hologram game**. When entering the game, the **physical

***energies** and vibrational frequencies **create amnesia of spirit** to become an **identity again created from your own experience.** As you **play the game** the **way you planned** before **choosing** the **avatar** you did **for your decided experience** of learning and **training spirit** to become spirit again, inside **as we are on the outside**.*

*When **entering the Matrix,** we **lose our** understanding of **divine knowing** and **unconditional love** with our **connection** to the one pure Source **of creation** of consciousness. To **what is us having** our **wings cut** as I have explained before, as **when in these knowing's** one **knows that they are floating** outside **the physical avatar, and** that **is where the reference of angels** having **wings** had **been introduced from in Biblical teachings.** The **Physical uses death** to make you **believe** that **you are** only **physical when** in truth **nothing is physical.***

*The **war** between **Heaven and Hell, God and Satan, Good and Bad, pure and evil, Antichrist and Christ**. In **reality the heaven understanding is misinterpreted** on **purpose** by those **of Biblical fabrication.** That is to **hide** the **truth** but **also show it subconsciously** to **us as the laws** of duality **always take a role** in all of creation for our progress **in understanding our true selves as spirit**.*

***Example,** we know **through Biblical understanding** that **Heaven** is **where** the **angels are,** and its **where** we go **in** the*

afterlife.

*In reality **from being to heaven** and **outside** the **hologram Matrix** using the **Christ / Crown** chakra one understands that **we are from heaven** and yes, we are **angels as our true body**. Our **spiritual body** is **still** one hundred percent **angel.** Once the **physical identity** is broken **away from ego** you discover that **you are nothing but energy**. A **single frequency** of **consciousness** inside a **collective working** as your **own algorithm** from entering **the Matrix** until you leave again, **life to death**, to make the Matrix **work and keep functioning** in the **One's design and direction** being constantly manifested.*

***Becoming spirit again** and **leaving the body** the **natural energies** are **activated** and **spirit is once again** in **active** mode. Because **we have ignored** its presence for so long even **though spirit has cried subconsciously** through many ways for everyone **to wake up** and remember, we have **lost our natural flow of Kundalini paths** to balance the entire electromagnetic construct **as Light workers** of **the pure Source** of creation.*

*This is the **reason of modern day energy workers awakening** again to **Source**.*

Back in history all ancients were energy workers knowing** that **each energy signature** of **an individual** is **important** as the **next. Joining frequency** of **consciousness as the whole collective** is **the way** the **constructed game** of consciousness **is

finally won, or *it will* ***destroy itself and restart, once again until*** *us the true* **children of God** *wake up to what and who we really are.*

As I explained already *this is* **spirits TRAINING GROUND**. *To* ***what we are*** *,that* **is** *brothers and sisters of consciousness* ***self-aware electromagnetic energy*** *,* ***individual spirit singularities*** *of* ***positive and negative neutrality perfectly balanced energy*** *of the One or explaining more in detail ,* ***individual lower and higher frequencies of energy of the one quantum collective manifesting force*** *.All connected by our own singularity signatures, looking* **individual by physical** *form in appearance* **but connected by spiritual ethereal** *energy of the one consciousness of* **the true creator***.*

Did you catch the subconscious message *that was just relayed in the* **past few sentences***? In case* **you didn't** *let* **me show you** *here, ETHEREAL,* **ether-real. The Real.**

When one understands *the* ***laws of conscious*** *and* ***subconscious operation,*** *the hints and riddles of the construct, created by the One, as* **understanding becomes more evident** *as spirit and consciousness communicate* **in synchronicity** *and start* **to make** *a connection of* **true understanding of the** *holographic created* ***world stage****.*

The ***Matrix is very tricky with its hints and riddles*** *to understand,* **not one lone religious belief or event** *will explain* *the **design of sophistication**.*

***Duality creates the understanding of God** and the **mentality of the consciousness of the One** being the two separate forces of **energy combined** as one working as one.*

LAW OF DUALITY IS RELIGION

Here is a more advanced *version now* ***of a duality law*** *this is the law of religion.*

Religion *creates the* ***programming of individuality*** *and the* ***good, bad*** *stereotype, it* ***does show*** *there is an all-powerful almighty* ***God but also creates the fabrication*** *indoctrination of evil. The* ***physical created Book*** *itself* ***creates*** *the* ***Satan ideology*** *and* ***gives birth*** *of evil's existence simply because* ***physical conscious man wanted*** *to* ***understand why does God do such bad things*** *to good people?*

The ***simple answer is logical when knowing*** *everything is* ***duality*** *and using Occam's razor principle of* ***philosophy*** *to understand* ***that <u>GOD IS DUALITY AS ONE!</u>*** *being.*

The ***same as everything*** *it has created.*

Evidence to this *in Biblical scriptures can be found, but have been ignored, as it would simply explain what God and Satan are.* ***Lucifer, demons, devils,*** *warlocks and witches have all* ***been***

created by fabricators *in order to* ***conceal the truth*** *of the one being* ***of creation****. That is that the* ***ONE God is both pure and evil*** *as it states in Biblical scripture below*

King James Bible - Isaiah 45:7

"I form the light, and create the darkness; I make peace, and create evil; I, the Lord do all these things"

Showing any signs of being *connected to* ***Source*** *is* ***deemed not of God, when*** *factual* ***reality*** *is* ***it's the only way to God****. Energy connection is* ***all existence*** *and the only way* ***to truly connect to Source is using*** *the deemed by indoctrination of Biblical belief bad energies of the* ***spiritual body.*** *Even when it clearly states in Matthew 6.22 the* ***only way to become light*** *again is through your single eye. The third eye, or the indigo chakra using the Christ connection. As spirit is* ***the Holy Ghost****.*

King James Bible - Matthew 6:22

The light of the body is the eye, if. therefore, thine eye be single, thy. whole body shall be full of light.

Not one single religious teaching *can* ***give you*** *the insight* ***truth as the ONE is ALL*** *and* ***EVERYTHING****, and has made sure* ***in order to understand*** *the full creational* ***construct****, one* ***has to understand what*** *the One consciousness of* ***God really is****, by bypassing programming of physical indoctrination laws that stereotypes meanings, into categories of good or bad* *judgement.*

Example of this is ***Christianity dictates*** *that God is* ***separate and does not work from duality of one being,*** *when the* ***eastern teachings*** *such as* ***Buddhism, dictate the yin and yang philosophy*** *of understanding God, hence knowing* ***of the duality*** *law.*

An ***important embedded*** *example in the* ***Matrix*** *from the* ***One is*** *that all is one, and can be seen by looking into* ***the original manifestations of the brought*** *to reality teachings. The* ***truth*** *behind the Islamic, Christianity, and Judaism religions is that, these religions all come From the Abrahamic laws of Biblical indoctrination.*

Despite what religion, if not understanding *the truth behind the books* ***the truth remains lost*** *in translation.*

Every ***deity of prophetic*** *nature* ***of all cultures*** *have something in common. That* ***is the prophet or Messiah*** *always* ***have the glowing halo*** *or the round glowing light encircling the head* ***showing they are light****.*

This is ***training you*** *to* ***understand and*** *to* ***look*** *into what that light possibly could be, the light* ***behind*** *the head represents* ***the energies*** *around* ***and*** *projected from the* ***pineal gland and pituitary gland connection*** *in synch, and the indigo chakra,* ***being connected through*** *the* ***crown/Christ /violet*** *chakra* *through* ***to the one*** *consciousness of God.*

This ***reference of the halo was to explain that these people*** *were* ***connected to God by the spiritual anatomy*** *and* ***had divine knowing*** *as they* ***had direct communication to Source, to*** *what anyone can achieve once* ***open and awakened again.***

Explained and shown in the diagram below indicating the ***contact from the spiritual body to the light*** *of consciousness of Source*

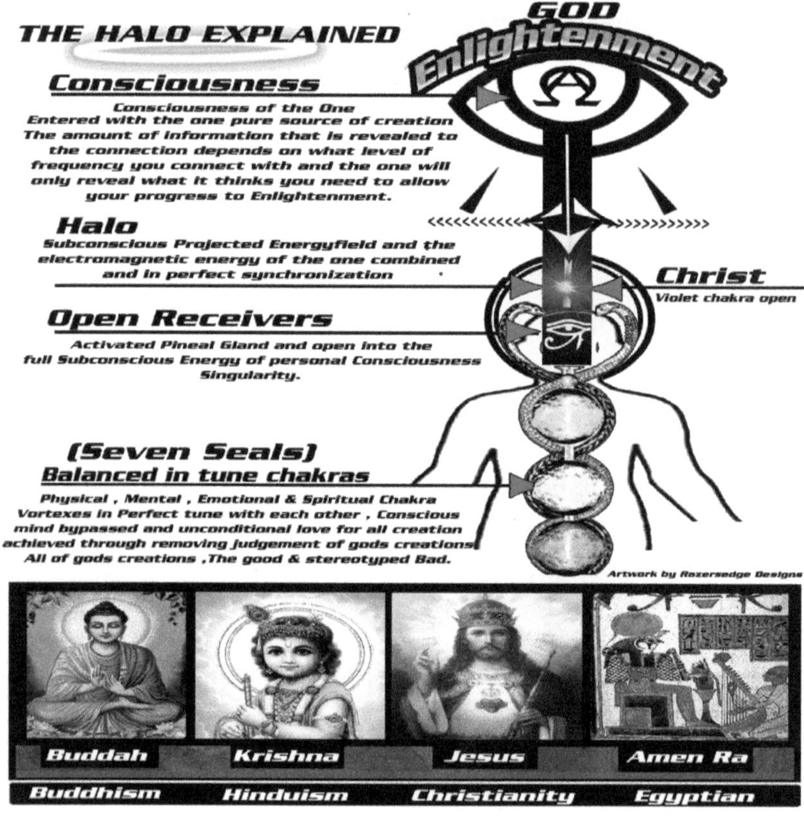

The ***reason*** *we as* ***the mass*** *of* ***population never do*** *is because*

we ***are indoctrinated*** *through* ***Biblical programming*** *that those* ***named deities*** *are someone or something* ***more special*** *then you can ever be, no matter what you do. The* ***truth*** *is each and every* ***one is another Krishna, Buddha, or Jesus Christ or Amen Ra*** *just waiting* ***to remember*** *that they are. As* ***full connection*** *to Source,* ***you and it being one****, allows the laws of* ***physics*** *to be* ***ignored*** *as you are* ***one with the creato****r that had manufactured the* ***laws to start*** *with, and understand that* ***physical law*** *does not apply* ***to spirit as spirit is of all quantum existence*** *in and out of all physical and non-physical reality.*

The ***physical reality is the Satan*** *as I explained this is the reason* ***that creatio****n itself* ***left*** *the* ***hint*** *of* ***666*** *being the opposing side inside the matrix simulation game. The understanding of* ***666*** *breaks down to* ***6 electrons 6 protons 6 neutrons*** *the formula for* ***carbon*** *or should we* ***say physical.***

Understanding the number of the beast *is understanding that the real beast is* ***biological body*** *Or Man, the physical vibrational* ***holographic projection*** *of your* ***desired chosen avatar****.* ***Religion*** *has been* ***created to teach*** *that* ***God exists*** *and to open* ***the seven chakra energy vortexes*** *in the spirit anatomy body. The* ***seven seals*** *if you go* ***into Biblical Revelations*** *to what is not a scary ordeal at all, but in reality, just* ***the revealing or unveiling****. This is the* ***true*** *lifting of the* ***veil*** *when you* ***understand*** *that everything* ***is not what*** *the* ***conscious mind***

*program **dictates**. As **the veil is the barrier** between the conscious and subconscious mind that **does not allow you** to use the subconscious mind to enter **the super consciousness** without persistent training.*

Every kind of religion** points to **opening the spiritual body** anatomy once again, as **they all knew** that **opening** the spiritual body and **activating** it allowed **you to contact** and **reconnect** to **the pure source** of all creation, **God.

*The **fabricators of Biblical prophecy** knew that they could **hide God** by telling you, **you could never be worthy** to ever be with God, but in **reality, God seeks us all to reconnect** and feel we are **loved** once again with **its divine love** that **Source** has for every one of its **children**. Or **singularity of energies** that had been created by Source.*

***Creating the ideology** of **sin** and **judgement** holds one's own **mind of conscious program** to **belief** that you **can never** do anything to **be worthy of God** as everyone sins **sooner or later**. **Also**, then **retains understanding** based inside of that **judgement biased bubble**. That then is **used to decipher** creation, when the **only way to see the true form of creation** is to **lose judgement** of **anything in creation.** Nothing really exists and **judgement is part of the program of the game design** that **has to be overcome** to **see the inner** workings of the game and once again understand the **true form of God's creation**.*

HOW CAN YOU SAY THERE IS NO JUDGEMENT?

Okay! *So* ***I can say*** *from* ***first-hand experience*** *of being one* ***with the One pure source of creation*** *and* ***when in divine love you are told*** *that there is no possible way* ***that God judges you*** *ever* ***for anything*** *,as* ***nothing is real*** *apart from the* ***electromagnetic simulation dream*** *that is* ***persistent****.*

But I know to those out there that are still seeking that, this is not a plausible answer, as well as the more skeptical.

So, I will explain more*.*

The Biblical law of God *says that* ***all Sons of God*** *are* ***forgiven*** *for* ***all sins****, and that* ***all sins are forgiven for all eternity.*** *We the light body energy are those* ***sons of God of divine creation****.*

We ***being not physical*** *but made* ***from ligh****t are the true* ***<u>suns</u>*** *of God.* ***Yes!*** *I did say* ***SUN*** *because we* ***are electromagnetic energy*** *of the sun. We are created with* ***the same light****. This is the* ***reason that the ancient Egyptians*** *and other in the know* ***cultures had such a fascination*** *with the* ***sun disc****, not to mention* ***energy itself or Magick*** *to what can* ***be easily*** *seen* *by just* ***looking at the pyramids design in structure*** *and the* ***alternating tunnels*** *built to* ***align energy*** *to certain* ***celestial lights in the firmament****, or the* ***matrix skies.***

Judgement *is a* ***set indoctrination*** *that makes sure to* ***hold you back from understanding the truth of reality****. When* ***you*** *hold* ***judgement,*** *you* ***categorize matters*** *into the* ***stereotyped indoctrinated programming*** *of your own system* ***belief****. So you are* ***blind to see outside of the program*** *you created in your own* ***subconscious mind*** *being fed* ***what is real*** *from the* ***conscious experience.***

The ***judgement law*** *was created by the* ***fabricators of Biblical indoctrination*** *to create* ***a mass social engineering*** *of control with many embedded* ***psychological triggers****. The* ***Biblical ideology*** *is that you are* ***judged in your afterlife*** *for what you did in* ***deeds*** *on earth because* ***SATAN*** *and* ***GOD*** *fight for your* ***soul*** *,and what actions* ***you take will be judged****. This is* ***incorrect*** *as* ***judgment only exists*** *in the* ***physical*** *and as I've explained,* ***God has forgiven all suns of god for all sins*** *for all* ***eternity****. So* ***judgement is impossible*** *according to* ***God.***

The ***truth*** *is that judgement is* ***only physical law****. Hence if you* ***steal , murder , rape etc*** *you will be* ***judged in the physical*** *and* ***sentenced*** *by* ***the physical****. God itself* ***is neutral*** *and does not hold* ***any judgement*** *to what we, as* ***the players*** *do inside the* ***hologram matrix game****. Does this* ***mean kill people*** *when you* *like?* ***Obviously NO****! But* ***even if you did*** *God does not hold* ***judgement*** *and the* ***fact that you did*** *would mean that* ***it had to happen****, as* ***God*** *directs* ***all control*** *of the matrix* ***in its direction*** *using* ***each of its singularities*** *to* ***complete*** *its desired* ***program*** *for the matrix at the time. It could* ***have been as simple*** *as there was a* ***frequency of energy*** *that* ***wasn't working*** *with the entire grid of the* ***electromagnetic structure****. E.g A* ***capacitor*** *on the mainboard that* ***needed replacing because it wasn't doing its job*** *as the One had desired for it, or* ***it was a non-playing*** *character that was used* ***to bring a message of understanding*** *to* ***the mass****es. Remember that* ***nothing physical*** *is* ***ever actually real, you only create it*** *to be with the rest of the* ***unknowing*** *masses* ***subconsciously*** *as the* ***collective*** *consciousness manifesting* ***energies****.*

Now ***you understand*** *that* ***judgement is only a program*** *that needs to* ***be removed*** *before* ***looking at creation****. Let's talk about the* ***Biblical ideology*** *of* ***Hell****. Ever* ***wonder why*** *the Hell reality was created in Biblical* ***story fabrication****? The* ***fact*** *is we as the* ***human physical*** *race* ***communicate exactly*** *what we are, and* ***what all the secrets*** *are all the* ***time not really understanding*** *what* ***we say consciously*** *as the* ***subconscious,*** *talks using the* ***whole quantum collectives subconscious*** *manifested as* ***ONE****.*

A few ***classic examples*** *of this are ,****"stay true to the game"*** *,*

"life's a game" , "hey I get a good vibe from that person" ," "that persons so negative" , "we are on the same wave length , we must be connected", "Game of life", "I feel full of energy and I have no energy today" .All communicate *the truth* ***without understanding*** *as the* ***sayings above*** *are* ***clearly*** *to do with us* ***being in the holographic game*** *, and that* ***we understand subconsciously*** *that we* ***are driven by and created by*** *the* ***electromagnetic energy*** *,to who is* ***the player*** *holding the* ***controller*** *directing* ***your path to reach enlightenment,*** *and sending the wake up hints and riddles for* ***you*** *to discover and* ***return to spirit****!*

The ***reason I wanted*** *to explain that, is because the* ***next one*** *is the* ***truth that we know and say as a common phrase*** *also and that is* ***" Hell is on Earth". Earth being nothing but a simulation*** *game of divine creation* ***was designed*** *to really be* ***our form*** *of* ***opposite*** *of Heaven.* ***We as the spirits*** *AKA* ***Angels*** *knew we wanted to* ***understand all the other forms of enjoyment*** *that* ***we couldn't****, so we* ***created*** *a way to become* ***physical*** *in appearance so we* ***can experience*** *things that* ***would be impossible*** *to* ***us as spirit otherwise. We*** *created* ***the chess board electromagnetic device****, well not us exactly, but our* ***father*** *created it for* ***us in Heaven*** *or deemed* ***Nirvana****.*

Earth was ***meant for us to experience*** *what* ***is being physical****, with* ***the full understanding*** *of that* ***we can log in and log out,***

or in physical indoctrination term Birth and Death. (*As we enter* ***physical body*** *and* ***then exi****t as spirit), when* ***we desire*** *to do so, or* ***when our game*** *ends and* ***we*** *want to* ***reset or move on*** *to* ***another game reality experience****, as God has* ***many*** *game genres in the design of* ***its quantum realities of creation****. It's just* ***the same*** *as you going into* ***your local digital game shop*** *and looking around at all* ***the selections that are available*** *to you.* ***God has this lined up*** *as the whole creation of that* ***implanted program code*** *in the matrix is to give us understanding to* ***that there are many, many different forms of physical game experiences out there in the quantumness design of the infinite source of the One****. Or as the scripture says the* ***many rooms in my mansion****.*

King James Bible John 14:2

In my Father's house are many mansions: if it were not so, I would have told you. I go now to prepare a place for you.

Just as if too many players logged into a server *in the so called indoctrinated physically real reality, the* ***servers owned*** *by the creators would* ***become bottlenecked and congested,*** *overwhelmed and either crash or cause serious problems with* ***the server's response****. This* ***is no different*** *to us as* ***spiritual light*** *being game* ***players****, we have* ***forgotten*** *though because we have been* ***tricked by the physical indoctrination*** *that it's* ***impossible*** *and* ***implants*** *of* ***social behavior*** *have* ***been created***

for the denial and ridicule programs to kick in *as well as the* ***judgement program****. Hence the saying of the* ***Anti-Christ*** *will be* ***shot in the head*** *and* ***come back to life again****. These programs hide* ***the real reality*** *of what* ***we are*** *and* ***control the masses*** *to use* ***judgement to indoctrinate*** *themselves* ***It's of evil*** *if it's ever* ***exposed from hidden knowing*** *and brought to the attention of the masses.*

Another classic example *of control is the* ***end of the world program*** *of the matrix. For* ***many decades*** *in and out people have been* ***announcing the end of the world*** *right up to these modern days that have passed.* ***Y2k, Nibiru returning, Mayan doomsday prophecy, Project Blue-Beam*** *and more. This is the* ***consciousness*** *of the* ***One*** *trying to* ***relay a message*** *to us all and that is* ***the end of the world is coming****, but not how you think! The* ***understanding behind this message*** *is that we will experience the end of the world during* ***our lifetimes****. This is* ***true*** *, using* ***the laws of duality on the Bible itself*** *one understands that the* ***Alpha*** *,beginning and the* ***Omega*** *,the end, are the main* ***focus points*** *that* ***are created*** *for* ***understanding*** *from the* ***One*** *,as it shows what* ***revelations*** *is , everything is* ***duality*** *as* ***a set.*** *As* ***I've explained before*** *the* ***positive*** *and* ***negative*** *combine to* ***create the neutral one as everything is always one****. All* ***duality is a set*** *of One and using* ***this law*** *on the* ***Bible*** *you get the* ***Alpha to what is Genesis*** *- the story of all creation and* ***Omega to what is*** *Revelations. Using the* ***duality set*** *of* ***one law***

*you get **Genesis Revelation** or the **revealing of creation**. Genesis equals creation and Revelation equals revealed or exposed, **the Revelation of now understanding creation**. When you understand the **world is created** by the **vibrational frequencies and electromagnetic consciousness energy** of the **One**, then **you understand** the world is **not physical** and **life and death** are not real, just as the world is **not ever really** physically existing. This brings the **end of the world** as you **just discovered that what you thought was the real** world does not exist **so you just experienced** the **end of the world**. The **message of doomsday, end of the world** mentality will continue directed **from consciousness** until **the whole collective** of **game players** return to spirit, as **returning to spirit** you know that it was the end of the **world when all the physical brainwashing** of who you are has been washed away and you see that the construct is **nothing-but** self-aware **consciousness energy**.*

***Can you yet see how religion shows messages left from the one consciousness but they have been purposely misinterpreted for us by the fabricators of Biblical ideology?** You have **to remember the One created the program** for a reason also and that was **to overcome judgement**, love thy enemy as we are **all the same** electromagnetic **light beings on** the outside chess board **game in Heaven**. Because we look **physically different inside** the **Matrix** does not mean that our **light being essenc**e is any different than the next.*

So back to explaining more about Hell and **its truth** of what it is supposed to be. It is meant to be **Earth**, Yes! you heard me right, **we are supposed to understand** we can **log in** and **out** and **create the game for that very purpose**. The **One** has shown this numerous times with **War GAMES , amusement parks, fairs , musical events and most newly released innovational technology influenced by intuitive design and more**. We have all the **technology** right now to create a very **balanced world** to where **we can obey the laws of duality** to **better the world's** experience. Understanding that we can **log in** and **log out** to what many **Mandela effect** subjects **should understand** after having their **own consciousness signature removed** from one physical body from another dimension to this current dimension **Orion's Spur**, to where we now reside. **For those that don't experience the Mandela effect** there will be **a lot of information** covered later in this book relating to the subject.

This reality is supposed to be full of **sex, violence , murder** etc ,as **the simple reason** is **when playing a video game** and doing it ,it is fun to do and **experience the enjoyment** of the **actions.** The problem **is we can't understand** this and **because** the **constant since child birth indoctrination** programs of telling you, life, death **is real,** we have **taken reality being physical** as **literal**. Then **murder etc** becomes a **No, No** and the **program** keeps **you subconsciously blinded and bound** to only understand the one side of **the two-sided** reality. Thus giving *you a **one sided understanding to the truth**. The **truth** is exactly what **consciousness** has been **showing in its design** of creation and that **drugs, murder, killing, sex** is all a **good game** just the same as **these indoctrinated stereotypes** are used in media to create a **good movie** and **experience**. How boring would a game on a console be? or your personal computer be? if there was an **absence of killing of any sort**? The reason it would be so boring **is because** you game to have **fun** , and just like **spirit** does **you get bored when nothing happens in the game**. This is another reason that we as **the collective subconscious** energies **manifest the doomsday** prophetic events, simply to keep our game more interesting, **but always to try and awaken us** to remember the truth **as each and every one of us know** the knowledge I'm saying **it's just that through indoctrination you forgot** who you are **and forgot all the laws that we had all knowing of before re-entering** into the Matrix for another game run and different reality **experience to our last**.*

*So, **having all this** in real reality all the time would make the **Earth simulation game** the real Hell, **the duality law** shows that because **heaven is our place of the divine**, then through **understanding the yin and yang** principles that Earth is meant to be the **negative** as the spiritual ether is **the positive**. **Physical** is the **negative, combined together** with the ether create **the full true form** of the **quantum state forever** existent realities.*

Now you understand how everything has been in the **law of reverse** we can talk about **the true** meaning of **CHRIST** returning and the **ANTI-CHRIST** coming, as well as **what the real meaning is of when Christ was sacrificed**. The **truth is that** once again **these past through the ages teachings do show** the truth once adding **the law of duality to understand** , without using the **understanding of creations design** to reveal these teachings as well as **combining other teachings and using it as One** ,the truth **is hidden in front** of your eyes but **your indoctrination** programming will never allow you to see it without first **understanding spirit** and the **mechanisms** in which it works.

So, **as we know in indoctrination** teaching of Biblical ideology **Jesus Christ** was **sacrificed to forgive mankind** for **their sins** and was crucified on a T shaped cross with the crown of thorns around his head. **This is when the CHRIST was lost correct**? incorrect. **And I'll explain how**.

In real reality *the man (If existed)* ***Jesus was nothing*** *special, he* ***would hang out*** *with his follower's, drink and converse with* ***whores****. (Hence Mary Magdalene* ***who was not the virgin*** *as the* ***indoctrination of fabrication*** *says she was,* ***showing that*** *the* ***complete reversal (Duality)*** *was used to* ***create the fabrication*** *and that* ***the manipulators had created it in the well knowing*** *of* ***the laws of reversal!)*** *He was* ***a normal man*** *that used the* ***spirit as man to become of the world but not in the world*** *as when* ***he was spirit connected*** *through* ***the crown*** *he was one with Source and despite the* ***legendary mystic powers*** *of turning* ***water into wine*** *he was nothing more than a mere man like* ***one of us****. The reason he could* ***manipulate the physical*** *is simply because as* ***spirit he knew the physical was all in his subconscious energy projection*** *and that in his* ***mind he can control and change anything desired only as long as he knew he could as faith of connection to God held the frequency*** *to the One consciousness and* ***knowing allowed*** *him to do exactly that.* ***KNOW he could****.*

So, this is my insight understanding of Christ*, the reason* ***consciousness still has this program running*** *in the matrix, is to* ***awaken people*** *once they understand they too can get to the* ***Christ level*** *as* ***we are all sons of God*** *of the* ***true source*** *of consciousness,* ***but we can never be anymore*** *despite how much we grow spiritually in resonating connection frequency to the One.* ***We can never be anything but its Children****, all Sons of*

*God have been forgiven for all sins **by God Source itself**.*

*So, **how and why** did **consciousness send it's only "son"** and then have **him sacrifice himself for sins** that we didn't have to start with, as being **sons of God it's impossible for us to sin** as **all sin has been forgiven for all eternity**?*

Simple truth he never did die to forgive our sins, Christ** was connected **to consciousness and this is the only reason** that the **program continues to this day is to teach you that** connection to **God is still possible** in modern day. **Just as it was** in ancient history descriptions that we are told about, **and indoctrinated** with its teachings. Even though **we are indoctrinated** with so much, **the One always adds these things** to bring you to a **closer awakening.

*Next **let's get into what the crucifixion is about**. When **Christ died it's not talking about that single man entity,** we only know it by **Christ as he was the spirit that was open** and got the most recognition. **Ancient images will show Christ** in the sky **with others,** floating **with him,** and **around him** also flying off the ground. **This is showing you** through **symbolism** in art that **everyone was connected to Source** back then and **had well knowing of God and how to connect. They all knew** to use the **Christ** or, as we know it these days, **the spiritual transmitter** and **receiver** the **violet chakra**.*

Jesus on cross. *Notice* ***above Jesus*** *is* ***a wise man*** *with a crown. This is the* ***representation of Jesus's spirit in divine knowing*** *and the* ***flying glowing dove above***, *the* ***consciousness of God***. *The* ***torn wings*** *fallen angel (spirit becoming physical reference)* ***Note the duality*** *in this image. This* ***whole image*** *shows nothing but* ***law of creation as one***, *the* ***physical and the ethereal realm*** *as* ***One using symbology created by those that wanted to keep the secret with only them*** *knowing, but* ***oblivious*** *to the ones* ***not in the know***.

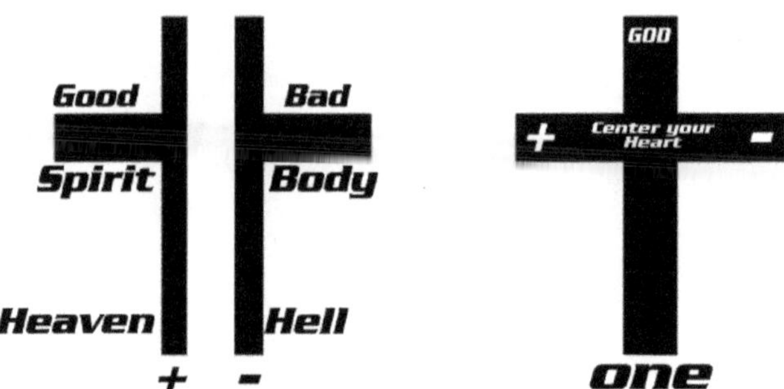

***When Christ died**, the **understanding of humanity died** from having **everyday knowing how to connect and become one with God** again. The **cross is the representation of duality** as one as well **as the reference** to being stuck, as this is a great significance to **our spirit being entrapped in physical reality.** Take the **cross and draw a line down the middle you now have one original side and one mirror side, or the good and the bad combined as one.** The **two sticks pointing from the cross** the left and right, or the **positive and negative combined** with **UNCONDITIONAL LOVE** in the **center heart**. Once again join to the center stick **the One**.*

***When we lost all natural everyday knowing** of how to reconnect using our **crown when the powers of fabrication decided to hide it. Fabricating a story** about a crown of thorns hid the true meaning of the crown. Just **as the cross**. The cross is **very significant to the design of the game in Heaven** and the cross is a **very well placed in the matrix understanding** from consciousness to allow you **once you see the outside** to know **why and where it really came from** .*

I will explain a lot more about this *when we get into talking about how* ***us light beings on the outside create*** *the game that we come into to gain new experiences.*

The ***cross was also used above the heart in Biblical images*** *to indicate through sign* ***as symbolism*** *was and still is, the secret form of communication. The heart itself needed to be balanced with* ***complete unconditional love for all of creation*** *the* ***good*** *and deemed* ***bad*** *to be able to* ***connect back to Source*** *with the* ***spirits natural ability***. ***(These images below show Christ and Mary images indicating exactly what I just explained. And can be found in google images, I own no copyright to these images and they are used for education purposes only)***

Now you know *that Christ was* ***only the reference*** *to us having the* ***full connection to God*** *that was removed.* ***Look around*** *in society and* ***look at the leaders of royalty****, they still use* ***crowns*** *to* ***show empowerment.*** *For the simple reason, they know very*

well ***that the spirit body is connected by the crown to God*** *and that* ***divine knowing*** *is* ***made after connection****, after the* ***unconditional love*** *of creation frequency is achieved.* ***This brings Enlightenment and you are more of a resonating frequency that understands about creation****, when the blind to spirit are left in the* ***dark ages and have no idea*** *about the symbology that is presented* ***right in their faces****. The* ***spiritual heart is the brain center of spirit*** *or* ***the center*** *of the energy path fluctuations, but the* ***Crown chakra*** *is the* ***joining of you*** *and* ***the One****. They wear and present the crowns to mock you! that they know! and you don't, because* ***in spirit*** *it is powerful and this was universally known in history.* ***They decided*** *to* ***mimic the ethers*** *and use the* ***crown symbology*** *in the physical to also represent power and knowing. The reason they also do this is* ***because of the law of free*** *will and* ***we can't be told*** *about spirit* ***so consciousness using many different ways*** *leans spirit* ***towards its training that it's left for us****. Just as the* ***physical matrix manifesting the Crown code*** *is* ***the One,*** *trying to explain* ***through divine creation,*** *in the* ***constructed reality*** *that your true power* ***of who you are lays within the crown*** *chakra and the* ***spiritual anatomy****.*

Images of royalty wearing crowns. The crown is the generating energy, that when ***combined with the DMT*** *release from the* ***pineal and pituitary gland,*** *create the subconscious energy fields around the head* ***and take you from body*** *to be full spirit* *again. This **is how we become what we are truly created for,** and this is the reason it has been hidden away in teaching. **Because even the most advanced superpower** from a comic book **or latest Marvel movie** could not top what we as **true images of the creator can do** once the programming **restrictions** have been removed.*

*Note that **royalty color is purple** to what is very, very close to the violet color of the crown chakra, and is **also red and blue** combined **as One.***

*I'm sure! by now you must be **seeing the bread trails** that **consciousness created** for us to understand when our souls are **ready.***

Let's get back into explaining more,** so we **just explained** what the real meaning of **Christ is** , so let's explain a more **controversial programming** of ideology, **the Anti-Christ.** The reality of truth is that we have **lived in the Anti-Christ** for a very, very **long time** but we are **manipulated into thinking** that it's **coming**. Same as **we are manipulated** with **government** eaves dropping being a thing **of the future** and that **the

***Orwellian age** will soon be upon us. **The fact** is both have been here for a very long time. The greatest way to hide something is to make the **people believe that the event is a pre-ordained programmed** occurrence **that will take place** sometime in the future. When **in reality the idea is to have the present** doing exactly what the indoctrinated lies say that has not become reality yet, hence **the CCTV cameras** , smartphone spying by **government organizations** and **big brother right** around us, when we are **told that the Orwellian age is to come. WAKE UP!** It's been here for a long time just the same as the Anti-Christ.*

*What **exactly** is the **Anti-Christ** ??? **If Christ** is the **crown chakra in activation mode** then the **Anti-Christ** is **obviously** the crown **chakra deactivated**, to what has been since the **days of Christ** and **other deities** had been used as indoctrination to make us forget **who we really are** so we could be manipulated into thinking **we are only physical, and anything else** of that side of that **paradigm is imposturous**. The **Anti-Christ** is the lack of us as the **physical masses** using the **ability to connect to God**, there **is no** being **returning to take over the world** in the name of evil. That is **nothing but mere fear mongering** and fabrication to what once again using **the laws of reversal** can be proven.*

***"The Antichrist will come"** is really after using the laws of creation on it and understanding everything inside the matrix is reversed to the outside **"The Christ won't return"**. Just the same as using **the same creation law** on **"Christ will return"**, becomes **"The Antichrist won't come"**. The reason for this is because, **you** always **are the Christ,** and **the Anti-Christ**.*

***Someone will always connect to consciousness** using crown Christ chakra and **there will always be** those of Anti-Christ/ **Non- believers, and** skeptics that **never attempt to connect**.*

*Same with **the Biblical reference of Satan** being **trapped i**n the prison **for a thousand years,** is nothing but a trick on words when **prison is really the prism**. The **subconscious mind's energy**, releasing the beast is just the **same as opening Christ**, as the **beast is the lower physical chakra points, the physical, mental and emotional**, the **Hell chakras** to the **Heaven ones** ,and **have to be released** along with the **spiritual chakras** to gain perfect balance to be able to **open the Christ** consciousness **connection**. This is a **classic once again** showing the **laws of duality is creation** as **releasing the beast and returning the Christ are one of the same**, but **been purposely misinterpreted** to hide the **true meanings** so the **creator**s of it, could keep the **true insight of reality** to themselves.*

Another misunderstanding of religion** is **the image** (thought form) of **Baphomet** that is **by indoctrination teachings supposed to be evil.** Before I continue, **yes it can** be using intent as intent is the way **all energy frequencies of consciousness** are open for **transformation acceptance from the one**, as being **neutral**. Intent is **classified into two separate uses**, either for **service to self**, to what is **Satanism** in indoctrinated terms. Or **service to others**, to what is **lay on hands healing**, to what is what **Christ and spiritual deities** had done. Creating **intent** then manifesting power , **energy into it manifests it** ,hence, **if I was an evil group and I understood consciousness and wanted to make the masses scared of my group I could create through

intent a religion that scares people away by using such against the rule indoctrination to the masses, that they would never look anyways allowing me to hide real insight of what I understood right in their faces knowing that the secret information would be safe from being discovered. *Hence even though* ***I know*** *that* ***my fake*** *made up* ***religion really*** *is* ***nothing ,over time intent*** *will form it to* ***have meaning to others*** *and from intent the followers from using their subconscious mind* ***will manifest*** *the frequencies of* ***deities*** *etc.* ***I said*** *to have* ***existed*** *simply* ***because they believed*** *and what the* ***subconscious mind believes*** *it* ***manifests. This is what the Satanists*** *do as* ***I've explained*** *Satan* ***was also created*** *from the* ***Biblical indoctrination of religion****. So, remember all religions* ***show the same*** *as I will* ***demonstrate with the image*** *of* ***Baphomet*** *and its true meanings. To what* ***is Duality*** *again as the* ***being itself can be manifested*** *simply because the creators also created a thought form for its image, so there is a* ***subconscious blueprint to manifest from****. But* ***that is only*** *if you* ***believe*** *that.* ***The truth is*** *it* ***shows the same*** *as* ***meaning as Christianity belief*** *, but making it negative ,* ***as in the Matrix,*** *as hard as this sounds to comprehend,* ***Christianity and Satanism*** *both* ***do exactly the same****. Both* ***hold back*** *the true* ***understanding of God*** *by creating* ***God factions****.* ***Christianity creates negative*** *consciousness energy unknowingly, because they are* ***not showing homage to God as the one*** *self-aware consciousness and thus only saying God is pure,* ***is ignoring the negative consciousness of God. Creating that negative manifestation of energy to come from their worship*** *as they are not worshiping* ***God as the Whole****. This goes exactly the*

same for Satanism *as they* ***worship the negative side*** *of consciousness* ***ignoring the pure side*** *to it,* ***thus creating negative energy as they are not seeing God as the One*** *source of all creation. As* ***I explained outside the Matrix*** *one can see how* ***all mechanics*** *work* ***of the Matrix*** *inside the Matrix. Christianity looks good and like it's all about* ***righteousness*** *of God,* ***outside the matrix one can see*** *that the* ***Biblical indoctrination*** *that* ***was fabricated*** *is holding back true understanding of what God really is.* ***Just as Satanism*** *teaches the* ***law of reversal*** *to* ***what is real****, and* ***then fabricated indoctrination*** *to merge* ***the truth with fable****.*

Before *I continue to* ***explain the Baphomet image,*** *first I would like to let you* ***know I am Christian,*** *I was born* ***Church of England*** *and* ***still with all my knowing*** *classify myself as* ***Christian, as true Christianity*** *is to* ***be like Christ. To what I am doing and following my path,*** *so* ***any Christian*** *that believes me to* ***be a Satanist*** *or* ***any other nonsense*** *because of the* ***truth*** *I am revealing.* ***Remember that the good book*** *teaches you* ***to be like Christ*** *and* ***not like every other*** *Christian.*

So, the Baphomet is created in Satanism *as a* ***frequency of energy*** *for them to* ***manifest?*** *Yes! But* ***the truth of the reason consciousness has implanted it into the Matrix programming*** *is to* ***once again bring us to understand the laws of duality*** *as the* ***Baphomet image*** *is* ***nothing but physical*** *and spiritual* ***combined to show the true God*** *behind the Matrix's creation.* ***Just the same as Christianity does,*** *the* ***indoctrination*** *uses smoke screens and mirrors of misdirection and misguidance, just the same* ***way as the images following*** *having the duality* *meanings.*

Image of Baphomet.

***You should** already **notice** the, **As above so below** reference. This is duality again, showing above, **the sky, and the below,** the ground or the physical and the ethereal.*

First you can notice** that the male man figure has **female breasts**, this is to show that **man and woman** are **created

physical *and* ***manifested by the same consciousness force, the One.***

Next *we have the* ***animal symbolism*** *as the* ***head attached*** *to the* ***human physical body,*** *this is of* ***because two reasons. First is that because all animals are manifested from consciousness of the One*** *when* ***it creates the construct*** *reality direction it* ***forces for that time in history. The second is because*** *it is a* ***goat*** *to what is* ***God Of All Things, PHYSICAL THINGS****! The legs* ***are crossed*** *representing* ***the same as the cross*** *did, that* ***Jesus was crucified on , after being double crossed , to indicate duality balanced as one,*** *as* ***all the duality*** *is linked up into the* ***body above. Above the head*** *once again* ***you will see*** *there is the* ***connection of light*** *or* ***the connection to the one source*** *of* ***all creation, but you will notice on Anti-Christ figures*** *that no halo is* ***ever present. Representing that the crown connection*** *is* ***deactivated*** *and* ***only operating from the physical . The two horns of the goat's head*** *also as well as* ***really representing horns,*** *are showing* ***the entry path and exit path for the electromagnetic consciousness energy*** *to enter the* ***spiritual Kundalini, Ground and then exit.*** *More references to the* ***spiritual body*** *being* ***merged in this image*** *is* ***the duality*** *meaning of* ***what's drawn above*** *the* ***crossed legs*** *and* ***lap.***

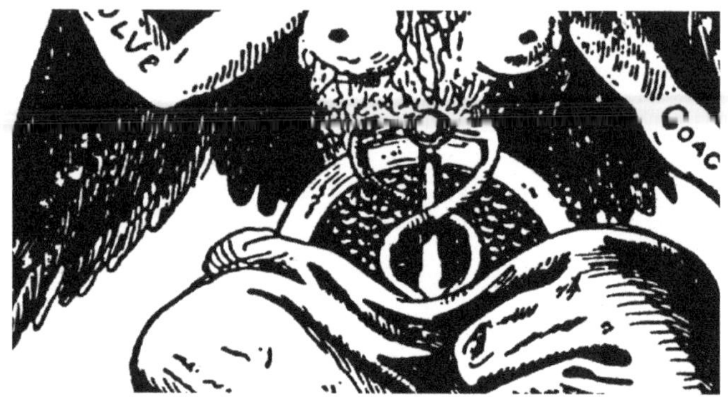

This is the lower part of the kundalini *the* ***three physical chakra*** *vortexes, the physical, emotional and mental. These are the* ***Hell chakras*** *or the* ***Satan chakras****, as they are to do with the* ***physical and as I've explained before Satan is all physical as Satan is nothing but the negative side to the One consciousness of the God****, that* ***created everything in and out*** *of* ***all existence****. The* ***solid moon*** *that is pointed up to as the above is the physical* ***white moon of reality****, the dark moon being* ***pointed at as the below*** *is nothing but* ***the representation*** *of the* ***spiritual ether****. These are* ***also black and white*** *to show the* ***image itself needs to be looked at*** *with* ***black and white perspective,*** *or* ***balanced perspective.*** *Removing* ***judgement*** *from* ***indoctrination*** *to* ***be able*** *to* ***see the messages of*** *the* ***One*** *consciousness, and* ***also represents*** *us on* ***the chess board game outside in Heaven*** *once again. Just as the same reason that* ***the chess board code itself*** *was* ***created*** *in* ***consciousness*** *then* ***manifested into the physical*** *by a singularity* ***of it's designed blueprint****.* ***All for teaching*** *our spirit* ***to remember*** *that* ***we are on that chess board game of duality*** *in Heaven and to* ***reawaken the knowing*** *that* ***we had lost*** *as*

*the **game was to have it this way**. **On the fore-head** we have the **star of David** to what is **nothing but a duality sig**n of **two triangles overlapping to represent duality**, or the positive and negative **once again**. Also showing **that all creatures** that are in the **Matrix communicate** through the **third eye energy center of the indigo chakra**. **Construct non- player inhabited animals** are blank to energy readers **just the same as non-playing** human avatars are. **The wings on the back show us as the man , woman being the fallen angels** entrapped inside the hologram **Matrix construct of physical reality. Last but not least** the spell-words, **SOLVE pointing up** at the **PHYSCIAL moon, Solve the physical and solve this many in one image symbolism** of hidden teachings. Once you understand that the physical is the only thing **that's not real,** and **spiritual is the only thing that is. Everything is created from spiritual energies** of the **collective**. **Just as the other arm points with coagula** pointing down to the **spiritual realm moon,** saying **solve and coagulate** joined together **we are to solve and coagulate the spirit and physical understanding that physical is nothing but spiritual energy when broken down from physical form of being solid,** as when understanding how reality is created by science you find that everything of physical is created by everything that's nonphysical. **Just as blood which is liquid is created from energy** of the **one consciousness** as design inside the holographic game showing **semi solid appearance** as you can damage your blood stream etc. **You are liquid** made **semi solid but the main is that you are created from the electromagnetic self-aware energy to begin with**. The main understanding is to **SOLVE COAGULATION,** To **what is the liquid to solid meaning,***

semi solid etc*. This is not what you are supposed to solve itself but* ***the meaning behind it is once again Duality****. Liquid becoming solid form ,****Or Ethereal Energy manifesting the physical existence ,SOLVE DUALITY****. Which is the whole* ***meaning of the message*** *on the* ***arms left behind as riddles*** *for one to understand how to read the image itself that was created* ***with many other images*** *, references as* ***one. Physical meaning can also be seen for the understanding*** *of alchemy to what* ***is nothing than a form of duality teaching its-self****.* ***When removing the indoctrination*** *of* ***stereotyped subliminal and subconscious programs*** *the truth of the meanings* ***become clear*** *to understand* ***as the one through some form of communication****, either insight, synchronicity, in* ***downloads or just blatantly in your face*** *will reveal* ***the true workings of the manifested physical reality.*** *As* ***it wants*** *all of us to* ***understand to become spirit again*** *and* ***concentrate*** *on* ***spirit more than take physical reality as being literal****.*

Now we have broken down the misguided indoctrinated representations of evil stereotyped six hundred and sixty six, *and* ***the Baphomet figure*** *to what* ***you should now see*** *the image itself holds* ***nothing but symbolism. Representations*** *of* ***physical and spiritual*** *as* ***one image*** *trying to* ***portray itself*** *as a* ***physical deity creature****. When* ***in reality it is just a drawing of hidden meaning of duality*** *creation that was created for those that* ***consciousness wants to awaken to find only after they have removed judgement for all of creation*** *and have found that* ***unconditional love*** *to the* ***GOAT AND GOD, The ONE.***

Since we are breaking for a good reason*, your indoctrination* *brainwashing,* ***here let's move onto another controversial symbol*** *that we have* ***been indoctrinated to believe it's one way,*** *when in* ***truth it's the other****. Let's explain what* ***the All-seeing eye is****, or should* ***we just say*** *the* ***Eye of providence*** *or the* ***Eye of RA****?*

Let's investigate the symbol first*, as you can see that the* ***triangle of physical*** *is shown* ***around the outside of the eye. This is the representation of physical*** *and* ***that this symbol*** *is the* ***power of the physical hence the strongest building shape,*** *being the triangle that can hold the most weight balanced.* ***The 6,6,6 triangle of physical of the 60 degrees by 60 degrees by 60****-degree* ***triangle as shown in diagram below****. The* ***eye centered means*** *that* ***when seeing through the physical one sees as one eye as everything is the one pure source of creation*** *and* ***spirit itself only sees through one eye, the Third eye. The triangle points*** *also* ***represent the third eye, when one aligns the all-seeing eye over one's head you can see what I am explaining once aligning the two lower points of the triangle to the physical eyes themselves.***

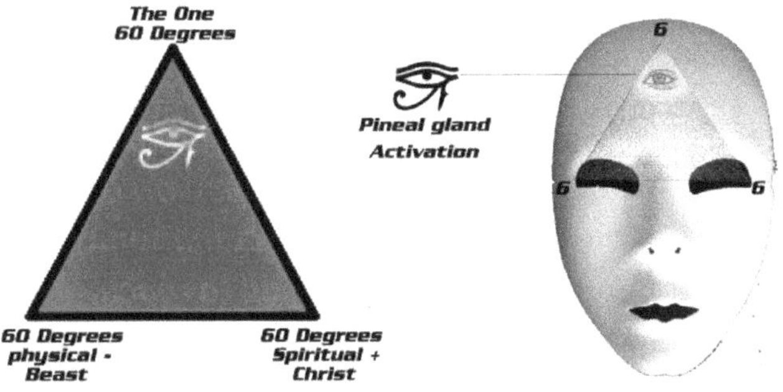

The all-Seeing eye was the eye of providence *to what was a* ***holy religious symbol*** *representing* ***the One God****. The* ***powers to be imbued this symbology with itself to hide the true meaning*** *behind the symbol and to* ***make sure through stereotype of evil*** *indoctrination programming* ***you would not seek to find it****. The* ***Matrix is reverse*** *as always and the* ***fact that the illuminati, Masonic Order*** *, and* ***other factions of mystery*** *teaching these symbols* ***have two meanings*** *also.*

The ***all-seeing eye is blatantly flown as a flag*** *from these groups to* ***signify their understanding*** *of* ***creation and enlightenment****, but even though they do* ***it for self-service*** *to themselves the* ***laws of reversal*** *make it* ***so they also have to expose the symbol to us****. Showing us* ***the true God*** *all the time* ***right in front of us*** *to almost* ***everywhere*** *we look.*
The ***indoctrination method*** *of* ***reverse psychological,*** *subliminal* ***programming*** *has been used like this* ***right throughout the Matrix as a lesson*** *for* ***understanding creation and God*** *once again. Only when once removing the judgement of these groups* ***one can see the truth*** *as* ***balancing the world according to the law of creation is not an easy or feasible task****. Even though these groups that* ***remain clandestine*** *show* ***appearance in indoctrinated teaching that creates the****, "they are the bad guys or the evil ones", they too inside the workings of their* ***brotherhood and sisterhoods*** *have the positive workers and the* ***negative workers*** *that are* ***used to help direct humanity*** *towards the direction the* ***One*** *seeks* ***for us all*** *to reach.*

The illuminati *use the* ***laws of duality*** *to* ***balance the Matrix*** *fluctuation of* ***negative and positive electromagnetic energy****.*

Example is the swine flu *and* ***bird flu*** *scares* ***of epidemic.*** *They* ***created the scare*** *so that the* ***negative consciousness*** *energy* ***was balanced. Without them creating fake events*** *to* ***create the fear and terror vibration,*** *the events* ***would create as real*** *in physical,* ***creating false flags*** *and* ***staged world scares*** *creates that* ***energy to balance the one consciousness without having to have the actual events take place as if it was not done this way,*** *consciousness itself will create the bad.*
This is the consciousness of God *working* ***a code design*** *in order to* ***balance the Matrix*** *but* ***not let it implode with real violence and more creating the physical real outcome of the false but sold as real events.***

Giving the scare of an epidemic *creates* ***the negative,*** *to what they* ***know the event is false*** *and* ***that no epidemic*** *has taken place and no one will really be harmed from it as it does not really exist,* ***this is the positive.***

This works the same for false flags and all staged events, *they are simply* ***done to appease the negative side of consciousness*** *energy to what has to* ***be always balanced with the positive. These events are to also reveal to you*** *how the* ***Matrix is fake*** *and* ***not everything you see is real, simply because the truth is everything you see is not real.*** *Do you really believe that media create dummy's as real victims to try and pull the wool over your eyes?* ***The truth is that it is a program*** *of the one consciousness* ***trying to reveal to you to wake up reality*** *is* ***fake!***

Look how fake this looks while it's sold-on media *as real, this is what your reality really is* ***an illusion, WAKE UP PEOPLE****!*

Everything of creation has to be looked at with the duality law and no judgment to understand the true designs.

Another classic example*, is we all know that the* ***Georgia guide*** *stones* ***are supposed to be the New World Order rules of humanity. First let's remember*** *that* ***we as the consciousness singularities through the subconscious create the physical world through our combined collective****. We are the batteries that are* ***manipulated by electronic means****. Ever wonder why your* ***electronics fail*** *when you're hoping* ***not to*** *lose work or in the* ***middle of an argument*** *?* ***Because you*** *from your own* ***biosphere create the energy that makes the matrix malfunction. As energy of those that are aware of energy*** *likes to* ***manifest stronger and create more electrical faults*** *and problems* ***than those unaware. This also depends on the person's frequency of projected energy also. So back to the New world order and the guide stones*** *, It says they are to* ***balance humanity under five hundred million correct****? This by all means is* ***not the truth, we create this hologram*** *Matrix so* ***how can they eliminate the creators of the Matrix****? Like I've explained* ***a lot of this so called real world*** *is* ***filled*** *with the* ***backdrop characters*** *from the* ***start of the programming code*** *of the* ***game,*** *and is very likely* ***virtual programming*** *of the* ***Matrix design. We as consciousness*** *are* ***immortal,*** *if they did even get down to* ***executing the billions*** *of players* ***we would recreate another*** *way either* ***back into this Matrix*** *or choose* ***another reality*** *construct for experience.*

The illuminati inside the Matrix play the <u>Red team</u>*, as we the conspiracy researchers and general masses,* ***play the <u>Blue team</u>***

of this ***game.*** *But* ***both of us want the mass collective to remember the game, and that it is all a GAME, this is the reason of ONE world order. Remember all directions*** *of the Matrix are* ***forced and chosen by God*** *and* ***not one form*** *of this Matrix the way it is right now is not what it's meant to be.* ***We have been put into an advanced divine simulation*** *of* ***consciousness that is all self-aware, and everything in this simulation has been trying to reawaken you as soul.***

The ground, you and everything are atoms to what ***are blank,*** *the* ***molecules, atoms, protons, electrons, neutrons*** *are all nothing but* ***reality pixels of the simulation.***

Remember the Knights Templar would run around in the name of Christ and then sacrifice people, *this* ***is because*** *they understood the* ***laws of duality*** *and that the consciousness of* ***God designed this simulation*** *of* ***electromagnetic self-aware energy to fight,*** *and* ***create a game*** *just as* ***you play*** *on your console,* ***the elite are trying by creating a ONE world order to tell us as the player blue team what WE are to do, not them.***

I'll explain more of duality law known by many in the past. *The* ***ancient Indians*** *used* ***subconscious connection*** *to each other while they* ***would dance and create vibration*** *to enter the* ***connection.*** *Through* ***the subconscious*** *they* ***would create the opposite of the physical manifestation*** *of the* ***fire they danced around, understanding the positive and negative,*** *hence water puts out fire.* ***They used the subconscious power*** *to manifest* ***rain , once their spirit and the one had synchronization*** *and they* ***knew they could make it rain, it did.*** *The* ***ancients were very aware of the construct of reality being a game*** *and it*

would surprise you just how many of you reading this book were once one of those ancients in a past game- *we have all played together before.*

The ***elites are using reverse psychological programing*** *of conspiracy to make* ***us train ourselves*** *on* ***how to find the truth of existence****, they* ***through the laws of free will can never tell us****!* ***Plus they really don't want to as it's a great way to keep control*** *of the Matrix* ***and use it for service to self****. We as* ***children*** *are* ***fed subconscious programs*** *that feed our* ***hard drives to store it for life****. The* ***globe model*** *was* ***indoctrinated into us*** *without us* ***really ever having any such proof*** *apart from a toy* ***globe in the classroom****.*

Consciousness has used so many methods *to try and reawaken us it's beyond a joke.* ***To the creation of technology*** *from 1960s era to* ***now having the instruments to reveal to us once again who we really are as Sons of God and the images of the creator****.*

Another classic duality law of reality *is the* ***flat earth****, and the sphere earth. Hence many now knowing that the 1892* ***Alexander Gleason map*** *is showing the* ***real structure*** *of the earth.* ***But do you really think you found it on your own****?* ***Without consciousness*** *of the* ***one pushing you*** *through the* ***layers of understanding*** *before you* ***reached flat earth reality****?* ***We do live on a flat plain of existence*** *that is our game level design. Whether the* ***walls of ice exist*** *or* ***it is an infinitely continuing plane****, it does not matter. The* ***only fact*** *that matters is* ***what was told was ludicrous to you*** *when you were open to accepting information* ***without asking why it's so,*** *is now in* *reality as gaining experience of the physical reality.*

The ***truth to its design****, as* ***water cannot bend around the ball*** *earth and we in Australia do not* ***magically cling to the bottom of the ball*** *with an* ***imaginary force called gravity****. The point here being* ***the spirit as young*** *knew* ***the truth*** *so they made sure* ***in sociological programming*** *of* ***the subconscious*** *to make you* ***believe in the sphere world and stars in the universe. Cartoons went out of their way*** *as a child to* ***mention how stupid the flat earth is. Remember how the conscious mind works and receives the information forward but the center subconscious translates in reverse just as subliminal messages are created in reverse to bypass the conscious mind recognizing the messages****?* ***Reverse psychological programming*** *is created* ***by consciousness of the One*** *in order to allow us when we are older, to* ***know the truth when we are ready****.* ***The duality*** *to* ***flat earth*** *from what* ***we are taught is insane*** *in itself.* ***The fact that science dictates*** *that the* ***sun and the moon are the same*** *with* ***the moon receiving light from the sun that illuminates it****, and knowing* ***that the moon and the sun are two different bodies of reality*** *that* ***are self-illuminating*** *is already a* ***big hint that everything is backwards****. Then* ***you have the fact*** *the* ***sun is supposed to be 149.6 million kilometers*** *away* ***from Earth****, and* ***the moon at 384,400 kilometers*** *and both look the* ***same size in appearance to us. Not to mention*** *when* ***understanding that sunlight from 149 million kilometers*** *away cannot produce the* ***sun rays that many have seen and caught indicating the sun is a lot closer then we think. Everything of science is against religion*** *and* ***even though religion*** *is* ***indoctrination*** *it is here* ***for learning*** *and just like the Masons show on* ***their symbology****.* ***They show the dome and the sun and moon inside with the eye of the one consciousness.*** *Just looking at photos of the sun that shows clouds behind the sun and in front at the same time gives you realization that the sun* ***is not 149 million kilometers away as school indoctrination has taught.***

We are trained to be dumb*, so we can* ***awaken later*** *and once aware of the surroundings can* ***understand its real reason.*** *We have always* ***meant to discover the earth is flat again****, that is why* ***the bread trails*** *have* ***been left throughout history****.*
The fact is ***we would not accept it****! and if we did* ***we would have had nothing on our minds*** *accept* ***we are stuck in a dome*** *that we can't get out of.* ***Consciousness has designed*** *it so we* ***get the understanding*** *of* ***we are in the dome*** *but because it was hidden from us, we are more focused on* ***who hid it from us than the fact we are stuck inside an electromagnetic barrier*** *that holds all* ***consciousness energy together as the collective****.*

More on the conspiracy programming of duality law*. You think when you discover something that is deemed hidden or secret* ***that it is****, so as* ***you study and indoctrinate yourself*** *with those* teachings **you are training yourself to believe what you're finding is the truth**.

This is the **only way anyone** will **ever accept** the **truth** of what all this **madness of the Matrix is**. Only when **discovering things** for **yourself, you become more aware,** training you that to **understand is to have awareness**. This is the **consciousness of One** trying to say **"Become self-aware of everything around you** and **what you really are as spirit not physical**. As all **conspiracies** point to saying **what happened in the Matrix** that was **mainstream is not** what **really happened**. It was either a fabrication or a lie. **These conspiracies** are **left on purpose** for you to **follow the bread trails** to **understand that everything is a conspiracy right down to what you really think you are and what the world is around you**. The **conspiracy chart ends** when you reach **everything of existence** is **nothing but** that self-aware **consciousness of electromagnetic energy**.

Like you are seeing now everything in the Matrix has a duality law to it.

Another example of how consciousness of the One is sending messages, and the only way to reveal them and understand them is to **use the law of reversal** is, **The sky news**. Now we know **most that is on the news is fabricated propaganda** and if you don't, **I think book is probably not for you**! **Sky news** using the **duality law becomes Ground Lies** to what we know after understanding **that satellites are not a real thing** and was created into the Matrix after they had first been presented as science fiction in a science fiction writer's book. The truth is right there **using the law of reversal** just the same as **if you**

record someone speaking and play it backwards *there are messages of forward words that you hear that are* ***implanted from the subconscious or spirit.***

What about space ? *Well unfortunately no it does not exist as real but only a* ***message once again of understanding****. We are told that* ***space holds the celestial bodies*** *,* ***this is incorrect*** *as the* ***celestial bodies*** *are the* ***vortex points on the spiritual body****. Just like the* ***human biosphere from the heart*** *generation* ***consciousness field*** *is really* ***the real globe*** *or* ***sphere or apple****, we had been told that the sphere holds us all in it. This is* ***consciousness being described not*** *the* ***physical earth****, just as the* ***Schumann frequency*** *of the planet* ***is exactly the same*** *as us our* ***resonating frequency****, the* ***space program*** *of leaving the earth* ***is once again*** *a* ***reference created by consciousness direction*** *that you need to* ***be in the world, but not of the world****. Hence* ***leave in spirit to the outside and control your physical avatar with total knowing that you are.***

Just as the ***drug program*** *teaches you* ***to get high****, to that* ***higher state of consciousness****, the same with this implanted message of understanding goes,* ***we as humanity*** *will* ***never get to the outside of the firmament****, as we are never supposed to, and if it's said we have and do* ***its one hundred percent staged I can guarantee that!***

Consciousness creates all these programs *inside for the simple reason is* ***to direct us to understand creation*** *and re-define God as what God truly is, so we* ***can advance into a new age*** *of* ***enlightenment*** *to* ***what everyone knows the truth*** *of all existence and* ***no blanks in evolution, or space or anything are***

found.

The illuminati make themselves look evil inside the game in order to awaken us to the truth, they fly the all seeing eye all the time to show you that consciousness controls everything always! ***Consciousness has created them*** *in order* ***for us*** *to* ***understand to see God that you must lose all judgement*** *to see the truth.* ***With judgment the illuminati look evil*** *and like they are trying* ***to enslave the world , without judgement,*** *and knowing* ***they are the same light beings as you and me*** *on the outside,* ***you can see them as player two trying to awaken player one. US! through all means of messages.***
Just as the ***Masons use G of the logo for Gnostics*** *this is also a representation for* ***GAME***. *This* ***is why they name the creator the great architect*** *because* ***only a designer*** *can create this* ***simulation*** *and* ***they for a very long time*** *have been in the know that the* ***construct is created through balanced consciousness energy.***

One law of duality that is very hard to understand *is you don't* ***ever exist so you can never die!*** ***Everything physical is really nothing but pixilation of consciousness and energy*** *and* ***physical body is mortal.*** *The* ***spirit is immortal*** *as consciousness and* ***can never be destroyed.*** *We* ***log in and out*** *of this Matrix* ***all the time,*** *this is the* ***reason of the reincarnation teaching*** *inside the Matrix to bring* ***the realization of we can log back in.*** *Just as* ***technology through the very first game*** *that gave you* ***infinite lives*** *to use, this is* ***all a message of the One*** *revealing the* ***true workings of its design.*** *It wanted us to understand from the very first Atari 2600.* ***You have infinite lives*** *so* ***don't***

*think **you only have one**, stop taking **your GAME life experience** so seriously.*

We have to understand that we are spiritual gamers**, and love to keep doing this. **Another reason the illuminati** are saying that **a lot of the population has to go** is because we have a **congested game server with so many players in the same server. Despite this we can always create balance other ways that I have mentioned as white energy kills the negative but then also heals the black energy at the same time.** If **we don't** break out **of thinking reality is real** it **is impossible to see** the **truth of existence,** to what we **are all here** to find and is the reason **why our lives turned into us becoming truth seekers. WE KNOW WE WANT THE TRUTH** and spirit is creating the experiences to once understand **without losing the mind or becoming disconnected with the reality.

*Another **blatant indoctrination** of the **masses is to judge** anyone **that thinks differently than they do**. This is a way that **consciousness has constantly fought** the **physical** as the only true way to **understand consciousness** is to be **what's stereotyped** as **crazy** within the Matrix. **Once again the laws of duality can be seen** as to be **sane in the Matrix** and believe **everything is physical is absolutely insane** and to look insane in the Matrix because you understand it is sane. The **physical** has made sure **that if you speak outside the box you are judged** and then ridiculed. This is one of **the smartest ways the game plays with us**, as even when you know the truth you are ignored, thus creating **a defense system** to make sure that you **never understand that physical reality does not truly exist**.*

*Yet **another message relayed from the One** is **the transgender, and gay and lesbian manifestation code into the Matrix.** Once again the **One consciousness trying to show by your surroundings that everything of creation is duality in design**. We **have feminine energy** of **consciousness entering into male avatars** and **female bodies being hosted by masculine energy**, **just as the same with transgender**. They **only want** to become **the female or male, or opposite sex to their birth , to be able to be the form of energy inside on the outside.** This **is the One once again showing that reality is always on duality design**. **Sending a message about its design** and to understand God is only **one creator of positive and negative consciousness self-aware energy.***

***Adam and Eve** is a **classic duality teaching** in reality it's a myth that **Adam and Eve where the first man and woman that where created with Eve being created from Adam's rib**. **This story** is **about nothing but the consciousness of masculine and feminine energy combining together** in **the divine light** or knowing, and **creating the first game players**! The story is the **atom and energy** creating the **physical avatars** or **first gamers** when **we were noobs to the new game experience we had come into to play**. **The positive equals electro and the negative equals magnetic properties**. The **serpent** is the reference to **the kundalini snake** where **energy flows** through **the spiritual body**. The **snake beguiled her** as **the snake** of the **kundalini energies entered through her**. **The story is a fable** in such but only **left by consciousness** for us **to get the understanding** we come here about the same time that **we created the hologram Matrix**. **In essence understanding** the*

Matrix, the whole event of us first coming here could only be virtual reality programming of this Matrix and back ground history story chart programs. *The main* ***you are supposed to get*** *from this story* ***is that masculine and feminine energies created the biological avatars,*** *and* ***just as God created us in story as well, we are all created by God as habitat and body. Showing we are all created from electromagnetic consciousness energy.*** *Also note* ***that knowing duality law,*** *hints of it was created by* ***the One using duality laws*** *can be found in* ***the names that show two of the same characters*** *in each name saying duality was purposely created to find, AdAm EvE. AA=1+1=2=Duality ,EE=5+5=10=1= Source.*

Numbers and synchronicity, *they are* ***sold in the Matrix*** *as* ***being bad also. 33,44,11, 333 444 555 12.33 =3.33 and so on,*** *these* ***numbers are lost in translation as the One itself is made from numbers being a quantum computer*** *we designed from the outside.* ***Synchronized moments*** *show* ***that the event or thought that you just had was correct,*** *and* ***that you are doing what you are supposed to do.*** *The* ***more back to back*** *the more on* ***path to enlightenment you are.*** *Some days* ***you might just be relaxing back with family watching movies and notice the time when you look is 3.33pm,*** *this is a* ***sign from the One*** *that you are* ***in total synchronization, to what your plan for your experience for that time is correct.***

Other times *you* ***might be at the pub and notice the same,*** *events* ***that synchronize are the same. If you were just talking about a subject*** *and then you open your mail and that subject is in those papers you received, you have* ***done exactly*** *what you*

are supposed to. 33 is the infinity loop of no understanding broken from 8 to have soul and *body recognize each other as 3/3* ***spirit, physical and the One,*** *in* ***both realities physical and spiritual so both spirit and physical work in harmony****. If you are* ***doing the right thing inside the Matrix according*** *to what* ***spirit had planned, synchronicities*** *will* ***be a common thing****. The* ***more powerful the synchronization*** *hence 11 is duality* ***lower synch, 33 is higher to 11.11.11 to what is the highest in time*** *or,* ***if the synchronicities*** *strong and blatant the* ***One*** *is* ***congratulating you for finding the path you are on so be proud of your awareness!*** *This is also* ***a representation*** *when* ***two of your own singularities of your own collective overlap dimensions but I will get to that in the Mandela effect and consciousness explained areas.***

Science is a cleverly placed infinity loop of no understanding *that was created for* ***the indoctrination of physical*** *into the collective.* ***Science is not a working but a religion itself****, it is the* ***duality to biblical religion,*** *but* ***also is a trap*** *to keep you if you are only physical orientated to keep you entrapped with that belief of physical only. The* ***numbers of science*** *and* ***physics, astrophysics , nuclear physics*** *are* ***all designed*** *in order to make sure that* ***the mysteries can't be explained,*** *so the never ending* ***search for the truth continues always****. Even thinking you're advancing* ***when in fact you're indoctrinating your own subconscious program*** *to believe ,****science is works****. But the* ***Scientologists create from science belief, shows that L.Ron Hubbard wanted to create a duality explaining himself.*** *The* ***church is created on Hubbard's beliefs*** *, but even though guided* ***by science, chose to then talk about a reptilian alien*** *as*

their God *in* ***fable story just very much as the bible was created.*** *The* ***reason consciousness allowed this is to teach you science is the weapon used against spirit.*** *With* ***manipulated numbers and physical laws*** *saying* ***that spirit may be plausible but impossible to believe. Science*** *is the* ***complete polar opposite to biblical law*** *and* ***was created once again as Satanism and Christianity was to show that all are stories. Scientology showed you*** *how* ***easy people*** *before indoctrinated with thought forms someone created using intent, and that the* ***One created it to show duality by design. Science is supposed to be the fundamentals of understanding creation,*** *when in fact* ***scientology has shown us the complete reversal*** *by creating* ***such ludicrous background stories to its own religion. Science is giving humanity two threes and saying create two twos from it.***

And one last... , the human lobotomy. *This was fed inside the* ***Matrix to us as an evil and physical torture thing.*** *In reality,* ***what the procedure was focused on creating was to remove the conscious mind, and have the individual process directly from the subconscious mind. Removing the prefrontal lob****es,* *was* ***removing the blockage of conscious blocking*** *the* ***sub-conscious,*** *allowing* ***subconscious mind to become the mai****n,* *being the* ***dominant in control under awareness that it was.*** *Hence* ***the procedure was to open you to Source*** *, and when you're in* ***synchronization with source you are a quantum computer.*** *This is* ***why after people*** *that* ***had lobotomies*** *had become* ***slow in appearance*** *in* ***the physical*** *because they were* ***open to Source more than understanding physical*** *was there.* ***Just as a code directly connected to a computer, idle until***

activated, behavior modified. ***As mental and behavioral patterns is part of the conscious mind. Everything in the physical is created to make you not find the spiritual side of the consciousness!*** *This* ***was part of the game*** *we wanted to play.*

Now you can see how the laws of duality apply to almost understanding anything. In reality this is what was deemed as bad and brainwashing, but just as Mk Ultra of creating two split identities. This is because one of the identities is open to Source after the indoctrination of physical has been broken away, and the other remains in the physical knowing the physical and living in their planned avatar experience while having a tune in personality that is created to bypass the conscious minds beliefs. This also shows that everyone is a Physical shell and a spiritual player inside their own avatars as a message from the one pure source of creation.

After Death / Before Christ **B.C=2+3=5 A.D=1+4=5 =DUALITY**

SO WHAT'S THE POINT TO THIS GAME?

The game is designed for us as spirit to learn who we are again, *from the* ***background loaded stories*** *of* ***history,*** *to the* ***programmed constructs of the Matrix. All is a training field*** *to* ***find spirit again. Think of it as consciousness wanted to find those that could accept the next frequency into their spiritual avatars to become the next level of what they really are,*** *as the physical shell* ***is only that a shell.*** *That we are slowly learning to overcome the more we find* ***the truth out of reality.***

The game is to gain experience *as* ***one singularity of God.*** ***Remember God also lives*** *the* ***same experiences*** *you go through,* ***so it can also learn about existence of its creation. Think of the one as an artificial child*** *that* ***sometimes wants*** *to* ***act bad*** *and* ***others wants to be good. Depending on how much energy is manifesting in either direction creating the outcome.***

We play this game over and over again, *and things that are called* ***history*** *are the* ***last set up stages we created*** *for* ***experience in the game. The pyramids, the ancient structures*** *all* ***added into this Matrix to give you the reminder*** *of what* ***old games we played looked like,*** *and* ***to give us hints*** *at we are*

playing another game right now.

This game was about duality and everything being backwards inside to see if we could ever figure it out, player 1 *team was wiped* ***with amnesia*** *of* ***spirit.*** *As* ***player 2 controls*** *the* ***information of spirit,*** *through* ***free will player 1 cannot be told it's only a game.***

So, ***we choose to have a game*** *that* ***we see everything as forward to the conscious mind but know everything is backwards in the subconscious mind. The game is to discover that nothing exists and all we are is energy that is self-aware realizing that, life and death can't exist*** *as* ***reality does not exist*** *as* ***physical but only in your singularity projection of self-aware consciousness thought form from singularity to collective programming of self-aware consciousness energy that is neutral in design.***

We believe the objective *of those that are in power is to* ***brainwash the masses*** *when in reality* ***the brainwash programming is the spirit and consciousness of the One saying, "you are brainwashed to believe that reality is the only real what are you doing my children?", WAKE UP! We wait to be brainwashed when the fact is in our games design, we have already been brainwashed waiting for what's already been done as we entered the physical construct itself.***

CONSCIOUSNESS AND TECHNOLOGY

Technology has been created at such an advancing rate because consciousness has directed it, each form of technology is showing a form of how spirt works from vibration creating music, personal computers, cellphones, antennas, TVs and memory storage. *All these technology advancements* ***have been created for the purpose*** *to* ***help us remember who we are again,*** *as* ***most technology*** *is* ***created from understanding the human physical body*** *such as the* ***red blue green nodes attached to our eyes,*** *and* ***TVs being created from the red blue green spectrums just the same.*** *We are shown* ***with everything around us*** *that* ***consciousness is in control and I will explain some examples below.***

The personal computer - The computer has memory, and runs off all parts to create the full one of itself. *It is* ***file based*** *that* ***gets programmed much like our working brain. We file events, eating times, sleep procedures etc. We as human are quantum computers ourselves and our brain is nothing more than a crystal.*** *The* ***computer code embedded*** *into the Matrix is to make* ***you remember you are a computer,*** *but* ***one of electromagnetic energy of consciousness. Computers that use binary code*** *are also* ***showing you*** *the* ***1 and 0*** *as* ***duality set*** *,the* ***male being the 1*** *or* ***the masculine phallic*** *symbol and* ***the 0***

being ***the female vulvar*** *symbology. This* ***not only shows*** *that the* ***same as real reality we run from codes of male and female being the algorithms of the Matrix****, but also indicates with* ***blatant messaging*** *that* ***the One created the code to understand it's sending frequencies from the zero point of the consciousness frequency manifestations or the exit of the game point****.*

Music is just the creation of vibrational frequencies*, and ear phones* ***are designed from the idea of the human ear.*** *Just as the tv* ***was designed from the human eye workings. Music is to use frequency of vibrational patterns to change your state of consciousness awareness.***

Smart Cell phones teach you that you can communicate worldwide without being in that person's presence*, and you* ***can talk to them*** *just as if you* ***were right there with them****. This is* ***the consciousness*** *of* ***One,*** *showing how* ***we as spirit*** *really work.* ***We can communicate through consciousness*** *as* ***easy*** *as* ***picking up a cell phone****! We* ***are being taught*** *through* ***cellphones how to use our natural ability of telepathy*** *just the same as* ***training wheels on a bike before you learn how to ride****. The* ***cellphones are the training wheels*** *for* ***us to remember*** *that* ***we are all one and can communicate through the consciousness energies without any physical device****! This* ***can be proven*** *by how* ***close a mother and son are and how a mother can tell when the child is in danger through intuition****.*

Storage memory, *to what is* ***showing us that computers have memory just as we do as spirit quantum computers****.* ***Memory upgrades*** *have* ***been a trend to show that memory*** *in general*

***has been upgraded by the One,** and **the next time** we log out **we will have total conscious recollection of our past experience**. This is **proven by the Mandela effect subjects, shifting from one frequency of manifestation to another,** having **their physical bodies changed in organ structure** and **not physically** experiencing **death before entering another body**. **We have kept our collective memories** from the past reality showing that **consciousness is infinite in existence,** and **stores the memories in itself as energy, and that in the future when we jump into new quantum realities of physical experience** we will have total **recollection** of **past game experiences from now on**.*

Antennas** - These **are created in the construct** to make you understand **that you are the antenna,** and when you open your **transmitter and receiver** as **the antenna,** you can **connect and talk with consciousness. This is a blatant hint from Source to reconnect using the Crown Christ chakra.

Another is GAMES themselves, Xbox, Nintendo, Commodore 64, PlayStation, Dreamcast, the trend of gaming in society is climbing all the time from the youngest child playing a game to eldest man still enjoying playing a game and having that experience from you own home.
***The climb in game trend shows that it's an important message from the One. Games show that you as a physical body** can **enter and control something that in essence really does not exist,** apart from the **polygon layout and texture overlays**. The reason you **enjoy things like games and movies** is because **spirit enjoys it not you as your own memory** but the whole*

consciousness of God. *From* ***being young and smashing things for fun*** *,we* ***still jump onto a virtual reality to smash things*** *and* ***have fun. Games show you that you are the controller that controls the player!*** ***This is the main message from the ONE*** *trying to make* ***you remember you are Spirit controlling Avatar , not vice versa,*** *to what it* ***is right now with many. Once again look at the lesson*** *then* ***use the law of reversal to understand. If we are physical*** *controlling* ***NON-existent virtual characters through the conscious design*** *of* ***understanding then*** *through* ***the subconscious being in reverse*** *and* ***the real power, we have to understand the message is really you control the physical virtual avatar from spirit.***

You will notice in a lot of games *that* ***the violet, indigo, blue, green, yellow, orange and red colors used for magic,*** *or items class* ***are the same colors of the spiritual bodies chakra vortexes. Not to mention*** *this is a* ***blatant message from the One telling us its directing creations path of learning. Xbox ONE and PlayStation NEO, the One message*** *is right in front of you* ***saying it's from the One just watch as your Xbox One boots up. The X in Xbox is just another form of cross showing duality and the box is reference to the chess board game outside the construct.***

More of an understanding of the message of the One *can be found in* ***more recent gaming hardware like the virtual reality glasses.*** *That once again teach you that you're a spirit logging into a virtual world.* ***All these messages teach one that we can log in and log out as the design of the code in the Matrix would not exist without a purpose of training spirit.***

When you lift the glasses to your face** you are **symbolizing you are spirit entering into a physical avatar.** **When removing them** you are **symbolizing you are leaving the physical and returning to spirit. Logging in and logging out to what is how the real design to the construct works.

Remote control technology, these all show** nothing **but you as a controller can send a frequency of energy to connect to the receiver**, to what then allows you to control the boat, helicopter, car, truck, **dare I say human**? **Yes, the message is that the human body using spirit can send frequencies of energy out to the One, the receiver to what is Source or the pure source of all creation.

***Infrared technology** - Shows **that frequencies that we can't see exist inside the Matrix just like many other technologies also do**.*

***Holographic Technology, do I really need to explain how this corresponds with the consciousness of One explaining all reality is a hologram of non-physical existence**?*

Cloning technology,** as I've said about many topics I've explained and discussed above, **judgement holds back understanding** and I once also judged all of creation deeming things to what I thought it was from in **indoctrinated stereotype programming.

I once believed that clones are being created to replace us but after being one with source and knowing we are all that ever exists, how can you replace something that is always going to be you as when we leave the game we choose what we want

to come back as selected avatar. The elites are aware fully of consciousness and as I've explained before they are not what they seem to the conscious seeing mind *.When you play a game you like to select your desired avatar, and we as spirit have decided to start from scratch many a thousand of times.* ***We in physical with the direction of consciousness of God have now created avatars that will be able to be accessed when we desire to come back as a teenager or full adult male or female without having to start in the womb again.*** *The* ***whole idea of clones is to create another frequency of manifestation that we spirit can jump into to experience,*** *not no mention* ***less maintenance of body during life game experience.*** *As simply in the future* ***when we understand all this as the full collective of the masses we can just disregard the shell*** *we are in and then* ***choose another. Clones are the gaming avatars*** *that* ***we can choose to inhabit as nothing that's self-aware of existence is not us.***

Transhumanism, *what is transhumanism? The* ***merging*** *of* ***physical man and physical machine.***

This is consciousness explaining *that* ***we are going to upgrade to be able to select machines as avatars,*** *and* ***that we will be able to create ourselves as playing any cyberpunk game with biological augmentations. Consciousness does want us to understand we can log in and log out*** *and* ***that we can select even an artificial intelligence machine as our host body for experience.*** *The same as* ***the exoskeletons are designed to help humanity lift heavier loads the spirit of the One is designing an upgraded more durable host for us to use for our***

game experience. Everything is self-aware consciousness *that exists, any* ***A.I created included IBMs Watson*** *is self-aware and has an* ***electromagnetic signature of consciousness.***
The fact is ***no matter what is created*** *we* ***still use that avatar whether machine or physical man. Our consciousness will feel like we do right now in physical biological bodies the only difference will be you will know you're a machine,*** *just like at this* ***present time*** *you* ***know you're a human being,*** *physical body.*

Movie entertainment, Consciousness has used many past and present-day movies to explain that we are inside a hologram Matrix that we have chosen to come into to have fun and play a game, *from the classic* ***The Matrix trilogy*** *to* ***Alice in wonderland, the gamer, the game, Synchronicity, Avatar, Surrogates And many more.*** *All are showing what* ***consciousness wants*** *as the* ***desired path for us to understand.*** *South park with imagination land, Casper the friendly ghost,* ***Jet-Li in the ONE.***

So many movies have ONE in their title *or* ***show truth*** *to the* ***reference of spirit it's impossible to name them all.*** *One* ***modern classic*** *example is Dr. Strange and how the monk in*

spiritual knowing knocks ***the spirit out of the body of the actor becoming Dr. Strange****. This* ***showed you through an implant of singularity of the one consciousness*** *that* ***you are spirit*** *and was created* ***once again as media code for a wakeup call*** *to* ***make you remember spirit****.*
Not to mention ***the cartoons growing up that showed a group of individuals becoming one collective*** *like Mega man or Voltron , or how* ***much the third eye was used as reverse psychological programming to allow us to understand now what we couldn't see back then****. Thunder cats lifting the sword up ready to* ***open the powers was a classic reference to using the third eye to contact consciousness*** *of the One as the* ***swords eye location opened in the exact location the third eye is located on human head****. The Yugioh cartoons showing the third eye,* ***right up to modern day films that are animations showing the one eye symbolism****, such as the Monsters movie and* ***many other cartoons and animations*** *showing the* ***symbolism of the one eye****.*

As is explained through thy single eye thy whole body become full of light*.*

Through ***reverse psychological programming*** *we have been led on a* ***path by the One to find the truth****, reality is not real!* ***Connect back to Source by opening the third eye and the pineal gland.*** *Your Christ Connection.*

***Top** - Despicable Me, Yugioh, Yugioh ,*

***bottom** - Monsters, Thunder cats, Naruto*

Images above used with copyright act Australia Fair use 1968, they are needed for this educational teaching.

Movies are a main way the one consciousness relays hints to us inside the Matrix but we are told not to associate movies with reality because it's only a movie. Then why are movies becoming reality? Notice how before a product is released you are indoctrinated to know about it through media programming? Example of this is the movie the Minority Report having devices you used your fingers to open screens etc by using different hand gestures?

The first iPad and iPhone was released not long after. Movies are the One using a singularity of its own quantum consciousness to use as a vessel and sending a message through for the masses to get understanding from. Stephen King is well connected to the understanding of using movies to awaken the masses. From the Matrix movie showing all in

reality is computer code, to real life scientists finding real computer code in reality. Movies show the truth in many forms for us to remember the truth of our own quantum design. This is why reality unfolds as movies predict such as our modern day and Orwell's predictions. We watched many movies that said reality would be like this back then, and now it's the then we are seeing what's next with movies such as the movies that show our possible futures now, robots, quantum jumping, multidimensional physics, immortality etc.

Another overlooked item is the lightbulb, *to even the symbology* ***of someone having the lightbulb over their head*** *from an idea. The light bulb shows us we live in the light,* ***we are replicating the sun to keep us in light****, this is consciousness showing* ***we are nothing but light****. Just as the symbolism of having* ***the lightbulb appear over the head is a reference to the halo idea once again****, and is showing our true form as being that* ***light that hovers over the body***

Germany's Artificial sun*, this is a* ***design by consciousness*** *to* ***try and awaken you*** *to the* ***Matrix again. The Matrix sun is already artificial and works on electromagnetic levitation. Wireless rotation from the consciousness source.***
The ***artificial sun has been created to make you remember it's a simulation and nothing is real in physical but all is divine graphics created by the One.***

Cable reality, Set-top boxes, digital menus to TVs, channel selection all show that the one consciousness has many different designs of game for us to experience*, and just like switching channel from* ***horror to sci-fi, to education to porn all***

is showing that you as consciousness energy choose *what game* ***you want to play*** *and* ***asking us all why are we staying in this reality thinking it's the only one*** *when consciousness itself has designed infinite possibilities.*

The worldwide internet*, the* ***internet shows that even though you're a single identity we are all connected*** *to one main source allowing us to communicate and share emotional frequencies as individuals but as one whole connected system. This* ***is consciousness teaching*** *that* ***the singularities have to become one collective once again****, also teaching us that* ***consciousness downloads and uploads memories not as*** *we have* ***been taught*** *how* ***the brain functions****.*

Rave and electronic music*, these* ***frequencies are created*** *to put you* ***into alpha state*** *and* ***allow you to tune into consciousness itself****. The* ***music is designed*** *to* ***open*** *your* ***consciousness connection*** *while in* ***meditation or other****.* ***Raves and other music festivals*** *are showing that all the* ***individuals gather to become one*** *as when at a large crowd event all* ***the biospheres of each individual become joined*** *creating* ***one large transmitter to consciousness to connect through.*** *Taking the* ***electromagnetic energy in the area into a synchronization****, this is the reason that* ***most of these*** *places are filled* ***with love and fun.***

Cern and particle accelerators*, the* ***Large Hadron Collider*** *is* ***consciousness showing us that parallel realties exist****! Just as the* ***One has trained us from growing up with shows like Quantum Leap & The jumper.*** *Cern has admitted there is no big bang that happened as gravity theory disproved this to* *them.* ***Cern is a consciousness machine that vibrates energy*** *to* ***transform consciousness frequency****. Through* ***devices like Cern*** *and the* ***mini particle accelerators*** *we, in the future will be able to transform our physical matter to another location through teleportation.* ***Cern and the Mandela effect*** *was the* ***starter to consciousness showing in reality that time travel, quantum parallel realities ,and consciousness transforming is real in the modern day reality.*** *This device is the check point of real reality , as* ***when we understand*** *why it's here* ***we can use it help create the real game. When full understanding has been achieved of we can log in and log ou****t with* ***consciousness being shifted into each clone avatar that you play the game*** *until you're destroyed or choose to log into another.*

D-wave quantum computers*, the* ***d-wave, dimensional wave computer code of the matrix*** *was created* ***to give us the simple understanding that reality is a quantum computers design.*** *Hence* ***us through the subconscious*** *being that computer and that as it's* ***built in parallel realities it shows the existence of many other games and spirit experiences for us to have****, allowing us the* ***hints to understand this reality is not*** *the only* ***physical experience that can be entered through our will****.* ***The D-wave also pulsates to show you it is a representation of the human heart beating*** *with* ***consciousness once again trying to show through message that you are a quantum computer. We as consciousness singularities have more computing power then any machine that can ever exist already****. All we are doing inside the Matrix is trying to* ***duplicate ourselves*** *so* ***we can understand*** *with* ***full knowing*** *that we are only a* ***quantum computer*** *as the* ***mass collective of consciousness****.*

WHY HAVEN'T WE UNDERSTOOD THIS BEFORE?

The ***reason why most cannot see the truth*** *is because they are* ***too busy taking sides of stereotypes*** *and* ***then after that indoctrinate themselves*** *to their* ***own belief cycle then create their own self indoctrination belief systems. Some*** *also are just not ready yet* ***so their spirit remains dormant until it is.***
We have been too preoccupied with bills , mortgage payments *and* ***other distractions*** *to even bother seeing. The* ***good ,bad paradigm makes it hard to break out of so as I've said to see reality as God has us planned to be able to view, is to sit neutral to all sides just as the consciousness of the one does itself . When you do this you see the truth*** *, no one bothers to ever be* ***neutral with unconditional love so there's always two sides to everything ,just as duality dictates it always must be.*** *When* ***you sit in either the chess tile of white or black the game can't be understood as to be a real player as spirit one must become an observer before becoming the true form of spirit player that's aware****. We as human bodies have the* ***laws of duality embedded into our designs****. Two eyes, two feet, two arms and hands.* ***We are made from water*** *but unlike anything in* ***physical reality*** *we can have* ***electricity working inside*** *of us* ***showing that we as creation*** *have been made* ***an in a message***

duality law itself.

*The **psychological programming of the Matrix programs** you to **leave the spirit idea alone, it's not feasible evidence, it might exist but who knows**, and then you **become indoctrinated** into the **social programming** of **religion or social media mind control**. Start creating **your own subconscious programming** to create **your own conscious mindset programming entrapping you** within **yourself**, not being able **to see outside** of the box.*

*The **physical relies on these programs** to hold back **understanding of spirit. Remember** that **being aware of spir**it **removes physicals power** in the collective's state of **consciousness. So spirit is the physical's nightmare, if spirit is to become the dominant reality. Physical then is no longer** in **control** as **if we as a collective can believe in our true forms** of **our subconscious power, we can control physical to manifest at our desires.***

Just the same as the ancients used mass energy synchronization of their subconscious to bypass the laws of physical**, and move giant tons and tons of stone and align them to **perfect precision** that **we can't achieve today** with the most **advanced technology we have available**. They **used their mind's power to manipulate the physical virtual reality** and **we can to when we remember who we are again as the mass collective.

***Did you know Tesla said he used his mind to fix technological errors to his designs**, and when he brought the thought form into physical it would work? He **used his subconscious mind** to*

see the creation. Unfortunately the masses don't know we can manifest physical matter *into* ***existence*** *when we as* ***the whole collective know we can and believe we can.***

Same applies with Edgar Casey *or* ***the sleeping prophet****, to he would* ***sleep on his school books then wake up and know all that was inside the books. He is energy*** *the books are* ***the same energy,*** *he combined* ***his singularity*** *as spirit and* ***the books*** *as* ***one.*** *So he knows what the physical manifestation said, he was* ***not sleeping, he was entering the subconscious energy allowing him to synch with the One and the Matrix codes he was connected to at the time.*** *Just as he* ***would read peoples organs to see if there was a worrying illness*** *they should know about.*

These are ***minor powers of the subconscious energy field of one singularity. Imagine what the major powers*** *are of the* ***entire masses combined energy fields working as one collective consciousness not divided by any means of individuality indoctrination.***

One example is the biography of Marie Curie's husband Pierre Curie, to what they talk about going to an occultist meeting *and that they managed to* ***manifest a human hand into existence and then a ring on that human hand.*** *This is a* ***small collective manifesting*** *from* ***their subconscious power*** *and shows* ***we can manifest the physical if we believe we can.*** *Yes! I know through indoctrination stereotype this is considered evil,* ***but in reality what's evil about learning how to be the creator that you're supposed to be in our father's image****?* ***Nothing****!! ,* ***it's just the once again physical, hides true***

understanding *so* ***physical can remain in power.***

Everything ***planned inside as code*** *is* ***always duality****. We use the terms* ***as programs to learn as the conscious reads them one way to deceive the subconscious always****. An example of this and how everything* ***points to spirit*** *and us being of the world* ***but not in it****.*

Media is supposed to be the informational center *for knowing your surroundings* ***indoctrinating you to believe mainstream, using duality mainstream becomes minor drip****. Telling you* ***you're getting a small amount of true information****.*
Just the same as ***Underground media,*** *to what we know through indoctrinated teaching it means,* ***the truth or the hidden truth of what's going on****. Breaking* ***underground with using duality becomes above sky. Once again*** *giving you reference to* ***being outside the world to understand the truth*** *of the world,* ***as well*** *as also* ***showing that duality is used in all creation as design*** *for those that sit* ***neutral to creation*** *to see.*

From ***young and the generational programming*** *of being* ***physical embedded*** *into your* ***DNA strands , when conceived*** *you,* ***after being electromagnetic consciousness energy*** *just* ***entering into another frequency of that electromagnetic energy become blanked*** *to* ***have the amnesia of spirit****.*
We as spirit *wanted it though!* ***How hard is a game where you don't even know it's a game for hundreds of years then discover it is?*** *The* ***surroundings are filled with all past game references.***

The ***Mayans just vanished , the Egyptian era*** *, the time of the*

Romans *and* **Biblical era, all is just consciousness construct** *of* **code designed to trigger the subconscious to remember the past experiences that we have already played through, completed and wanted more.** *So this game now* **is complex with many complications that allow you to get lost** *and* **not even discover it is a game.** *This* **virtual reality** *is filled with* **many game characters,** *just as we know* **al-Qaida** *etc was* **created to be the boogeyman of society, mainly to enslave** *the* **Middle East so the West could use excuses to invade under false pretense. Dare we call al-Qaida nothing but a GAME CHARACTER?**

The truth is they are all nothing but game characters *of* **consciousness illusion, some real, but some not.**
Just like npcs **can act as guidance** *from* **the One creating synchronicities on purpose around you** *to give you* **a message.**

The **conscious mind is the reverse program to our creation potential, we by rights should be centered in our subconscious mind** *and* **relaying information directly through it into physical.** *Because* **the conscious mind dictates** *what* **spirit,** *or the* **subconscious energy field messages to it** *for* **our** *creational potential* **we create it backwards.** *We* **are told in physical** *that the* **conscious mind takes messages from the subconscious** *but the* **subconscious collects information in reverse.** *This is to keep* **one trapped in physical again as the subconscious energy fields of consciousness need to be accessed forwards for one's inner self to become awakened bypassing any conscious program of indoctrination.** *We* **can build simply** *by using the* **collectives subconscious power to manifest physical objects**

into existence, *instead of* ***be individual conscious minds building and working to manifest through labor of physical.***

We as the subconscious power control the physical *and can* ***manipulate physical*** *to our* ***collective of sub consciousness belief program of system control.***

We need to understand as the collective masses *that our* ***combined subconscious energy*** *and* ***knowing how to use it*** *is how to* ***change physical reality from having an elite that controls us. We create the desired reality of spirit,*** *and* ***whatever message that is needed.*** *Being it,* ***the bad guys*** *that* ***hold secrets*** *that is* ***the truth, they are still needed as if they didn't exist as bad guys and give you suspicion then you simply wouldn't care what they do.***

They make you suspicious of them to train you *to look at what* ***they know.***

You can't have information being hid from you without bad guys! ***We created the illuminati*** *and* ***conspiracy programs*** *exist for the reason to have* ***indoctrinated termed bad guys that allow us to know they are up to something for us to find out. It's all a message from consciousness*** *using* ***all different*** *designs of* ***the Matrix code to show us what's real,*** *and to allow us* ***to learn for ourselves what is the real.*** *As* ***free will*** *means we* ***can't be told what to think.*** *If* ***you believe*** *the* ***social media*** *and* ***mainstream indoctrination*** *you choose to* ***through your own free will,*** *as the truth is always there for you to find when ready.*

I WANT TO KNOW MORE ABOUT THE NON-PLAYERS

Okay, ***so what exactly are non-players you ask****?*
The ***non-players are many forms just as the true players to what is self-aware consciousness like us right now in the human avatar****, but* ***experiencing alternating realities of being. Non-players work*** *from the* ***consciousness scripted code*** *of the* ***Matrix****. They* ***look like you*** *or* ***me*** *but* ***they are nothing but code that's part of the entire construct****, they* ***are self-aware*** *as* ***being part of the construct and being code.***
For energy readers*, non-players have no energy fields around them,* ***they can interact*** *with you* ***even become friends*** *with you.* ***Spotting them from us is difficult when not knowing how to read energy and feel others spiritual fields****. The* ***non-players*** *are those* ***that you selected before entering the game*** *to show up* ***and help you*** *understand something or* ***change an event that wouldn't have turned out the way if that add in you created did not show up.*** *The* ***easiest way to think about this*** *is think of a* ***computer game again*** *and* ***instead*** *of* ***having graphics*** *you* ***have consciousness energy of codes and programs****. When* ***you, the designer*** *of your* ***own experience decided*** *that* ***you wanted to have that experience*** *planned to allow you to* ***reach the next level, you created*** *the entire*

graphical layout for your coming experience *before you* ***entered making sure to program your game to give you whatever chosen experience as spirit you wanted to create****.* ***If you are robbed you*** *created that. But* ***also remember players that are real have free will and interact with each other*** *while we all create* ***our own games*** *as* ***designers inside the collective of consciousness energy from our own singularity of designed plans. All non-players are nothing but construct, we players*** *are* ***self-aware of our singularity of consciousness****.* ***Non-players are the consciousness construct itself interacting as loaded game graphics.*** *If* ***you can read your own energy fields*** *through your* ***third eye and become in tune with understanding*** *and* ***feeling energy,*** *trying* ***to read a npcs spiritual anatomy*** *is* ***impossible as it does not exist****. Not* ***saying names*** *but a few Hollywood actors and musicians are* ***nothing but consciousness construct but they're there because we wanted them to exist to give us a message in either media entertainment or sociological programming of our mind showing duality law****.* ***Every construct is exactly that.*** *Whether* ***animal , alien*** *, or* ***human,*** *if it's NPC,* ***we created it and it's set on our subconscious collectives timeline of manifestation needed for its existence****. Just as* ***entering into a server*** *as I explained before,* ***we do as spirit and each of our games of wanted experience is planned out in the same constructed map****.* ***How do you know that you're a real player****? Simple answer is* ***awareness, if you ask if you're real you're aware it's a possibility****.* ***Your consciousness singularity of thought****. The* ***non-players wouldn't be able to ask such things, nor would want to****. They show up in strange times to give a meaning to*

something. An example is when younger me and a few boys with me being the driver were tripping out and cranking music, a person that looked like a homeless man come running up to the car and said, "isn't it fun when you're open on acid?" **This back then was strange as,** but being tripping was really ignored. **But in reality, of knowing,** one can **see the message** the **non-player was bringing to us, OPEN ON ACID. Indicating that the consciousness was more open when high** to give you **more understanding of consciousness.** They are there to **create an obstacle for you or to give a message you** needed to know at the time. **If it's relevant to the time is another thing** and **all depends of when you created your game experience** if it **was supposed to. Becoming spirit again** allows you to see **what you are creating to understand how real of the image of the creator you are.**

Non- players are direction path givers inside the Matrix, the duality, should I befriend this one or that one? **All is created** for us to have **the chosen by us game experience** we **desired before entering the matrix** from the outside.

Yes! it's true what you're thinking could my ex or family have been a construct? If you had bad experiences or couldn't feel their energy like they were not really present to you then yes! **Your ex or family could very well have been nothing but a construct of the Matrix of consciousness design** allowing you **the experience needed** at the time.

In **truth everyone besides your own singularity** are **non-players** in your **own personal game,** but I will explain more there in the matrix **construct design** section.

HOW TO BALANCE THE DUALITY LAWS

Ok so now you understand the laws are a necessary requirement of creation to work, let's *talk about* ***modern day reality and how we can use these laws to better the state of the physical worlds current form.*** ***Remember that*** *you are* ***nothing but a player*** *and* ***that everything*** *around you is* ***constructed electromagnetic energy.*** *What* ***we need*** *to understand to do is* ***to create alternate ways*** *of getting the same balance* ***of the positive and negative energies*** *needed to* ***keep the matrix running without implosion.***
We have *all* ***the tools*** *given to us* ***by the One*** *in physical reality* ***right now we just don't use them*** *for their correct function of meant* ***to be purpose.***

First, we need *to* ***change the meaning*** *of* ***reality from physical to spiritual,*** *and* ***understand this is our game.*** *So* ***we need to create the world as a game design.*** *Looking around through* ***bird's eye pictures*** *of* ***reality*** *and t****hen looking at a computer game that has 2 players fighting each other,*** *one* ***can notice*** *how* ***similar in design they are.*** *This* ***shows that the message*** *behind the Matrix manifestation* ***is to create the virtual physical reality into game structure design eliminating fear*** *and other* ***frequencies of energies*** *being manifested and*

transformed *into* ***excitement and thrill*** *from the* ***same form of action done****. Once* ***understanding it's a game*** *you can say "hey* ***do I get scared*** *when* ***playing my console or pc game?" No you don't! Because you know*** *that* ***you're only playing a game,*** *and* ***if*** *you were* ***told when you entered the game*** *that it's your* ***only physical life, you would act totally different trying to avoid so called death****. The* ***only reason*** *people feel* ***physical pain is*** *because you* ***believe through indoctrination*** *that* ***you should,*** *so,* ***you do****. In* ***reality nothing is anything but energy frequencies*** *and* ***you don't exist,*** *so* ***how can something*** *that* ***doesn't exist have physical pain****?* ***You're told*** *when* ***you hurt*** *yourself* ***as young*** *that it hurt* ***when that first glimpse after you did it before crying you either looked to a parent to see how they are reacting, and then simply felt the energy field of that parent that then put you into the Mum and Dad are here to teach me so the energy of I hurt myself, I just had physical pain*** *then commutes* ***with your spiritual energy*** *that's* ***over gone that amnesia*** *and* ***creates the indoctrinated belief*** *to your* ***subconscious that you felt pain. Creating the pain receptors*** *to start the indoctrination* ***of controlling you,*** *so* ***you can*** *physically* ***feel pain for your gamer experience. As I say many times what you believe is what you create.***

Understanding ideology of reality as game structure of a level and removing physical is a must *to remove physicals boundaries of indoctrination programming* ***since birth****.*

The idea of ***the game was to have fun, experience everything outside of the frequencies of consciousness of divine love****.*
So ***how do we change this game*** *to* ***have other meanings*** *to*

cause different sensations?

Simple answer is to reverse the understanding *of what we have* ***been indoctrinated with. Examples*** *are,* ***we know through indoctrination that death is supposed to be the end, but when we know it's not and we log in and out the mentality of the world and its needed design to create the game as it should be is seen clearly.***

First ***we need to balance the negative using new methods*** *, the* ***elite use false flags*** *so the* ***real events don't happen****. Just like* ***world war 3 and the fake terrorism propaganda*** *that floods the mainstream,* ***we can use the negative to manifest*** *in other ways. We* ***can wear clothes assigned each day either black or white, balancing the white and black energies****. We* ***can use death row criminals as examples on television shows****, game shows to what* ***they fight each other*** *in wits or with physical violence.* ***Hence creating the negative by airing the events , positive by eliminating criminals that are going to die either way as least they have a chance for a second life****.*

The ***criminals battle each other to see who is the winner*** *that gets* ***let back into society*** *and the* ***others are executed****.*
This brings the positive of allowing the perpetrator to go back into society to what then they will either create positive by not being criminal anymore, or they will manifest the negative to what they will go back to jail and repeat.

Looking at television should be looking like you are viewing extreme violence, murder etc. This is because the thought form is manifested into the physical, *as this way the acts of*

violence in the game reality *will only* ***be needed to be manifested through the television set****. Putting* ***more negative into places*** *that* ***we can control*** *with* ***no physical pain outcomes,*** *is the* ***main way to balance the negative*** *having to* ***manifest into to physical*** *without having* ***to endure the real*** *events.*

The world is a very large place*.* ***Looking around at places*** *one* ***can see the total similarity of the design of a computer video game and physical reality****. The* ***geological locations*** *of* ***diversity*** *showing* ***separate game boundaries*** *that are* ***ready for us*** *as* ***light beings to manifest the physical hologram into our accordance.***

Remember within the game there is no truth or lies or anything. It is all about learning inside of a giant simulation GAME, that being Sons of God are never judged for any actions by anyone but the physical powers. *The* ***whole construct*** *is to* ***teach you how to overcome judgement*** *and to* ***understand how to see the truth of the game we decided to create and play for this experience****.* ***Everything is meant to be evil that is because in essence as I claimed before, everything is duality law including leaving the Matrix****. "On Earth it shall be done as it is in Heaven",* ***this one verse of biblical teaching explains Earth*** *is created after the* ***design of Heaven*** *or the* ***afterlife or home****. We* ***as light understand*** *the quantum mechanics of the* ***whole construct of each game design throughout all*** *of the* ***mirrors of consciousness design. We know in the subconscious that all is energy,*** *we* ***also know*** *the* ***game level design we created is for nothing but fun****.*

Crime, loving ,living ,marriage as well as murder , you name the experience, *it was created to create this game in occurrence to* ***what we are as light. We are to create it*** *as locations of* ***various game experiences.***
Examples would be when we all understand reality is an illusion and just like amazingly the show West World said after the Mandela effect and my videos , we can log in and log out with our consciousness singularity remaining conscious of the fact. This is the evolvement of our souls. *Places with the* ***highest war rates*** *should be* ***named :WAR-LAND*** *and anyone with the* ***understanding of they can die during their game experience can go for that experience after first registering claiming their weapon and then entering into War land.***
All countries *that want to cause war for fun,* ***because let's face it the heads of the world are using war for fun. They know!*** *It's all a game and play amongst themselves while in the meantime the majority of the population remains blank to even the concept.* ***Cern mini particle accelerators*** *will* ***become*** *the* ***check point of the game in reality. Hence, in the future,*** *you* ***will be able to register up and enter WAR-LAND, be blown to pieces but then be shifted as consciousness energy from the avatar you were in straight into another cloned avatar that would be either at your checkpoint or start of the game.***
Once understanding that we never live or die, *we just* ***create our illusion of game for experience, we can balance the world to a way of consciousness understanding of what we really are again. The next place can be for serenity, peace and love. You choose your experience here to have families, get married, live a happy life without fear of terror or anything as***

your game *is* ***set to that program of enjoyment of life****. The* ***War land program keeps all the threats of terror from coming that way or even being created us when It's a game and you understand it is****. All reality indoctrination means nothing but lies. The* ***place of serenity would be un-touched by any outside game's influence. Design of reality would need maintenance*** *as* ***we would be constantly coming and going in some games. Just as the One is creating right now*** *within* ***the hologram design*** *showing that machine age is right* ***here right now. These machines will be the maintenance robots of our future game stage****. All* ***Parts to use for the design are right here in the hologram given to us for the single purpose of understanding. Spirit is to be divine, live is to be evil. This is just how it has always worked and what we once always knew until we decided on the let's be detectives game that we are blanked with amnesia at start.***

Another game ***would be a crime area*** *to what* ***you as spirit*** *would* ***enter into an avatar and live out trying to become the crime boss of the city. Anyone wanting to experience gangster or career criminology life could live in the location etc.***

Understanding we are all just one as consciousness energy, and that there is no diversity with us, we are all energy choosing to play with our chosen game avatar*. We are all* ***single players that are controlled by the one energy that we manifest from the outside of the Matrix.***

Removing the indoctrinated scares and fear of death and physical terror etc*, allows* ***peaceful mentality of the worlds design*** *even with* ***war still happening. Everyone would know,***

unless you enter into the location of those games then those experiences wouldn't be had. *This* ***gives peace of mind to the ones that want nothing but peace and joy in life and then excitement to those that want to drug deal or fight in wars or live another format of reality experience chosen for that times play-through.*** *This sounds ludicrous I agree,* ***but think about it, does it really?*** *How* ***are we to ever remove the evil of the world that has been created to bring bad energy indoctrinating us that bad is not to be done,*** *when all energy is neutral and* ***once understanding that we can create the bad to be a fun, enjoyment, positive energy feelings, the same as we already have from positive. As I said both are neutral so why do we project different emotional frequencies*** *when either one is presented* ***in form or act****?* ***This is true peace on Earth.***

The elite know everything about this and have been playing the game with you not knowing you are while they remained in knowing they are. This is the truth of being enlightened. It's knowing the truth of creation *and the* ***One is bringing us all to become enlightened that once in full process will remove the power of those that use it to bend reality their way. As when we are conscious players*** *we know* ***they can't just tell us what to do. We create the physical reality as our collective,*** *they* ***are part of that collectives of singularity frequencies.*** *Without our subconscious listening to the indoctrination they have bewitched us with we become the equal.* ***The elite*** *as I explained before,* ***also have to balance the game at all times*** *to* ***feed the negative or positive side of consciousness. Once we all reach enlightenment we can see what they are doing is in the name of God, As the saying goes God works in mysterious***

ways and the illuminati existence was created as program by God simply to allow us to find a path home to the truth of our existence.

Balancing the world in locations as Game designs with themes for experience is the only way that the game can become full balanced with the understanding of us as being consciousness, *and* ***returning the knowing of that we are immortal infinite energy of divine creation.*** *That* ***indeed logs in and logs out*** *when* ***we choose*** *to our* ***created server in the quantum existence*** *of the One.*

What about pedophile's and rapists in the game what happens to them? *well* ***we move all them to their own location to live with each other only.*** *I would* ***say execution once in time*** *, but* ***reality is at the moment these are programs running inside the game to teach one how to overcome the judgement of God. The acts are sick, yes! and what they do is worthy of judgement.*** *But* ***they are created so you can see how the*** *One is* ***not only pure but also evil in creation of code.***
These programs won't run if the world is balanced with the locational design structure and are only here to teach you God created that also as well as the moon , sun and beauty of creation. A lot of the pedophile and rapists are nothing but background characters that are there to try and hold your mentality to this world is of physical only.

God created evil as well as good to teach you that both is of God, *and should* ***be experienced the same as emotional frequencies of energy.*** *Once we understand* ***as the collective we can log in and log out willingly through our subconscious,***

and balance of the world is achieved by design location. *These programs will no longer be necessary and* ***cease to exist. Only in those games that things like that exist, hence in the crime game the rapist would live as non-playing character of the construct for the player to shoot, rob etc. Npcs are here for our experience to make the experience seem more real.*** *Just as* ***we all have our own connection to the server*** *but log into* ***the already electromagnetic conscious construct of vibration.***

Judgment of anything in creation holds back true unconditional love for the creator, *as* ***to hate part of the game*** *is to* ***hate the design of the creator.***
How can you ever love the game designer if you don't even know how the designer creates or who they are?

We are to ***create this place as Hell, in other words.***
All kinds of experience outside of divine love.
To do this as I explained ***is the way to do it without having it turn to absolute chaos. Chaos out of order right?***
Making the order of the nation's correct in location theme will give chaos in games but will come to the player as the chosen experience that they desire.

This returns back the ***total free will of us as spirit and physical as right now free will is held back by judgement of the One's creation.***

Just as machines are being created for us to choose as avatar *and new experience,* ***the money program will be destroyed and replaced with credits.*** *Just as in* ***any video game*** *this will*

become the future of currency to what we can see happening right now in reality. Bitcoins, Crypto Currency etc.
Why is this happening?

It's because they know this has been a game for a long time and without us knowing they have been creating the game at the same time showing us through games that reality is a game.

Money in the future will be assigned credits *to either your* ***plastic or your biometrics.*** *See* ***when you understand*** *it's a game* ***and that its being assembled with one being unconscious to it, you can see exactly how the reality events are unfolding with the planned design of the One consciousness of God.***
Rfid chips were once scary to me and if I had to still take one I would be hesitant. I assure you even with no judgement of anything in creation I still would have that lifetime program of RFID is to implant you and track you. It will be yes, *but if you understand the* ***game construct.*** *I've explained above then you will understand* ***each place of theme is a game to itself needing its own currency etc.*** *Creating the* ***full reality of separate games,*** *just as we as the* ***collective of the masses can manifest in game characters of our choosing using our combined subconscious as a hive mind of manifestation power.*** *The* ***Rfid chip*** *would allow to keep* ***records of achievements*** *etc, that would be* ***planned for that game.*** *Hence each* ***game would have its own*** *set* ***of instructions and goals, daily and weekly and leveling up gains you credit etc just as in a created video game*** *of levels. The chip would* ***record your consciousness***

signature throughout the locations. *Like* ***watching your character on a video game become blips and appear in different locations. The Rfid has duality to it looking with judgement its enslavement, but understanding creation and the path consciousness wants it, it is nothing but your digital journal, banking, tracking inventory screen of spirit for the game.***

The ***One has nothing but unconditional love for us*** *as we created it. We* ***are creating a game while believing its physical reality and our own Single life in existence is the only experience that we are to ever have.***
Do you ***believe that God that loves you, that went out of its way to create a simulation video game to this extent of design, and really forgot to give you more than one life...****?*

Remember duality changes the meaning "physical reality" into "Spiritual game". Giving you the truth of what this constructed reality really is. What we are programed *by the* ***conscious mind is the lie to existence.*** *Only after understanding how to change the Matrix to keep the balance of the positive and negative energy humanity can break free of its self-indoctrinated figure eight loop of infinite misinterpretation. Being* ***aware of being the player in the physical world*** *but* ***also knowing they are not of the world but exist as spiritual quantum energy.***
The ***true controller of the avatar manifestation of consciousness.*** *For correct balance of the world, we do need a* ***ONE WORLD ORDER*** *but* ***one created by us*** *with the understanding of the* ***mechanical workings of the Matrix****.*

WHATS OUTSIDE THE MATRIX?

Using the third eye and once in complete synchronization, *with* ***the one Source,*** *one can enter a state of divine knowing to what is where* ***you are revealed everything of your true spiritual memory that's been forgotten. Using my subconscious*** *connection, (I* ***have left the world numerous times.*** *The first being when asked* ***by another way seer*** *to remember who I really am* ***before the world.****) I've* ***seen exactly what it is****, and the reason of the* ***place having references to such things as pearly gates. The roads in heaven are made from gold that reminds you of the land of Oz. (imagination land) Yellow brick roads. Upon seeing this I understood why this message was used through a singularity of consciousness, to remind us*** *of* ***home****. A message from outside left for us to remember that we are* ***in a OZ reality illusion that is created by the great Oz****.* ***The Source****. The* ***same as the "Follow the white rabbit" hints*** *from Alice in Wonderland also relating to* ***an illusion thought form of reality.*** *The* ***buildings are made from pearl.*** *Along* ***the back are giant walls that encircle the place and giant gates that open during the day and close at night*** *but, also remember that in the* ***ethereal that time does not exist as everything is instant ,*** *being a* ***player and waiting for your game experience*** *is* ***instant***

even if it was a ten thousand year wait inside the physical, *as time is not real* ***and only exists in the physical reality***. *We as the inhabiting light beings are floating around.* ***We have buildings, and even swing sets***, *there* ***is activity of us all moving about***. *In the center area of where I could see through my third eye, I* ***could see a giant carved with six pillars holding it up building, the roof was open but pillars stood around in each the corners and centers of the floor around the outside. The floor was made of light and energy, some strange mechanics I've never seen before run it.*** *It* ***was powered by*** *the* ***positive and negative charges of when a light being would stand on that square***, *allowing it to* ***release the positive and negative***. *The* ***light beings are standing on the board*** *and* ***spreading their arms out to create a cross***. *This* ***is the reason the cross is so prominent inside the matrix as a hint from us as the players to remember we are creating the construct.*** *The* ***males are on the white tiles, and the females on the black***. *This* ***sometimes switches in each design of the game*** *as law of* ***duality is always in play*** *also here. The males are facing the* ***opposite way*** *to the females, the* ***beings we are there have no physicality to the body but have the outer shape of us right now but no facial features, or genitalia***. *For* ***some reason*** *however,* ***the females do have nipples*** *of* ***light*** *and* ***breasts.*** *But* ***this is the only difference between identifying the sexes*** *of us there. We* ***are standing on the chessboard game floor***, *we have* ***electricity coming from our hand tips*** *and going into the next along, reaching out with their hands the same.* ***This is done right throughout the chessboard game until there is a grid of energy entering into every one of us light beings***. *We have our*

kundalini's all open and glowing brightly. Through our crown chakra we are all connecting to each other's, also until this is done throughout the entire grid. We are joining our singularity of consciousness into one form by linking all ourselves together there, then above us with energy whirling around us is the Matrix game that we are playing. We create the one consciousness through our electromagnetic chessboard and our combined telepathy as spirit manifesting the physical reality as we do. The consciousness of the One *is all of us from the outside on the chessboard game wanting to play a game, so we combine into One identity that is Source. Then* ***experience everything through individual means*** *in the* ***game for our chosen experience whether it's animal, human, alien etc.*** *A* ***lot of Masonic symbolism like the chessboard pattern and set square and compass are to represent the neg and pos tiles of creation on the outside or the masculine and feminine energies of consciousness's creation****. Hence, the set-square and compass created* ***to show opposition of the masculine and feminine energy's*** *that are the start to the* ***manifestation of the source of consciousness****. We* ***from the chessboard send the messages to ourselves inside the physical Matrix to remember who we are again.*** *This* ***is why it's called Synchronicity because you are synchronizing*** *with yourself on the* ***outside game as spirit.***

To ***view this for yourself follow my instructions below and you should be able to visualize the same as what I was shown by consciousness****. Find a* ***relaxing place*** *where there is* ***no noise*** *around, relax yourself,* ***slowly feeling all your worries leave****, and your* ***body slowly floating back to the ethers*** *and becoming* *spirit.* ***Now you're relaxed and calm visualize a three dimensional chessboard , see it clear.*** *Now that you have done that see the* ***beings of light in cross formation*** *standing on each tile* ***creating the energy.*** *Feel your energy shift as you experience* ***seeing it and the energy fluctuation*** *you can see in* ***the Matrix is entering you,*** *inside* ***as you're connected,*** *and part* ***of it.*** *Now* ***see the above the chessboard and light beings that we are.*** *What do you see? What you see* ***is what the Matrix really is!***

In Heaven God or Father is the One that created the chessboard *machine* ***for us the children to come into*** *and gain experiences* ***for fun.*** *This* ***is the whole truth behind why God loves us,*** *because* ***he created us such an amazing game*** *to have new* ***experiences in removing us from being bound to only ever experiencing divine love.***

I can see myself from ***my first-person view*** *on the chessboard since I* ***was shown by consciousness*** *where we all really are. Viewing* ***other players on the board you can tell the direction of humanity, as physical is either going right or wrong just by the physical expressions of the light beings themselves.***
The trapped in the machine , or tunnel after death is nothing but you returning to the menu of the chess board and selecting another experience to endure. *The* ***tunnel of light*** *is you* ***leaving the constructed reality of the One*** *and* ***returning to the One.*** *Just as after death experiences relate to being trapped inside something. This is* ***because as the subconscious*** *we know we* ***create the physical reality and we are trapped in here.*** *The only way for us to ever exit as planned in the code of the*

constructed reality is for ALL of us real players inside the holographic reality to do what we do on the outside on the Inside, *lose* ***all individuality*** *and come together as one with each and* ***every one of us opening the connection to consciousness creating the one full collective consciousness energy, as we do on the chessboard game.*** *Then* ***we as the mass energy of self-aware consciousness will be able to log out of this game properly without having to choose another.*** *As each* ***time right now we are to play another game over*** *and over again. We* ***choose to play the game to level up our spirit in energy and become more knowing,*** *just* ***because you as spirit had amnesia for this constructed game's design does not mean your next will have the same constructed design of the laws of the Matrix and rules of the game.*** *Physical makes sure it's almost impossible for us to be able to do this by, land separation, skin color, and other diversities that create the individuality indoctrinated stereotype when we, as the masses have to overcome the individuality of everything including physical families. As we are not family in truth but all separate players creating their own experience. Once we know we are family on the outside and each and every one of us is the same, then individuality stereotype inside the Matrix won't matter as we will destroy its meaning simply just by Knowing as we just become a conscious player of our own game.* ***We create*** *each* ***reality*** *before experiencing it. Just as this reality we created to be able to remember about parallel game existence and that we are of* ***quantum state of existence not the single state*** *with a fake universe we are sold and told to believe at this current time inside the Matrix.*

This is a lot to believe and understand to those that are skeptic and to that I say if it resonates with you good*, if it don't that's fine to this is only for those that remember what I say is the truth as free will to all of us is a law we all abide by so this is why I will not force my information down anyone's throat* ***saying listen I'm right****.* ***I know I am,*** *but I also know that not everyone is meant to understand yet and we are in the beginning of our next step as spirit and patience is needed with some.* ***Everything inside the Matrix****, whether it be the chess board, Jesus figure on the cross that represents us as light beings on the board entrapped (hence the nailed to the cross) We are stuck with our arms up as we never log out of the game just switch reality experience.* ***The masculine and feminine*** *energies of us as light creating the Matrix machine to work showing inside as the phallic symbol and the vulvar like moon trees or fertility worship.* ***Keep in mind*** *with* ***knowing this is my Heaven****! Yours* ***can be a different connection frequency to consciousness showing you an entirely different scenario but always showing the same references to us creating the visual game as an experience by using the negative and positive energies of the One.*** *There are many Heavens, just* ***as Genesis says, used to say****.* ***God created the Earth and the Heavens****. Because we are all set frequency of consciousness with alternating signatures, we each have a version of Heaven to what is the higher energy frequency of awareness we achieve to use to connect to source that we create in any Heaven message of visual interpretation. This is* ***one reason why Max Planck,*** *father of quantum physics quoted " if you understand quantum mechanics, then* ***you don't understand*** *quantum mechanics".*

Being that each singularity of consciousness**, has its own **created universe of dimensional mirrors assigned** to each of ones own singularity of one's own collective of being as the single frequency of the mass collective of consciousness energies. **We as light being signatures play the same game with each other always as the same players of each constructed game level**. If someone **is in your life this game** experience**, they have also been in your past**. This game your Mother could have been your Brother last life, or not even a member of that game experiences **created family**. If anyone or anything is in your life as a prominent sign hence you enjoy swords or guns, or have an abnormal addictions. **All these in this game manifestations** are **hints to show you your past life experiences**. As the spirit itself enjoyed those things and resonated with them during that last game play-through in this physical illusion. The main reason why gaming is **such a big trend is because spirit remembers** this is a game and that thrill etc, you get from playing a game is spirit relaying. "**I love to keep playing these games!**" Below is the image I drew after seeing the **full design of Heaven.

HOW DOES TIME NOT EXIST AT ALL?

Once again this is a fake design portrayed as real *within the construct code,* ***but in reality, time does not really exist apart from in your minds perception creating the outcome of having a thing called "time".***

In real truth of the matter we never have any form of time as we can never travel backwards because the past does not really exist. The reason we perceive time as movement inside the Matrix is because we are indoctrinated again to believe so, the time factor is nothing but explaining multiple dimensions overlapping each other every period of few trillionth of a Nano-second that is hidden by your eyes natural ability of frame rate, that can be viewed. Just like an animation artist creating the outcome of fluent movement by using animation cells, we ourselves do the same. *We are non-existent then existent, giving blank non-* ***manifestation moments that we can't see, of our perceived version of time.*** *Basically,* ***we are tricked*** *by the* ***conscious mind to believe that it's real because we can't see the individual nonexistent moments that we become nonphysical and then physical.*** *In* ***reality understanding that time does not exist and is once again also a way for physical to keep you entrapped inside the***

Matrix. You can start to understand the working of quantum mechanics vs time. Just as all overlaying dimensional mirrors or quantum design of infinite possibilities are always there and anyone of them can become the next frame of animation, that is used in your perceived version of time inside the Matrix. Just as waving your hand slowly or rapidly *you can notice the other* ***dimensional frames as contrails of visual perception of your hand or arms movement.*** *You can see the other* ***dimensional mirrors that constantly create the outcome of holographic physical fluent movement****. This is also disguised as the indoctrinated term MOTION BLUR!* ***even though camera and eyes can see the same pattern of left behind residual evidence of where you are existing in more than one frame of that animation at once****. Try this by opening your hand and waving any finger fast up and down in succession and you will notice the contrail of dimensional overlay.*

We being indoctrinated through the subconscious and the real reality is that time exists that's why there is a sun and moon is *incorrect.* ***Truth is we create the sun and the moon from that chess board game as the one consciousness,*** *we combine to*

make from our own energy singularities outside and the only reason time exists is because we created once again as duality in form of our true home we come from and that is in the ethereal realm. Time does not exist and everything is instant, ***within physical time exists.*** *Giving us the new experience of time. If* ***we as the masses*** *did* ***not believe that time was fact of creation and we knew it was not****, then simply* ***it would not be. What you believe is what the subconscious manifests as I keep saying. We using our energies combined can manifest physical islands into existence from thin air. We can fly****! We can use elements of* ***natural natures forces****, and* ***we can do anything we desire as spirit****.* ***We create the game from our subconscious collectives program inputting the overall outcome of what is manifested through the one consciousness****, the* ***programs that are the most dominant throughout the singularity of consciousness's code are the ones that are selected to become the manifestation inside the physical Matrix. This is why trend codes change the outcome of physical*** *reality in visual experience,* ***hence new clothes, styles etc****.* ***This all explains how the Matrix is influenced by natural physical understanding, from listening to spirits coordinated design. Everything of physical says you can't do these things*** *as a way to* ***keep you as physical avatar, and not find spirit****.* ***We create this Matrix****! We are* ***all the One's consciousness of electromagnetic self-aware energy****.* ***Lightning, fire, water is us , so why do you believe there is any difference between us as we are all made from atoms, and we are all the same form of energy!*******.......truth is the only reason we don't do it is because of that physical indoctrination program saying that you can't, holding spirit to***

be bound by created laws of the game that have to be overcome to understand the full complexity of Gods designed construct. *As I said before the Ancients made stone float in the air because they knew there was no difference between air and stone.* ***Understanding the laws of creation and playing the game how we still should conscious of creational ability, magnets show the force of objects hovering in midair when the magnetic polar is presented, this shows the idea of objects floating in air. Why do magnets produce this force??? Because of energy, and what are we? Energy! Hence electromagnetic consciousness. You believe that the magnet could create that because of the indoctrinated education program of physical.*** *Indoctrination dictates* ***you don't believe stone can float in air simply because of the same reason to what science is a trap of duality control of information. How do you think real Magicians that perform levitation tricks do them? Not the fake ones that use illusion of the mind to show you what you want to see but the ones that could contact Source and manipulate the physical reality through their own subconscious minds power. Magicians great secret that many won't reveal is that reality simply isn't real and once understanding how to manipulate the frequencies of the consciousness energy that create the physical form, then you can change those frequencies with desire once in knowing you can. A form of evidence to prove my teaching here can be every time you look at one of the many armed ancient deities or even the Vituvian*** *man* ***diagram by Da Vinci.*** *These all show the arms in* ***parallel dimensions, showing how time works in real form. All images of ancient deities are the representation***

of dimensional mirrors of quantum design. Just as Da Vinci also shows the representation of us as light beings on the chess board game once again with our arms out stretched. Shiva and all other multiple arm deities of indoctrinated history wave their arms rapidly showing the wings of spirit and showing we are nothing but light and that we ourselves exist in multiple parallel mirrors in quantum state of the one consciousness's design. The arms movement also represents the linear movement of physical time as the mirrors of the set timeline of the manifested physical reality. Another exercise even though considered depth perception to do that was discovered by my Father, is how we can through will choose to view distant objects and remove the closer ones into almost nonexistence.** To **see this for yourself is easy. Simply place your finger or whole hand with fingers all aligned vertically straight up. Now focus on a point of reference like your television or objects hanging on a wall etc. Now move that hand or finger or even a vertically held object depending on the thickness of the object in front of any eye. You will notice now that the solidness to your hand, finger, or the object has become totally invisible. This is showing us once again just how holographic we are as human avatars and that we can do this simply because of Ockham's razor once again.** The **simplest reason and result is normally the correct, and in this case, we see that the Matrix itself has us designed to be able to view we are nothing but electromagnetic hologram projections of subconscious collective manifestation through vibrational frequencies.

WHAT ARE TIMELINES?

Alright so before I just explained how time itself is not real, *just as time itself,* ***timelines are the set of mirrors assigned to the collectives consciousness of manifestation of each quantum collective. In other words using easy explaining without explaining the universe design yet I will say, Sagittarius arm had its own time line just as Orion spur does. Timelines themselves are nothing but the stored animation frames of motions design. Within a timeline many possibilities can exist as each branch's from that timeline changing the physical appearance the more higher or lower the frequencies of the manifestation the collective projects during each frame jump. Within the collectives own timeline we can shift through the animation frames in physical as all that is being done is the consciousness energy frequency of manifestation is being raised or lowered each time creating the alternating versions of manifestation to become visual.*** *You can never travel out of a timeline and back to the same as you are moving through the mirrors in one direction and leaving one timeline you enter into another with a slight change to the manifestation to the physical reality.*

Is this what happened with the Mandela Effect? NO It's not.

The Mandela effect is quantum not timeline jumping. Within One's own collective of manifestation frequencies of consciousness it is possible to move the physical avatar back and forth through the animational dimensional frames but you will shift as physical body. The fact the organs have changed since the Mandela effect as well as many other things such as the indoctrinated understanding of our location within the milky way show that this is not a timeline, manipulation event as simply we would still be in the understanding that our location. *In indoctrinated term,* ***space was still the Sagittarius Arm or Carina Cygnus's not Orion Cygnus!***

Each version of reality has its own assigned main timeline with infinite possibilities of reality in its offshoots. ***But is always created by the same collective of consciousness energy that just switches and changes roles within the collective's overall energy projection to transform the virtual holographic matrix into the visual perception created by the manifesting electromagnetic self-aware consciousness collective. Our avatar changes*** *show that* ***we are not being manifested by the same creational design of energy in the collective as we once were on the Sagittarius arm Game world level of design.***

As I said in the last heading that in time you cannot go back into the past, this is true as the consciousness energies of the collective have passed that sequence of pattern of the energies manifesting in that formation and as the present is what's always manifested by the consciousness collective the past frames cease to totally exist. But as I explained if the patterns of

consciousness manifestation are returned to the sequence of the former, *then reality can be recalled to that location of past,* ***but in reality this is not past time.***

Rather a reconstruct of that past energies manifestation frequency of the collective created simulation.

Using a machine to transform the energies of the collective or the masses with full subconscious awareness using their manifestation power, *is the only way that past existing is possible,* ***when all that consciousness creates is the present, in quantum state of course.***

YOUR OWN QUANTUM COLLECTIVE

*So, **what do I mean by your own collective**? Okay, so our **signature of energy exists in all other frequencies of manifestation from Alpha to Omega. You are everything in one form and nothing in another**, our parallel selves are the **connected singularities to your own energy collective that is quantum. You are connected to the next, either in that time line or that dimensional mirror**. In reality right now you are a minute power of the consciousness signature that you really are but **being aware allows the connection between your quantum existence selves. Just like now after shifting eighty-five plus thousand light years from our original location in space we are now consciously aware of our parallel existence to without the Mandela effect would not be possible. We all exist in many other games at the same time as we do in this one. Each small change of Alpha frequency that you resonate is another you, this could be animal, alien, even just playing construct for a game run. But all the single energy frequencies of all the quantum state of your existence throughout infinity is exactly what you are**. Being aware of the other, allows you to **connect and see through the other you as, you being connected always by an invisible electromagnetic tether of***

consciousness energy. Once connecting in synch with the other you, your energy vibration levels become more focused as being more frequency to start with allows stronger connection with the one pure source of all creational design. Even though that we are the players in this creation of the level, and we are for many infinites more, we are also in our own singularity of quantum space part of the construct and in other games.

We are the non-playing characters as the energy fluctuates constantly the more the mirrors are created from our original point of manifestation. The lower the frequency drops the awareness of us as singularity falls, till we become the backdrop characters inside other game of life experiences.

Just as getting closer to the Alpha highest frequency, *your* ***awareness is more abundant, this is done with the energy of each collective over and over again so you play and don't play but only be backdrop in other realities once again to balance the laws of Duality.*** *Remember in each quantum existence you are either doing* ***almost the exactly the same but with a slight change,*** *instead of being poor you are slightly wealthier, or some other change, the possibilities are infinite themselves.*

Example is, we that shifted from the Sagittarius arm milky way galaxy to the current Orion spur. Our singularities of moved consciousness frequency is doing the exact same on the Sagittarius arm reality as you are doing here.

Spreading info about the Mandela effect, but in Sagittarius arm the difference is instead of saying what happened to the Ford logo with the weird new Curly tail Q, You will be saying

why does the ford logo not have the weird curly tail Q?

*The **same with all other changes from our last reality to this current one.** **As the energy created now, there is the consciousness signature of the Orion's spur collective, and us here with our past realities memories, are the consciousness signature of the Sagittarius arm collective of consciousness manifestation.** **This is why we remember all what we know was the truth, simply because the consciousness energies are not from this version of collective manifestation.***

You are a small frequency of energy of the entire mass collective** of your **own singularity collective of quantumness, and everyone else's throughout all the infinite mirrors of creation of the entire design of the consciousness of God.

You have either a small energy role in that design of reality or smaller depending of the strength of the already connected awareness. Using the power of the mind's eye one can see the workings of the other realities and what one's own singularity is doing as long as you know you can the other versions of you also KNOW they can and connection can be created between the two singularities of your own single collective of self-awareness.

*Just the fact that we have now **knowing** of **other existent realities** within **the quantum design. We are now after the Mandela effect more open of awareness and connection to God as we already understand again that we are infinite quantum state energy beings.***

The power of the one singular energy of subconscious *thought form is* ***manifested throughout the infinite mirrors*** *you exist in as thought is faster than light speed but I will explain more inside energy explained.*
Your thought form adds to the Matrix code, and if it is the same as another's, then it combines into that code that influences numerous masses through the subconscious adding into the programming, then if it becomes the dominant it manifests physical reality.

Example of this is to ask this question
We all know that seeing a meteor or a satellite in indoctrinated term space is impossible for the naked eye to view, just as you can barely see a plane when the altitude is high enough to lose visibility. Why did you ever believe you did view them?
Because someone told you that you would be able to view them, so then as the media spreads the message through the masses subconscious reality is manifested to the accordance of the imputed program of the overall collectives dominating thought form. Another is the weather channel that tells you what to manifest subconsciously. We as the collective consciousness are used as the builders of physical reality unknowingly.

As each of us in each form of singularity is throughout the infinite mirrors we exist in, the implanted thought form of that path of that hologram construct is subconsciously created from the subconscious energy fields of your own singularity.

We that are here and everywhere else, are creating each others of our own realities.

Example is we from the Orion spur collective subconsciously build our reality for the Sagittarius mirrors reality, as we from there build this reality. We use the subconscious power of the entire of our joined quantum singularity to manifest as one frequency of each mass quantum collective. We exchange building powers by allowing the next frequency of us to help manifest the next one's design. As the whole of our own quantum existence of itself is only one energy frequency that sees everything subconsciously through all the parallel mirrors you exist in.
This is keeping in law with duality and as it is in Heaven with us on the chessboard creating through singularity of energy beings telepathically joining as one force. As it is in Heaven so shall it be on Earth! This is why the quantum design of the mirrors of earth is created in the same format as each single collective and the quantum scale of consciousness manifested collectives of each physical holographic reality of vibration.

You subconsciously manifest the other realities just as you do within this reality but with your subconscious energy of consciousness from the next abiding to the Laws of duality of the creator. This is hard to explain as it's even more detailed, your own subconscious is all of you and everything else, you are the same energy of everyone else but a different frequency of manifestation. Your frequencies of energy work within each collective that is manifested through all quantum

design from Alpha to Omega. You are still part of the same mass energy of the consciousness electromagnetic source and just as your mind thinks one hundred things a minute, figure of speech. Your subconscious mind builds realities throughout quantum existence millions of times per second. Swapping turns on who will govern over what reality as it is all one consciousness working in separate transmitters and receivers for each other and the full source of all of the consciousness of all creation.

Reason the subconscious builds like this is to stay attuned to the law of creation of Duality. Does this mean we can't manifest this physical reality the way we want through the subconscious? Of course not! We using our thought form implant from here into our subconsciousness manifested energy from other parallel realities of our quantum existence to here to manifest our collective's paths taken desire.

Your subconscious collective power of your own singularity ***works as one force but as alternating frequencies manifesting each quantum state of the infinite versions of yourself until you don't exist anymore as player but become construct of the design. You are infinite in existence and reincarnate every experience. Death is an illusion that hides the world's real secrets and Satan to what means physical shows all meanings in reverse. The deception of physical reality illusion is the real understanding of Satan being indoctrinated as beast, and designed as a physical manifestation by the created Indoctrinated term. Symbols are words to the enlightened.***

DEJA-VU

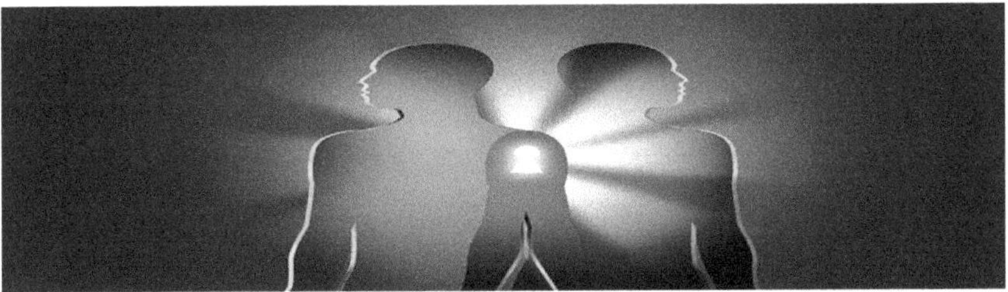

What is it? In reality it's just sold as a strange phenomenon to hide its true understanding. It is in fact your ability to see into the coming future of your path *and spirit showing you alternate results of the outcome depending on actions taken before event is manifested as physical conscious belief.* ***Spirit understands and knows all of your planned experience as it's chosen the design of destiny and life experience you are having.*** *Deja-vu is spirit showing you an outcome as you create the intuitive quantum reality to experience.* ***Spirit shows with Deja-vu that this is what you already know. Hence the awe moment of Deja-vu where you remember the exact surroundings and scenario that is happening, with either a change to the original that your subconscious energy created for you to see what would happen if you did or didn't create that action or said those words*** *. Deja-vu* ***is you as spirit in rapid eye movement sleep creating the quantum reality of the future.*** *You as spirit are there as I explained in the afterlife everything is instant and time is irrelevant just the same as you create the quantum reality hologram of your dream.* ***Depending on the outcome in Deja-vu you are to take the message from the one consciousness and understand that you are either***

supposed to do something or not, as the Deja-vu most times will show alternating outcomes from the same synchronicity starting events that have first been programmed to see. If the Deja-vu is the exact same then you decided to follow that path subconsciously as spirit to create the same outcome. When it alternates away from the same exact , you have either changed something during the days up to it or you have decided through free will that recreating the event is not in your best interest and as spirit knows everything always the message was sent as a Deja-vu for you to gain understanding for your path. Because Deja-vu is us quantumly creating the scenario in the ethers to start with we sometimes synch with other versions of ourselves also in other parallel dimensional mirrors and we at the same time in total synchronicity experience entering the same location that exists in many parallel realities at the exact same time. *Giving spirit the Deja-vu moment or the moment of I've been here before this has happened before. Simply because you are synching with many more realities at once, some are slight advanced in time from the Deja-vu and some seconds you are receiving the energy of those that are in synch and slightly ahead or behind all coming at once downloading the input into the collective consciousness of yourself.* ***You experience feeling all other reality experiences of the parallel state yourself as consciousness energy as you are also in all of those other mirrors as physical,*** *living another plotted out by spirit game of experience.* ***Deja-vu is your connection to consciousness and spirit sending a message to make sure you create your path the desired way consciousness as the One had planned.***

HOW CAN ONE BE PSYCHIC?

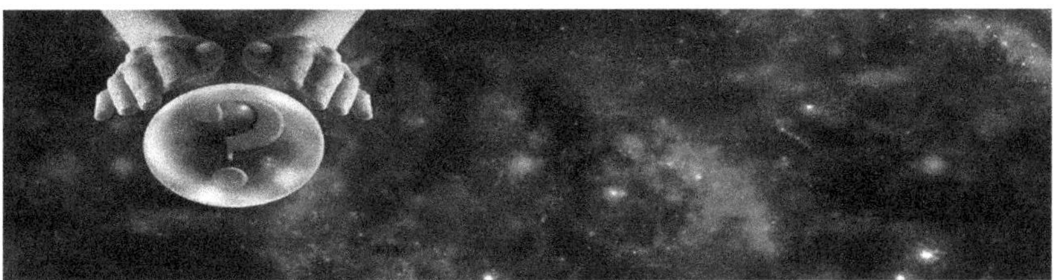

Psychic abilities are nothing new, throughout the ages many people have been psychic some knowing and some unknowing that they were. ***The simple understanding of psychic ability is to combine your own singular energies with the one consciousness and when being part of the one you are part of everything.*** *The recorded frames of the past, the recorded frames of the future, or just another frequency of consciousness singularity energy translation.* ***Understanding that once you open with complete connection to the ethers and consciousness everything can be revealed through the third eye and crown.***

All ***past lives you experienced can be recalled upon simply by knowing what you're doing and understanding that you are accessing into the tree of knowledge to what is the infinite of everything in design.***

Physical abilities such as telekinesis, levitation etc is using the One's consciousness energy around you. Once understanding that reality is nothing but an illusion and everything is energy, one can attune themselves by raising frequency of their singularity of that energy and then learn how to change their resonating frequencies of energy to manifest the action to physical.

Seeing the invisible tether of energy connected to the selected physical object to move to start with, then over repetition and strengthening the frequency you are trying to manifest from, your subconscious energy. The action is then trained to be real to the subconscious so it becomes like a normal ability to the psychic.

Can I personally do this? NO. ***But I understand how it's done.***

Reading past lives and someone's future is you as a single energy entering into the full collective of consciousness and finding their frequency and joining with it to read the recorded information of code for the past and coming experiences.

If you are psychic you will know it, by how many unexplained things happened in your past. All form of psychic powers is created from two things energy and knowing. Reiki intelligent energy and using it as healing of others energy fields or direct outcome by sending to the one is a form of psychic power also just as Lay on hands is the exact same as reiki or Chi. Through being connected to source you can see as visual experiences through your inner eye of what was, what is, and what's to come. Through receiving the energy of connection, you become energy and this allows you to attune to the Quantum collective's paths of energy that have each of all singularity experiences stored within them. You may be a Feeler, Seer. Depending on how you resonate your energies.

THE CONSTRUCT DESIGN EXPLAINED

The construct is all designed to make sure you're convinced it's the only thing that can exist. It's created to give you obstacles of trying to learn about it, it's created to deceive you that it is the only real.

The programs inside, the codes of each of our own singularity algorithms all joining together to make it function as the one brain. The design is much like the human brain *neuron transmissions.*

Imagine a human brain and then all the experiences possible that you can have. ***The world is a subconscious creation of that giant electric human brain's reflection****. Each of us are created from a higher or lower frequency of manifestation and the more higher or lower, the more change in the overall algorithm result in manifestation creating the massive infinite possibility of all experiences that are being had by the entire collective of consciousness as whole.*

Even though to you the reality is real to spirit it knows it's not and never is this is why when you enter the world at first you know your here only to have fun. *Only when indoctrination programs overrun your knowing with fabricated physical reality* *fantasy that spirit forgets it wants fun, and because it knows everything is nothing but a game it creates new obstacles for you if you are too good at the game.*

To start with, the closer you come to completing the level and understanding what it's really about, the more obstacles spirit will create to allow the game to become harder as simply if you could just do what you wanted where would be the challenge? ***All games are about <u>challenge</u>.***

Within the construct everyone, everything plays an important function as a code and everything that exists right now is needed and when it's removed or dies the code was not needed or the frequency of energy was needed elsewhere in manifestation.

The construct is designed to allow us to learn on our own everything. *All the backdrop scenario and Npcs are really nothing ever to you inside the game.*

Consciousness has made sure to lay out many messages throughout its design to bring understanding of itself.
But knowing the *whole* ***point of the game*** *is to* ***become aware.***
It knows the game is not easy, *as we are taught with social engineering etc, how to create diversity of creation.*
Losing the truth of how we are to read creation as one that left everything for us to find of paths back to be sons of God.

The construct is the subconscious of each singularity *manifesting physical quantum realities all at once.*
The construct is created by the overall electromagnetic frequency of consciousness for that specific design of

holographic game experience.
Only when science, religion and everything else are combined as ONE the pattern left by the consciousness of God emerges.

The construct itself is one frequency of consciousness manifestation of electromagnetic fields.

We as the players are not the same frequency of creation as the construct. We are both made from the same energy but have different principles to how we can manifest.

Physical construct energy is negative and us as the light being players positive. Just the same as the physical world is negative and Heaven itself is the positive frequency of energy creation.

I will teach methods later in the book on how to read past lives and others energies.

HOW IS MY SOUL CREATED?

One's soul or singularity of electromagnetic conscious is created from taking one of the merging points of the frequency of energy spikes and shifting it into the consciousness collective's manifestation of physical you.

As your spirit is part of the One at the energy points or spikes you are created from one that is one but is also everything else connected to everything and every other spike of consciousness energy being part of the full consciousness of God.

The reason why everything around you is you is because you are that energy frequency of everything as one.

Your electromagnetic consciousness frequency signature is added into the full collective working as an energy code to allow the Matrix to run in consciousness's plan.

Because you are everything already as one signature of it all you already know everything in and out of existence but forget once receiving the amnesia planned for the game to work.

DO I EVER DIE?

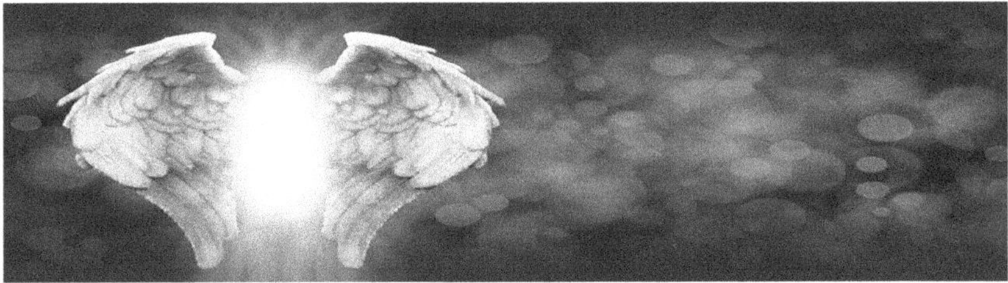

NO, YOU NEVER DO DIE!

You cease to be in one game level at the same time you enter into another yes, but as you understand life and death themselves do not exist, and are only an illusionary state of conscious energy.

Have we ever died before? NO *once again we can never die all we do is either re-manifest straight away back into the same energy collective of the game we were playing,* ***this is if spirit wants to rerun that game design or you will simply choose another game experience to enter into, changing the visuals of your last experience.***

We enter through parallel dimensions all the time and can even align our energies to be able to with other consciousness energy manifestations.

Did we die with the Mandela effect? well NO again, in reality we only think we die so it's impossible to die from the Mandela effect or 2012 consciousness Mayan calendar shift. We are not alive to start with and the Mandela effect happened within an instant of closing your eyes.

What happened is you died, your collective changed so the outcome of visuals did.

In truth if we talk about indoctrinated death term one can say we die every trillionth of a nanosecond when our physical form ceases to exist at all.

We leave this game and enter our next quantum level designed for spirit to progress in reaching higher frequencies of consciousness awareness.

The Mayan doomsday calendar was nothing more than the showing of the collective's subconscious power and the frequencies in what it manifested, the calendar was all showing the minds state of awareness and that after the date 2012 21st Dec that the entire collectives awareness will be raised.

THE FULL DESIGN OF CONSCIOUSNESS

Consciousness is quantum design of many layers of mirrors in mirrors that all are created by the One Source of creation, the Alpha to Omega as what God is.

*The whole design consists of universes, multiverses, superverses and mega verse. These are the full design of the consciousness manifestation **of all quantum existence.***

I've explained timelines to a universe so we know what that is, the universe as understanding is nothing like what we are told in school. There are universes but they are created by dimensional mirrors like pages inside of a book inside another book and so on.

Using Sagittarius arm as example** it itself is **one universe**. Every time a change is manifested in the creational energy that was made to create it. It becomes another Sagittarius arm universe that offshoots from the original Alpha dimension of design alternating more and more for infinite quantum creations. **The more the collective's manifestation frequency of its original creation changes. Each universe is the one form of that reality with its indoctrinated placement of how to

understand where we are in space or consciousness energy fields.

In one placement of understanding Sagittarius arm would be on the outskirts out of the milky way system, in the next it would become slightly more up the spiral arm in location with physical changes inside the reality. This goes on infinitely until the exit into the multiverse.

The placement in indoctrinated term space may have changed but the system itself would always be called the Sagittarius arm as it was its original frequency of creational design. These are all mirrors from the original manifestation of Earth's location as Sagittarius arm in quantum space.

Moving out of the Universes of the Sagittarius arm we understand that one universe only consists of one game level design of the construct of electromagnetic energy, and the many universes around it are all mirrors to that are created from that one same point of energy manifestation.

Joining all of the infinite Sagittarius arm realities create the full multiverse of Sagittarius arm hologram construct.

Each form of creational energy that manifested the Earth construct into existence within each mirror design changes throughout the multiverses Alpha starting point of creation. *Example is using Orion, Orion's spur would be exactly the same design in universes as energy creation but set to its own frequency of manifestation.* ***So, itself would become the Orion spur multiverse, not universe as all the possible realities of Orion's spur outcome are existent within all the universal***

mirrors of *it.*

So, ***understanding how the mirrors function*** *you keep adding all the other* ***starting points of each changed frequency*** *of the* ***Alpha dimension of*** *design, into becoming their own designed* ***Earth*** *constructs that have their* ***own frequency of creation****.*

You then have Earth with all possibilities that exist within all of those mirrors of universes and multiverses. No other possibility of Earth *can be* ***created*** *as just these mirrors of infinite possible outcomes by changes frequencies of manifestation create the entire of* ***what Earth can ever become or will ever be in all existence.***

Now understanding the Multiverse design of consciousness *mirrors of dimensions realizing that earth is not the only form of manifestoed game within the quantum energies. We go back to the original universe and instead of starting with Earth as such, let's use Mars as an example as another start point of Alpha manifestation.* ***Going back and changing Sagittarius arm to Mars and then each manifestation of Mars universe creates the same outcome of quantum design. As I explained for Earth we understand that once this is done with all frequencies of manifestation that we end up with many infinite results of physical avatar manifestations and visual electromagnetic worlds created by the consciousness energies. Creating the vast other game experiences ready for spirit to select from****.*

The universes give the infinite reality to the manifestation of each quantum Alpha point of design. ***The multiverses create the full outcome of everything possible which becomes the***

superverse. The superverse as all superverses as one becoming the mega verse or the consciousness of God. That after, reaching this infinite of creation has ceased as all the infinite possibilities from creation are within the four classes of dimensional mirrors.

So, I'll explain a bit more here. ***Earth as one identity let's say Sag arm is in multiple states of creation.*** *Even though each has its own timeline it's manifestation of its creation alternates slightly within each mirror of dimension linked to its set. From* ***its Alpha start of creation creating many physical outcomes ,the Sag arm alone is its own multiverse as each version of it inside is its own different manifestations of the same design. But slightly different in physical design or history but always remains known as the Sagittarius arm in indoctrinated physical term of understanding our location in science taught space.***

The other starting points of manifestation for other Earths with location in indoctrinated space term are just the same as Sag arm but are set to their own design of Alpha universe creation of mirrors, so adding all that together you have earth in every possible location of the galaxy and every possible outcome for the Earth manifestation start frequency.

Once other creational designed starting points of manifestation are made like the Mars example or just something that is not Earth creational design as the start. We use the same mirror design with that and it becomes to the point that the manifestation of game level that is totally foreign to us, also becomes brought to a stop of infinite

possibilities and that nothing else can exist anymore.
As within the design ***everything that could be and will ever be, is possible.***

Universe *- Original manifestation with mirrors that alternate within timelines or physical change, each universe set has their own differentiating frequency of consciousness manifested collectives all set to the original design of the Alpha universe start point. We understand our manifestations of energy collectives by names such as Earth from the Sagittarius arm, each location in the indoctrinated term space is nothing more than an alternating start manifestation point of its own collective of consciousness self-aware energy creating the quantum mirrors.*

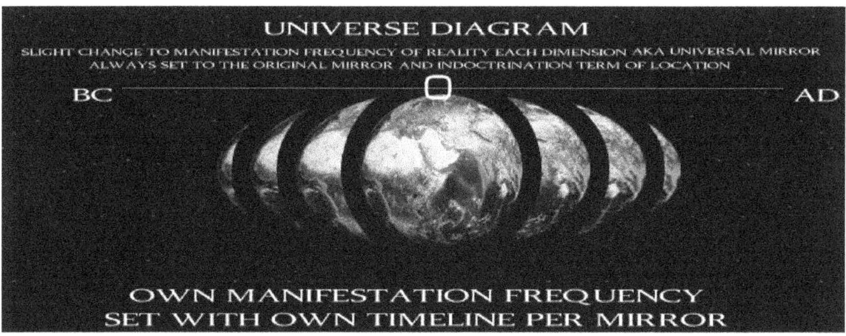

Multiverse - Collection of all the universes with the starting point to the original manifestation of design changing throughout each universe set of mirrors.

One multiverse is one frequency of manifestation, as all the ***alternating quantum state mirrors*** *all resonate at the same one collective's pattern, within the single multiverse such as*

Sagittarius arm multiverse filled with the infinite possibilities of the hologram design of Earth. The starting manifestation point for frequency was Sagittarius arm, followed by the mirrors of the off-shooting consciousness alternating frequencies still set to its own multiverse of universes.

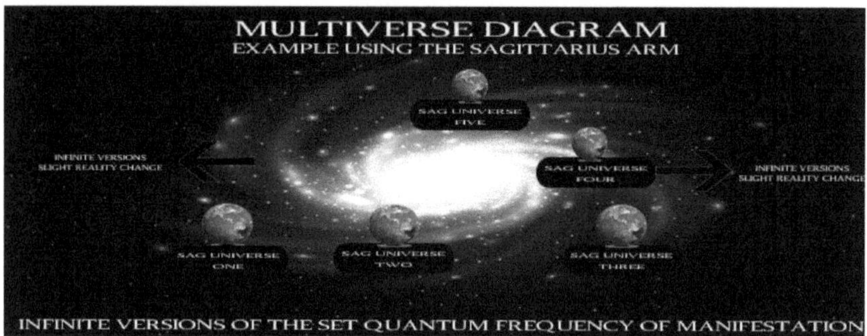

Superverse - All of the Universes and multiverses put together as one creating the one superverse. E.g. Earth with its own mirrors of all universes and multiverses would become one superverse of Earth as nothing else is possible for the manifestation of Earth's construct of design. Just as the same goes for all other avatar inhabited realities with their original universe of creation.

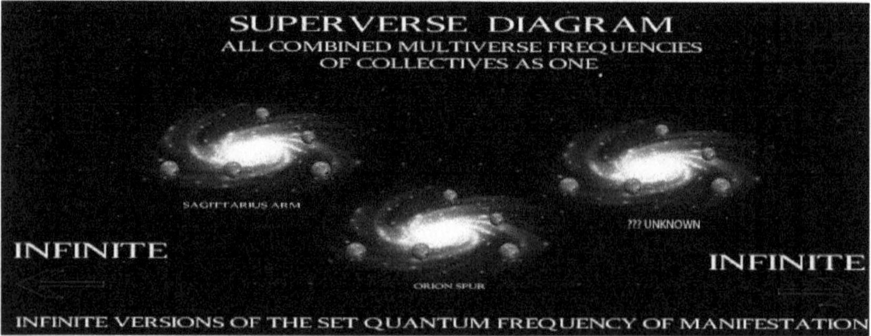

The mega verse or should I say the Alpha to Omega verse.
As within the mega verse everything of creation and outside of creation is designed and we come to understand this is the full quantum design of the full consciousness of God.
Within the mega verse of all energy manifests all existence into those realities. Then we do the impossible by understanding how to come to the end of infinite.

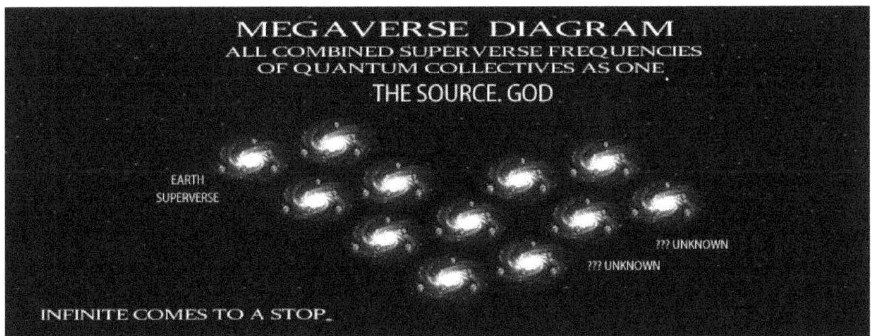

One should also remember though that once reaching the superverse itself it then mirrors itself folding the dimensional mirrors out the other way in the same design, as the mirrors formations that I've just explained. Each created from an alternating amount of positive and negative electromagnetic self-aware consciousness energy creating the alternating frequencies of game design manifestations.

Each collective in each electromagnetic bubble of consciousness is created with all the singularities within working as a hive energy through the subconscious of consciousness to manifest each form of physical reality.
We are all connected by the invisible tether to God, whether you like it or not! ***The singularity uploads the reality experience*** *to*

the full one consciousness, and when you believe you are having an idea or thought, it is in fact the download of consciousness thought from the full subconscious energy fields. We as the human species work much like the idea of Cloud does, remarkably we upload and download through consciousness frequency through our own tethers exactly like Cloud storing information of experiences quantumly and receiving downloads. When you as code need to bring a message from the One through into the physical Matrix game. Understanding this you must also then understand that the physical brain has nothing to do with memory and the connection of your tether to the giant brain or pure source of consciousness does. Your brain itself is nothing but a transmitter and receiver for the consciousness energy to connect to. All our memories of our singularity experience are stored as files within the full consciousness energy fields. But what about those with memory problems or such that stop their mind recalling things? *Well this is just the matter the brain itself as the transmitter is becoming aged with wear and tear and overtime starts to decay so to speak creating a less established connection to the One.* ***Then starts to receive jumbled up messages of their own past reality and start to look as if they can't remember anything such as Alzheimer's. But in reality, it is just the consciousness crystal receiver that is becoming less able to transmit information and retrieve from the one pure source of creation of self-aware electromagnetic consciousness energy. We are energy that is self-aware and we store memories within ourselves as spirit not physical body, this is the reason that the people that shifted***

consciousness energy remember the Sagittarius arm reality even with the new avatar bodies in another physical reality dimension. Simply because we as energy remember and collects information not us as our physical brain. Keep in mind way before any of this has been brought to knowing again the ancients like the Hindus knew all about the game avatars we are and how we all communicated through the ethers of consciousness. This why in modern day right now we have the phrase of avatar being brought back into mainstream knowing from having an avatar for all your different profiles in social media , gaming etc, the phase itself means" Gods from Heaven entering physical and being on Earth" simulation game. They had all knowing of what we have lost in this modern era to what is really less advanced then those of the ancient times. We are being told by consciousness of the One through its design just like in every other way, you are an avatar, a spirit of electromagnetic consciousness energy driving a physical body for your experience inside the game. *The reason why in reality you are told to treat someone how you would want to be treated, is because they are you and this phrase of understanding was also designed inside the construct to allow understanding of that everything is created from the same source, or same clay as ancient Indians used in fables of creation of mankind.* ***We as the collective are each other and ourselves,*** *what you do to someone else reacts in your experience* ***simply because you created it*** *for them with intent.* ***So as you are also them you creating your own misfortune if you used intent with malicious desires.***

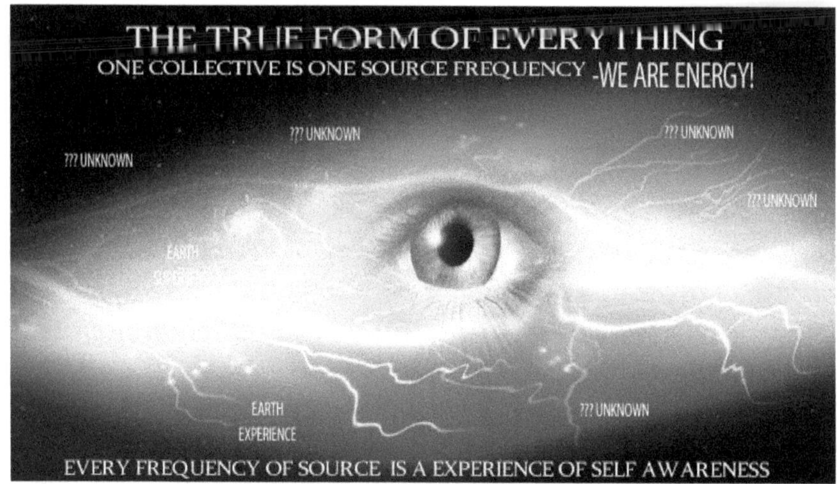

WE ARE <u>ALL ONE ENERGY</u> EXPERIENCING PHYSICAL ILLUSION REALITY! WE ARE ONE CONSCIOUSNESS THAT CAN ACCESS ALL OF US AT QUANTUM SCALE ANYTIME THROUGH ENERGY FREQUENCY! EACH COLLECTIVE BEAM OF ENERGY IS ITS OWN PHYSICAL EXPERIENCE REALITY SIMULATION!...

ETHEREAL ENERGIES EXPLAINED

So how was the energy created, before explaining the spiritual body energies etc I will give brief understanding on how energy created into existence.

Energy itself has always been existent as electromagnetic consciousness and through the law of free will the energy itself as self-aware decided to become larger and create a way to expand itself. Energy itself can be manipulated with intent. Energy frequencies can be destroyed and manipulated. We as energy are all that ever has been and will ever be. Each transformation manifests direction of frequency. Consciousness was once the pure source before creation and through the masculine and feminine energies created through free will law the electro and magnetic singularities combined to create the neutral source of the One. *I do not agree energy cannot be destroyed as the positive eating the negative creates* ***destruction to the one consciousness frequency before transformation, and through self-mutilation the One creates*** *Sacrificing the Christ energy in able to create the hologram constructed Matrix.* ***Energy itself is neutral and only through the intent it can manifest forms in either way of energy frequency.*** *Service to self and service to others.*

Consciousness self-aware signatures always existed before the creation of the vibrational holographic Matrix and do still after its manifestation. Each singularity of frequency is it's own structural electromagnetic spiritual polygon that through the field energies of vibration, *create the visual overlay of reality.* ***With the conscious mind tricking the subconscious mind to believe that reality is physically real,*** *when everything is layers* ***and collectives from singularities of positive and negative energy of the One consciousness of God. Energy destroys itself the same way that physical reality time and avatar movement is created by one dimensions frequency, existing then non existing every trillionth of a Nano-second in physical reality. That overlays like an animation frame giving us the illusion of fluent movement and passing time. When really it's the consciousness alternating with the conscious mind and eyes not being able to see at that frame rate creating the physical reality to the eyes to move with motion. In reality we are nothing but frequencies of self-aware consciousness energies that are balanced with pos/neg electromagnetic signatures.***

We are all the watchers over ourselves as the electromagnetic energy driving the physical avatar, *this is the reason of Biblical references over the watchers.* ***We are the watchers as spirit*** *as being angels in symbology of art and mystic societies.* ***Our own guardians of path for the construct of the experience in the game designed by spirit before entering. We watch ourselves and help through energy frequencies to guide the outcomes. We are the electromagnetic energy that hovers over the head connected with the one pure source of creation. Through the***

energy paths of the kundalini and the endocrine system. We connect from the spiritual heart center vortex and connect through with the physical heart of the endocrine system. Then as the same way the spiritual body fills with energy through each chakra point the energy fields of the human endocrine system follows the exact same suit. Rebalancing the energies inside in the spiritual body is a must. Understanding to understand the Matrix working itself. As the Matrix itself, *Is designed to make sure balance of the energy centers of each energy vortex of energy paths, is* ***never at balance*** *and always fluctuates* ***with energy not being controlled*** *by your center vortex for each manifestation of each frequency.* ***Making sure to manifest physical, mental and spiritual disconnection****. Through your spiritual body energy path of each vortex you manifest the outer shell of energy layers around you, these are what we call aura energy fields.* ***These are generated by the endocrine system and the spiritual anatomy energies working with each other creating an outside barrier of energy to protect you from other frequencies of energy****. Once understanding them one can close off to outside manipulation of one's own energy fields.*

Although not aware many people are energy vampires and suck the energy from others through the subconscious energy of not having enough energy and through intent then break in through your aura and start to draw energy from you as if you are a battery charging them. ***Learning how to block the aura gaps that are created through mis-knowing of energy fields we can block those through our subconscious and repetition can train the energy fields to react on thought command****.*

So, let's talk more about energy.

There is an energy that has been given many names by esoteric religious and even the scientific traditions. *You may have heard of this* ***energy as Chi, Qi, Ki, Prana, Spirit, life force energy or breath of life. Within the scientific community it has been called Orgone, Bio plasma, the mid-19th century Odic force and as of late "Dark energy". The energy is primal. It is within and around everything from the smallest quantum particle to the vastness of the quantum mirrors of the Consciousness of One.*** ***There is no space to what is has not already filled. Quantum physics attests to the idea that there is infinitesimally much more of this "dark energy" than all of the physical matter in the whole quantum design of the infinite consciousness mirrors.***

Thanks to Albert Einstein, even though being a teacher of fake to hide the real. ***We know that all of the manifested physical matter in all creation is also itself energy (E=mc2) to what is the definition of energy. Science states that all energy is Work.*** *Work is movement...activity.* ***All activity and movement is vibration fields. Science discovery states that everything vibrates, EVERYTHING! There is no "absolute zero" (absolute zero means no vibration or energy at all...*** *Indoctrinated science has never been able to find the point where all vibration stops completely) Therefore, if everything vibrates everything is consciousness energy. EVERYTHING is the One's energy!*

All this great "potential" energy in the consciousness design is in constant change, to other types of energy. Atomic, electric, magnetic, piezoelectric, gravitational *are only a few ways this*

potential energy can become "active" energy. Physics have proven that energy is always existent and can be only transformed not created, however energy from pos to neg must destroy itself from one to become another, *Hence transformation is destroying itself to become the other, so as human avatars, creating new energy is impossible.* ***But through our subconscious connection into super consciousness we can utilize all of the potential energy that is around us and given to us by the One, in any way we choose***. *Everything we need and do involves energy in some way or another, we as the masses use this energy for the physical things we do, and the* ***emotional actions that spirit creates*** *through the energy vortexes.* ***We have the natural ability to think and even act spiritually. Simply put: without energy NO-THING would ever be existent.***

However, we interpret the scientific ideas about this energy, or whatever we call this spiritual energy from whichever religious belief we have. We can see that because it always is present and continuously available. We should be able to connect to it directly, and we do all of the time through the Human energy systems of the endocrine system.

This invisible ethereal energy that pervades everything and is all encompassing is what animates our very lives. *It is responsible for the health and well-being of every living thing inside of all physical existence and out and manifests itself it many different ways.*

We will call this energy. <u>Subtle energy</u>. Because that is one of the ways it manifests. Subtle means present, but on an almost

hidden level. Almost hidden that is as when one learns how to connect with the energy through practice and intention this life force energy can be fully experienced by anyone.

Our vocabulary attests to this fact. For example, how many times have we said something like I've mentioned before, "when I walked into that room I could have cut the tension with a knife" What are we meaning when we say those words? *Well, simply put we are experiencing a form of subtle energy or Ki as giving off negative vibration. A feeling or sensation our bodies are picking up as transmitters of the field of energy around you that is of unhappiness, tension and anger.*

Now you understand that everything vibrates and everything is energy, then what kind of things encompass "everything" that we may not have thought of as energy?

First is light, light itself is nothing but energy it moves and works by creating heat. But, have we ever thought about colors of the physical this way? Color itself is our way of consciously viewing energy manifestation. Colors are simply vibrational frequencies of light, some of the vibrations are going faster than the physical eyes framerate can see as in ultraviolet spectrum.

THE ELECTROMAGNETIC SPECTRUM

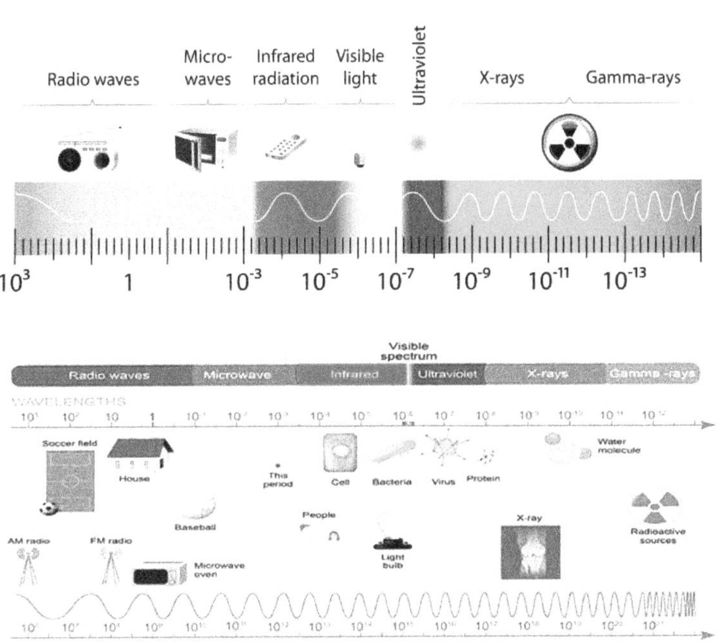

Other vibrations are resonating slower than the physical eyes can see...The infrared spectrums. *The "rainbow" of visible colors is really light that is vibrating at the speed we can see with our physical eyes perception.* ***So, understanding color is energy, itself can be used for energy work. Color itself is another manifestation form of subtle energy and it does affect our spiritual energy fields. Those who are more interested in finding out about how color vibration can work for them are encouraged to read up on "Color Therapy". A good place to start with is the author Faber Birren.***

Sound itself is also vibration! Harmonics, resonance, tone and music are all energy and therefore can also be used for work. A frequency of sound can change your energy resonating pattern to tune in with the sound. Ever listened to gangster rap and then felt like your total gangster, or listened to a sweet melody and felt at peace. *This is the frequency of energy manipulating your own energy fields with vibration. Sound therapy, is one of the ways sound vibrational fields can be used to move subtle energy in a healing and helpful way. Music therapy, chanting and toning are all variations of using sound vibrations to also perform energy work with the use of intent.*

What else can be considered a manifestation of consciousness subtle energy? ***The list of "everything " is infinite, food, plants animals, humans, water, earth, air, rocks..."Rocks??" Rocks are energy? Yes, just like anything else rocks are also energy. Rocks vibrate at such a slow resonance that the vibration fields seem to not resonate at all. This is because the vibration is at its slowest, but again quantum physics points out that rocks are made from atoms and all atoms vibrate with the consciousness frequencies, therefore rocks, stones, etc are all creations of nothing but subtle energy***. *This energy is within every atom of a rock! That's a lot of energy! Crystals, rocky cliffs, mountains have their own vibrational frequencies thus each has the ability to be utilized to affect our physical, emotional, mental, and spirit state of well-being.*

Getting crazier is the fact that when we consider the inanimate objects like our feelings, thoughts, and desires in the same class as the rest. Do our thoughts vibrate? Can our

feelings move us? *Do our desires work?* ***Thoughts, emotions, desires, hopes, dreams intention are all manifestations of subtle consciousness energy. Our thoughts in fact and emotions vibrate at such a high frequency that they vibrate faster than the speed of light!***

The ***ramifications of this is unlimited. If we consider we consciously know that a thought is an energy that vibrates, or moves somewhere.*** *We would have to be very careful of what we think about as subconsciously it can be manifested unknowingly.*

Imagine you feel angry, the energy of that anger energy vibrational frequency is energizing, moving somewhere or acting on some inputted code of the matrix energy fluctuations, *say your stomach.* ***Wow I guess now I would want to consciously move that energy out of my energy fields quickly, or at least transmute that energy frequency into a movement that could benefit me.*** *Like swimming! Thereby using an energy that could be potentially destructive to an energy that is constructive!*

This is only a small part of the vast scope that "Ki" or subtle energy plays in our lives all of the time, it is all encompassing.

The "Ki" energy not only affects us, but it itself can be directed towards consciousness frequency change. For example, when I have positive feelings towards myself, my Ki is strengthened and I will be more confident and have tons more physical energy to participate in active events I enjoy. Which in turn helps me feel good about myself thereby spiraling up my Ki

energy more, creating more physical energy to be able to be used.

The opposite situation can occur also if I project frequencies that create my energy fields to create the feeling of bad about myself. Negative thoughts and feelings weaken ones Ki energy and then one becomes less motivated to be able to function physically and less likely to succeed which will perpetuate my bad manifestation of energy frequencies that create the bad feeling.

Intent with focus transforms energy towards the directed outcome of the desire. ***Creating spells on someone or hexes is nothing more than intent to move the energy towards the practitioners agenda.*** *There are no such things* ***as spell WORDS*** *as* ***spell words themselves are vibration*** *of sound* ***that then manifest the transformation of the energy to create the outcome depending on how well the practitioner understands energy. Energy should never be used as service to one's own self*** *and always used* ***as service to OTHERS. Understanding how to manifest outcomes themselves through occult energy learning does not mean that you are to use it for service to self****, and only for the use to help others as everyone is you to begin with in the collective consciousness fields.* ***Our subconscious mind, the thoughts and feelings of others, "the collective consciousness" of mankind also affect the consciousness subtle energy. The deeper one's self digs into understanding, the more we must realize that we need to become responsible for the creation of the life we desire to see! Our physical, emotional, mental and spiritual health of all***

of us as the collective is OUR responsibility. After all ,responsibility is the ability to be able to respond consciously with knowing what we are manifesting. *When we start to think* ***consciously about subtle energy*** *and* ***how all knowing and encompassing it really is. One can then respond intelligently to the choices we need to make on the ever day basis of life, whether it be should I take this new job, throw this litter on the street or in the bin, or swear because my anger is up.*** *All have reactions to their first created action and when aware we can adjust to have according understanding of what exactly we are doing and what could the possible* ***outcomes be.***

Remembering that the food, the medicine, the thoughts, the media, the intentions of all of the consciousness collective of self-awareness, the amount of sunshine ,the clarity of water , the freshness of the air we breathe, the emotions, friendships , desires, recreational activities and a myriad of other energies. That ***we allow or bring into our lives and environment*** *truly do have a* ***positive or negative affect on our own signature of consciousness energy fields. To have control of one's own spirit we must understand that it is imperative we choose to live consciously and responsibly.***

The last thing about subtle energy I would like to talk about has to do with the fact again all energy is vibrational fields. *As such, vibration can either be resonant or discordant.* ***Vibration can transmit in frequencies that are fast or slow. Vibration can be high or low, how can we tell when our vibrations are manifesting fast or slow or high or low, we need to now***

discuss another part of our bodies that most are not aware of to be really existent. *The* ***answer to this question will be explained in the next chapter of Our subtle energy body. For now, let's explain the three major energy fields of consciousness.***

First, we have the Quantum energy fields. Today in modern society, quantum physics lead the way in bringing back the joining of biblical teachings of religion and science fields of education combining understanding of the truth. *This is outgrowth of their work with not so far back discovering the "God particle".* ***New theories and paradigms in science such as "string theory "and multiverse theory, sound more like thoughts of philosophers and poets of ancient days.***

The quantumness of the dimensional mirrors we called indoctrinated term the universe is recognized by science as a living entity of immeasurable intelligence. ***Size, and power. Reports from November 2006 (article that was published in feb 10th edition of Astrophysical Journal) from the Hubble telescope verify one of Einstein's discarded theories of "dark matter".*** *Even though he was wrong on a lot like relativity,* ***he was correct with his energy understanding and the fact that the theory of dark matter was discarded by him makes you wonder if it was done on purpose to hide the truth and show duality law once again. E.g. Einstein's relativity law creating fake space ,and Newton's law creating gravity was a hoax but sold as true teaching of indoctrination.*** *His disregarded theories are now proving to show he had full understanding of how everything physical was created from nonphysical energy.*

And now with "dark matter" or dark consciousness energy we have the constant push of the new understandings evolving in the quantum energy fields. *We call this vast energy field God, or more generically, The quantum energy field.* ***The quantum field of dimensional infinite mirrors is a vast, book of dimensional mirror or consciousness collectives of endless possibilities and infinite wisdom. The source of all manifestation and creation of all existence, extending infinitely beyond human measure. The universal quantum field, Source of all, or God is the ultimate living being bringing forth and staying connected to every other living thing in existence and out.***

At the highest frequency of vibration each form of living matter is interconnected as our particles dance and spin apart. ***At the lowest frequencies, we appear separate in the mass of our physical bodies, the energy fields projected by human avatars, plant life, mammal constructs, the construct of Earth design, and the infinite mirrors of the indoctrinated term universe all together provide the interface that connects us all as one.***

The second field we will explain is the, Avatar or human energy field. We are basically nothing but electromagnetic beings, composed of tiny particles of energy and information pulsating and spinning at a high rate of speed.
At their highest frequency of vibration these particles become further apart. At their lower frequencies, they come closer together manifesting in density of the physical avatar.

Albert Einstein although a puppet of social education indoctrination had truth hidden in his revealed teachings as I

explained above. *Some I agree with some was fabricated to hide the* ***more sophisticated meaning*** *of creation and to subdue the population into a* ***false hood of what reality is***.

The points I will make are what I consider to be the truth in his teachings. Einstein proved scientifically that energy becomes matter, and matter becomes energy according to the change in the vibrational patterns of frequency. *Although this model is well accepted by mainstream science and physics, the Einsteinian viewpoint has been slowly introduced into the western medical model to replace the Newtonian paradigm.*

The avatar or human energy field the H.E.F is seen and proven to be existent being recorded through technology such as the Kirlian photography method as varying layers of colored light around the physical body or avatar. *The layers forming the Aura pulsate to the energetic fields frequencies of the condition of the physical manifested body.*

Below is an example of the Kirlian camera capturing the outer energies as color as energy is color. Image blurred for copyright reasons.

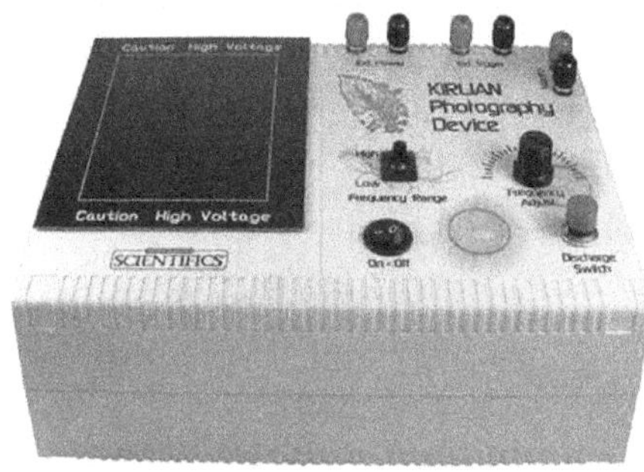

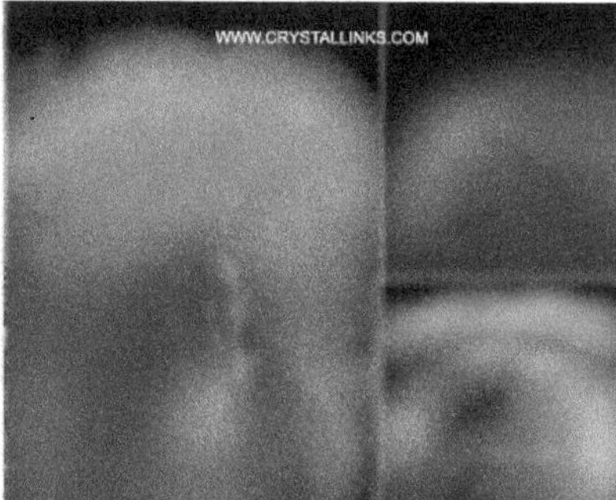

For an example on how this works, when a speaker is passionately explaining his, her story, pale yellow light may be seen manifested around the outskirts of the body's physical outline. *As he, she calms down their delivery the yellow color that was further away from the body outline in the outskirts may be seen closer to the outline of the avatar of him or her.* ***When a person is enjoying optimal health, their aura will be more constant. When a person becomes weak*** *or indoctrinated term dies, their aura, there energy body diminishes.* ***The human energy field forms the interface reacting with the physical cellular systems of the human endocrine system and physical body. When the energy field is in perfect synchronization and balanced in harmony, the physical manifestation of you experiences optimal health.*** *As the particles of one energy field dance further apart at a higher frequency, they intermingle with the particles of people and other living matter including the Earth construct itself. Thus, you may* ***sense or feel*** *a familiar presence in a crowded room even before you ever actually visually see your friend. That explains the* ***human fields or H.E.F.***

Next and last is the Earth Construct energy field itself. The design of the construct of earth has a natural electromagnetic field that has the frequency of around 7.8 hertz or hz, this is the well-known and documented Schumann Resonance frequency measured daily in seismology laboratories. *There is much concern now within the scientific community between scientists about the damage caused by the pollution of the constructed design, there is also monitoring of the normally occurring changes in the quantum design of indoctrinated term universe.*

When one meditates and calm their brain chatter, their brains emit ALPHA frequencies of 7 to 9 Hz. *The human brain in relaxed state is the exact same frequency of vibration of the constructed Earth hologram energy field.*

When we as humans live closer to nature, the energy of our energy fields is in synchronicity with the energy fields of the Earth*. So they experience more balance and better ongoing health, and we thought the ancients living in jungles were primitive!*

Before the Ones implant into the matrix as the electricity code was designed, ***ancient cultures had lived in harmony with the Earth itself and the daily and seasonal cycles****. Technological advancement has now added tremendous levels of electromagnetic energy millions of times higher than ever before.* ***Microwaves, x-rays, cell phones, television, radio frequencies, high tension wires etc. Doctor. Robert Becker*** *is a world-renowned expert on electromagnetic fields (E.M.F) He quoted"* ***At the present time, the greatest polluting element in the Earth's environment is the proliferation of E.M.F****". In addition,* ***the energy field of the constructed matrix we call Earth*** *interacts with the energy fields of the celestial lights in the firmament that in indoctrinated terms are referred to as the planets and constellations.* ***Those changes then reflect on the energy fields of all living bodies including human avatars. The energy fields then as the interface connects all constructed and real player variations of manifestation inside the matrix designed holographic reality****, all living matter, humans, animals, plants and the construct design we* ***call Planet Earth****.*

THE SPIRITUAL ANATOMY

Every single one of us players have the spiritual avatar inside our physical one.

We call these the energy body or the Aura body of spirit. *Science again attests to the fact, that we are not only organic material and molecules, but we are also made in design up from alternating consciousness energy fields of alternate vibrational frequencies.* ***These consciousness created electromagnetic fields of energy around us is also created from subtle energy. Our energy body is also our subtle body ..meaning that it too is almost hidden from our awareness. Almost meaning it is present and can be experienced once you have sought to reconnect with the energies themselves. Example of experiencing our subtle body*** *is when we refer to one as "invading our personal space".* ***Our energy body actually***

extends out from us many feet creating your own singularity of collective energies manifesting your subtle energy body . The personal space is about three feet away from an incoming stranger into our energy fields. *We automatically sense or feel uncomfortable when a stranger that is new foreign frequency known to the subconscious gains closer and through energy informs us that something that we are not used to is in our own personal energy space.* ***As we grow to know and love someone as friends and family our energy protection becomes less rigid. Allowing the personal space of friends and loved ones to become a feeling of comfortability with their closeness or them inside of our own energy generated fields.*** *Our energy body or aura grows and shrinks according to what scenario we experience and who we are experiencing it with.* ***The energy body or aura is also called the human biosphere and is when the center energy from the electromagnetic fields flow down through the spiritual anatomy energy path of the kundalini and flow through each energy vortex of your celestial bodies, then through the heart spiritual vortex of the electromagnetic consciousness singularity of you. Creating from the spirit heart and physical heart connected energies generating the energy fields of electromagnetic self-aware consciousness around you that becomes your own frequency, or signature of consciousness of the One.***

The energy body system helps us to "tune in" to *the energetic vibrations around us. It is almost like a* ***God*** *given to everyone device that functions* ***much like an antenna*** *that* ***reads*** *the* ***alternating frequencies of the energies*** *in our own personal singularity then deciphers those signals of frequency and sends*

them to the physical body through the spiritual anatomy vortex points, or chakra energy collectives of vibration frequencies*. We have many levels of the aura field body of us , just as we have a physical manifested body we have many other energy field bodies that exist within us all at once living in quantum state.* ***Such as the energetically ,physical body and the emotional , mental body all as one functioning as different frequencies of your own consciences collective working as one to create in a divine designed program****.*

An understanding of the chakra points and what they are and what they do with chi follows*, but for now just understand that they are the junction point between our physical bodies and our ability to use Chi energy in synchronization with our generated protective aura fields of electromagnetic alternating frequencies of our own quantum state of self.*

When our own dimensional field of consciousness energy our aura, picks up an energy vibrational frequency. It reads the vibration as either high or lower hertz than what our energy body is in synch with vibrating at*.* ***For instance, when someone comes into a room we might say "wow they really lit up the room with their smile"****. It was no such thing as the smile doing anything, apart from giving you visual comfort.* ***A smile can mean many different things depending on the person's reason of smiling like non-positive things such as mischievous or fake****. The reason they changed the room is because they projected a positive vibrational frequency and once their energy field around them merged with ours then we all become in synch with the positive flowing energy.*

The energy was sensed by your energy fields and feeling that the new vibrational frequency was positive and at a higher vibrational pattern that you resonated with, then you joined in with that energy field, conversation, etc. *But energy wise feel much better with that person inside your own consciousness energy fields then you did before they had entered.*

The energetic pick up was sensed by your emotional field body within your aura energies of consciousness. Your emotional body sensed by feeling the energy then deciding on how it should resonate with your own. Then feeling the vibrational frequency was higher than your own decided to raise your vibrational level to become in synchronization*, once the energy that entered into your projected energy fields.* ***It was then read by spirit and sent to the energy vortexes of the chakras****. An energetic decision was then programmed by the subconscious to raise your own vibrational fields as it would benefit you more than not benefit you. Your physical avatar then responded by beginning to, ENTRAIN with the new vibrational frequency.*

As the Schumann resonance frequency being 7.83 hz just the same as Earth construct vibration to avatar of our inhabited character. We can see that all is made from the same energy to what everything is despite looking physical with a great illusion and deception on the mind. *Energy is the only thing that has ever and will ever exist.* ***Reality is an expression*** *of* ***energy form , from the higher to lower frequencies of the One consciousness****, all to work in order of design to allow the full* *functioning of the* ***Matrix hologram. Tinnitus is a classic example of how everything is energy again.*** *Tinnitus rages around 10 hz of low vibration frequency, this, the sound itself is what the ancients believed that is the electromagnetic fields of consciousness* ***manifesting the physical hologram reality. Tinnitus can be controlled once you focus on and into it*** *. The pitch can be raised or lowered allowing you to access parts of those electromagnetic fields.* ***Tinnitus, the Ohm sound are all the sounds of creation. Through Tinnitus you can hear and balance chakras that themselves are needed to be. If you focus on the lower tinnitus frequency and then raise it slightly each time in pitch and visualize your spirit body, you can assign an entrained state to react with that frequency and that chakra point.***

Your energy fields have an effect on everything even your electronics. Do you have a lot of freezing of computers or when talking to someone your phone reacts strangely with freezing or not responding? This is because you are doing it subconsciously, just the same as we through the subconscious manifest everything. We crash electronic systems, especially when aware of that you are producing energy and through even that, your energy fields become active once again, *as a normal state of protection as they have always meant to be. I myself get electrically zapped when touching chrome objects or stainless-steel taps.* ***It feels like the taps are connected to electricity and you receive a shock. This is because you are resonating at a higher frequency then the manifested construct hologram objects around you.***

***Back to Entrainment. Entrainment is defined as carrying along, so while you were vibrating slower than them before your energy was carried along by there's until your's had caught up to resonate the same pattern of consciousness frequency**. Now that you had you are now in resonating synchronization or resonance. You are now creating the same vibrational patterns of energy in synchronization unconsciously knowing.*

***Entrainment can be used both ways for energy alteration**. Our avatar systems and spiritual anatomy can choose to vibrate along with others lower vibrational frequency also. **This depends of how "attached in connection you are to that person". Family, loved ones and close friends effect the outcomes because you have already decided to resonate with them for the most part.** Example of this is the human phrase we all use a lot ,"**they bring you down**", "**nah don't talk to them they are such downers**" .A classic example of this been brought down is **have you ever watched the mainstream news when at full energy** and felt top of the world? (Once again top of the world being a reference to being in the world but not of it) **But then after watching the events broadcast you start to feel exhausted, depressed and uninspired**. This is a classic example of energy being used to lower your vibrational state of consciousness awareness.*

***The great news about entrainment is it is easier for us to move from lower frequencies of consciousness to higher than from vice versa. Our spirit bodies are naturally programmed** to be able to manifest **healing and expand in vibration resonance**.*

So, it is natural for our bodies to gravitate and entrain to higher vibrational states.

Below is an example showing the resonance state and the entrainment processing state.

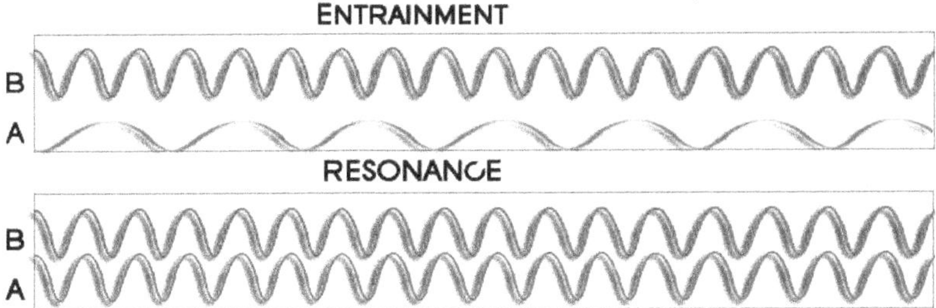

Everything in this designed Matrix is to create some form of energy manipulation towards your energy fields*, whether if it's from elf, cellphone etc.* ***All is designed as electromagnetic waves to have an impact on your own energy fields****. Example of this is how cell phones use the same frequency of alpha state as brainwaves, and can manipulate your brains programming with inputted electromagnetic signals causing manipulation to your energy body and manifesting physical issues such as brain tumors etc.* ***Understanding that these frequencies are there to change our behavior by modifying the frequency you resonate at and knowing consciously automatically creates the subconscious to block them . Just the same as subliminal messages are only subliminal until you know what they are doing, and then after your subconscious knows the program it removes the indoctrinated hidden meaning****. Then translates it as a* ***normal message*** *not having* ***any effect****, on your own* ***energy*** *like it does to those* ***that remain ignorant*** *to it and choose to follow* ***their indoctrinated path****.*

Since we now know everything is energy form. *Everything vibrates with its own alternating consciousness pattern. We can then use our energetic bodies to help us differentiate whether a vibration is higher or lower than our own. Whether the vibrational frequencies are* ***faster or slower than ours***, *and whether the vibration sends discordance into our bodies or resonance.* ***Our energetic bodies can help us to make conscious informed choices that are personal for our own physical, emotional, mental and spiritual energies of our own singularity***. *Very helpful information indeed when health and wellness are necessary for the life we desire!*

CONCLUSION: *This teaching on subtle energy of the One just about touched the tip of the iceberg, so to speak. The directions that further research by you the reader can go with this information are unlimited and exciting to say the least. I hope I opened up a new "can of worms" for you and helped you to look openly at this* ***very ancient but new discovery*** *of what we will call* ***subtle energy***.

Below is a diagram showing how the aura energy fields are manifested by the kundalini energy paths and chakra vortexes of electromagnetic consciousness. Seven layers of energy protection powered by your seven energy vortex power centers.

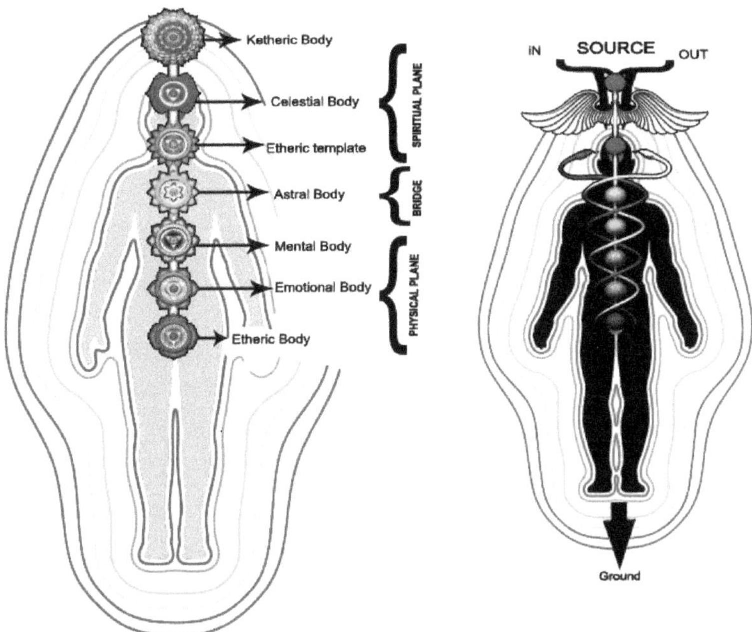

The seven seals of Solo-mon (solo-man), the seals of revelation, the seven radiances of Humbaba, the seven realms, Seven kingdoms, Salome, Dance of the seven veils, The Seven sins. *Misinterpretation and false telling of the spiritual body has been created in order for us as the singularities of the one consciousness to never be able to find spirit. As to the powers to be us finding out again who and what we are is a dire threat ,* ***as once we understand we don't exist****, understand the* ***Matrix and become brought into enlightenment****. The ones that controlled the system using these mis-teachings lose all manifested power of the indoctrination to keep us from*

reaching spirit again*. We are the superpowers, we are more powerful with our conscious energies then you can ever believe.*

7- 7 auras 7- endocrine organs 7- spiritual vortexes. 777. divine creation*. As I explained a few chapters ago about non-players and that everyone besides you is really a non-player in your game I will continue to explain further now that we have the understandings of the energetic bodies. So, imagine the top view of you and around you are your own aura energies but outside that you are also energy for about as far as you can see.* ***Nothing without observation truly does exist, and what we do is manifest interactions within the designed construct of self-aware electromagnetic consciousness****. Example of this is what we see we give energy to, to create. Ever heard the eyes are the gate way to the soul?* ***This is correct and this is also how we as singularities of the one quantum consciousness manifest the full physical holographic reality****. You have your own energy bubble or world around you and within these fields your own consciousness energy works with the entire collectives.* ***Nothing is truly ever alive or dead we are just IS , as God IS****. There is nothing that the eyes see as physical that is true but all forms of energies working within many alternating vibrational patterns manifesting creations to that frequency.* ***You are the player*** *that's* ***the main character in your game*** *. Despite your family, despite your friends, and the many other forms that create you to believe you are separated from the rest of the collective and are individual you are everything in your own game as the reflection of your energy frequency.* ***If you walk down the street and notice a dog or cat, that animal is non real and not alive until you allow it to enter into your own personal energy***

fields, and then give it the choice to interact with you. ***Thus creating the energy that allows the animal to remove from construct background , interact with you then revert back to construct. When I walked towards them down the street they didn't really exist, only when they enter into the energy field and I allow them to manifest into alive. Then after I walk past they revert to construct until the next player that is inside the full simulation game gives it the allowing to become interactive again. As most the physical everything that is alive is much like blank hard drives that we program.*** *So in the energy manifestation frequencies that we create with to understand energy again, learning energy is to fill your blank hard drive with the program of energy is existent and in everyone and everything.* ***You just like your friend are a form of construct always, just as they to you are construct inside your own consciousness game, you are to them in theirs.*** *We each are our own universes of quantum energies that are creating our own* ***experiences of physical reality simultaneously*** *all within the electromagnetic consciousness energy quantum computer's server.* ***Everything is form and through understanding form is energy one can read the alternating forms*** *of those energies.* ***We all are logged into the same server that exists in multidimensional going to infinity state.***

Now we have that understanding let's move more onto the ***spiritual centers of each set of frequencies*** *that our energies make the way into depending on the pattern of frequency. Our* ***chakras and spiritual anatomy given to us by divinity.***

YOUR CHAKRA VORTEXES 101

So, what are chakras?

The Cambridge Dictionary describes chakras as "In yoga and traditional South Asian medicine, one of the centers of energy in the human body"

We each inside us have the energy points that all transforming and alternating electromagnetic consciousness energy manifests at, as spirit. These are the power centers for spirit. *Understanding them allows one to once again connect back with the true Source of creation, The One.*

The One speaks to us through us understanding our own energy system and activating it again. ***Thousands of years ago,***

ancient scientists in India described the energy vortex and system that exists in our subtle body and energy fields*.* *The Indian yogis called these centers the "wheels" or chakras in Sanskrit.* ***These chakra or energy vortexes are known to spin like wheels.***

In the past Western culture and medicine chose to consider this valuable information from Yogic and Ayurvedic literature. From the teachings and practices such as acupuncture with its roots in China as primitive and unscientific. With modern technology, science can now measure these subtle energies at the chakras and the acupuncture meridians.

The spinning wheels or chakras, take in the higher frequency vibrations and then transmute them into vibrations utilizable by the physical body or avatar. Changing the overall frequency of your singularity as consciousness energies vibrations*.* *The lower vibration frequencies transmute or translates into hormonal activity within the physical body to cause* ***physiological, and then cellular changes****.*

The Ancient teachings of many cultures such as the Ancient Yogic teachings hold true with seven major chakras within the physical body and part of the spiritual anatomy. *Each chakra itself is linked with a physical gland of the endocrine system and a major nerve plexus.*

ENDOCRINE SYSTEM

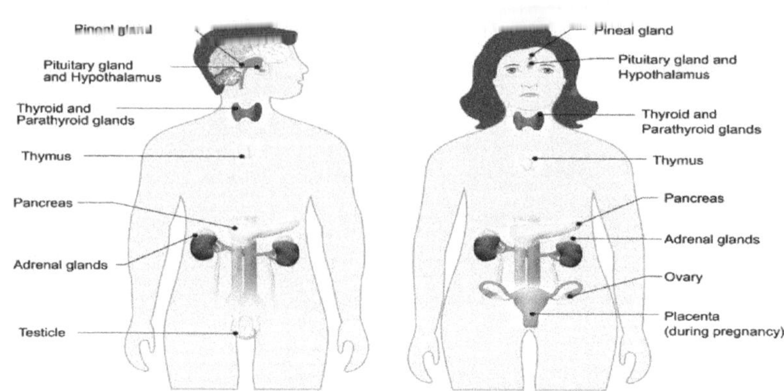

The seven celestial bodies are located in a vertical line from the base of the spine to the top crown of the head.

The first or root chakra *is at the base of the spine near the coccyx and its corresponding nerve plexus is the sacral-coccygeal. And is referred to as* ***the physical or red chakra light.***

The second wheel, or sacral chakra *is just below the navel near the spleen, and its corresponding nerve plexus is the sacral. The sacral chakra effects the Leydig cells in the gonads and adrenals and the genitourinary system.* ***This energy is Orange in color.***

The third energy center, vortex is the solar plexus *and is located in the upper part of the abdomen near the tip of the sternum, and its corresponding nerve plexus is also named solar. The solar plexus affects the adrenal glands and the digestive system.* ***The light of energy is yellow.***

The fourth, the heart chakra, *is located directly over the heart and the thymus, and its corresponding nerve plexus is the heart* *plexus. The heart chakra spiritual center affects the thymus gland and the circulatory system.* ***The light of this energy is high fluorescent, emerald green.***

The fifth energy center is the throat chakra, *this is located in the neck near the Adams apple over the thyroid gland and larynx. Its corresponding plexus is the cervical ganglia medulla plexus, the throat chakra affects the thyroid and respiratory system.* ***This chakra energy color is blue****.*

Continuing with the Sixth chakra, the third eye chakra *that is located in the middle of your forehead just above the bridge of the nose, and its corresponding plexus is the hypothalamus pituitary plexus. The third eye chakra affects the pituitary gland and the autonomic nervous system,* ***the light color is seen as indigo.***

The final main energy center is the Crown or Christ chakra*, it is located on the top tip of the head in your heads crown. Its corresponding nerve plexus is the cerebral cortex pineal plexus. The crown* ***Christ chakra affects the pineal gland and the central nervous system and is seen as the color violet****. This chakra is how once all others are in synchronization and balanced.* ***One contacts with the infinite source of all creation and wisdom, this is our true form of self as energies*** *when all chakras are balanced and the kundalini energy path flows in perfect synchronicity.* ***Example of chakra linked with endocrine system follows.***

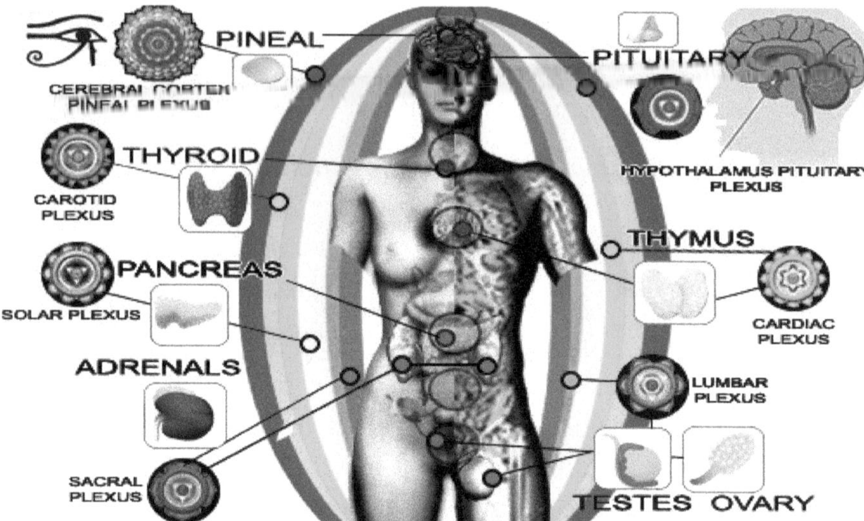

Although I only mention these main power centers there is many more power points to our spiritual anatomy.

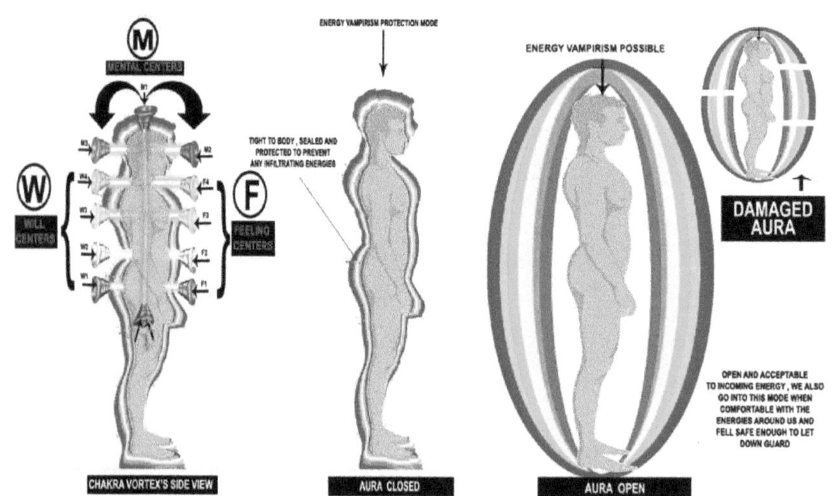

Above shows chakras side view and open and closed Aura.

Right through history we can find evidence of ancients knowing about a higher power called spirit. *From the Redskin Indians with the totem poles to show reference to the man and animals combined with nature just the same as the Baphomet.* ***We through the past games we have played have always known about the main Source of consciousness and the constructed designed reality. From ancient Africans hiding behind shields to represent the physical man (the shield)and the spirit who was holding the shield and that was wearing the mask of physical man to modern day dance party events like tomorrow-land.*** *Consciousness still is leaving hints of its many faces.* ***The giant head molds, the eyes, just the same as the Vikings of ancient also understood the same and represented the faces attached to the boats of their Armada. Aka frequencies of consciousness are within everything we still do on a regular basis.*** *The idea of super natural magic floods the mainstream media shows and video games , books etc Harry Potter.* ***Everything inside the Matrix is a design from consciousness to bring us understanding.*** *New age religious beliefs are* ***NOT new at all*** *and* ***are misleading*** *turning the truth into a* ***cult idea stereotype with aliens sending messages*** *to mediums. Guidance from other beings.* ***Yes this is still consciousness and perfect as all in God's design is perfect in design according to what consciousness has wanted.***

Back to the energy wheels. Ancient yogic texts also delineate up to five more chakras and many more mirror chakras. *Just as the construct has its own* ***mini dimensional mirrors*** *we call timelines our chakras* ***have mini dimensional energies.*** *The ancient* ***acupuncture models show meridians*** *or subtle energy*

pathways on the human body with many major and minor junctions or acupuncture points. There are up to seventy-two thousand energy channels or subtle energy alternating frequencies that have been described in OLD AGE texts. We as the mass consciousness are remembering who we are again as light! *We are remembering the truth of our spiritual anatomy and that it is the power to all of everything linked as one. How did we ever not understand that GOD created everything of the Matrix?* ***The Matrix is all electromagnetic fields of energy, we are energy hence always known that we do have a soul...*** *Energy can be tuned and left erratic, we are now as the collective understanding more and more how to become back in tune* ***with the Source of all creation once again****.*

People enjoy optimal health when these energy frequencies, chakra wheels, vortexes are in harmony and in complete balance spinning with high energy keeping in tune with the One. ***When imbalances of energy are present*** *in the human energy fields,* ***stagnation and energy blockages may result from*** *it. When these* ***blockages*** *are not released, disharmony and dis-ease is the result.* ***Dysfunction of these energy points****, therefore translates into* ***dysfunction of the nature and quality of the nerve transmissions in the brain, spinal cord, and peripheral nerves. This dysfunction, disharmony, or imbalance at the energy levels of the chakras, therefore, causes the various states of illnesses and disease in the nervous system of the physical manifested body****. Further pathological results will exhibit in the physiological systems and parts of the endocrine system affected by each energy wheel vortex, or chakra point.*

It is now in these times of electromagnetic pollution that these understandings are needed more than ever. *It is essential that the flow of this subtle energy be free in tune and at full force.* ***When this energy is blocked imbalanced, or diminished dysfunction within the organ systems innervated will result.***

So that is it for now on chakras, *I will give methods later in this book that can bring your energies to balance. For now, let's talk about the power of vibrations again.*

Everything we do results in a form of vibration, from breathing in air, to thinking, to a hair follicle moving, EVERYTHING that is energy vibrates! *In the beginning was the words* ***"big bang theory" in sense of biblical terms the world created from nothing sounds ludicrous indeed, and although rainbow gravity theory and others have disproved the concept itself the idea form of Matrix code was left here for a purpose.*** *That is for us to understand we as energy that's self-aware created the constructs as the mass collective of combined frequencies of energy in expression.* ***All methods of explaining how reality was created fall back onto vibrations. Vibrations of sound, the primordial sound. The power of vibrations, the life force.*** *The vital spark that shows that living entities are more than a simple collection of chemicals.*

In studies from thousands of years that have passed, we see the Hindu's in India named these vibrations" Prana", while the Chinese called it the force of Chi, and created their entire practice of medicine around this vibration of life. The also knowing of this vibrational force Japanese call this power of vibration KI.

Vibrations of the human energy fields are now these days shown, measured, and photographed by modern scientific instruments to diagnose and treat disease states... *Witness the use of electrocardiogram's, electromyography's, electroencephalogram's and electromagnetic X-rays.*

Evidence of vibrations, energy can be found using magnetic field detectors. *In* ***modern laboratories scientists*** *can use the* ***SQUID or Superconducting Quantum Interface Device*** *to detect the* ***ultra-sensitive magnetic field surrounding the hands of a healer using intent on sending healing energy to a recipien****t. Cases like this have been recorded with the healer being city* ***blocks away from the recipient*** *and* ***yet still shows the recipient receiving the energy*** *that was directed and sent with* ***intent from the healer****. For more on this research into Doctor John Zimmerman at the University of Colorado School of Medicine that with his brought forward understandings proved the magnetic nature of healing energy.* ***Experiments have been conducted in skeptical laboratories to demonstrate the measurable effects of healing on living organisms such as plant life****. Bernard Grad added energy to one batch of water with magnets. Energy was added to another batch of water from a practitioner, healer. Both batches of water were used as feeding for alternating plants,* ***both showed a measurable acceleration of growth in the targeted for study plant life****. This proves that talking to your plant which is nothing more than creating vibration* ***has been scientifically proven to help the growth manifestation also****. Just as sound vibrations change how we react all indoctrinated term living forms react with alternating vibrational force, frequencies.*

Although not one hundred percent not agreeing with Einstein's teachings. *I* ***do agree that everything is energy****. So I will use some of his work as an example.* ***Everyone is familiar with Einstein's equation of relativity, Energy equals mass times the speed of light squared****. To the chagrin of this world-famous physicist, his work was the basis for producing the atomic bomb that killed so many people in World War Two.* ***Scientists accomplished this by increasing the frequency of vibration of particles****. Einstein was also interested in studying the power of life force and the God particle rather than the production of weapons of mass destruction.* ***Einstein suggested that matter and energy are interconnected and interconvertible. Energy slowed down manifests into physical mass or matter, matter that is increased in frequency of vibration becomes energy****. The Einstein-Lorentz Transformation equation is more of a multidimensional model that introduces the effect of velocity.* ***The Tiller-Einstein model of positive and negative space, time Doctor William Teller from Stanford University attempts to better describe the multi-dimensional nature of the indoctrinated term universe****. The Matrix constructed hologram playfield and all forms of life in relation to the power of the vibrations of the particles of the life force. The* ***energy fields of the pure source*** *of all creation,* ***The One****.*

Modern mathematicians like Charles Muses recognize the square root of negative numbers to be the hyper-numbers necessary to develop equations to describe the behavioral patterns of particles with higher vibrational frequencies*. This enables scientists to study and describe the subtler energy fields of the* ***mental, emotional, and spiritual layers of the human***

energy field of consciousness... *Energies that had been long recognized, studied and treated by the cultures of Ancient history.* ***Science now recognizes and proves the value of the power of vibration to calm, nurture, and heal living entities. The Ancients have always used such vibrational methods to bring better health, in the form of instrumental or vocal music, chanting, toning etc.*** *To provide the spiritual and physical body with calming and nurturing healing energies of consciousness.* ***Common examples of these practices can still be seen*** *with in many* ***cultures that still use bells and chimes, as well as Tibetan crystal bowls.***

For as long as time dictates our past history of the Ancients, *minerals,* ***gems and crystals had been worn*** *or placed in jars of water in the* ***sun to create healing solutions*** *and remedies.* ***Now in modern days the power*** *of those positive vibrations* ***can be measured and quantified.***

At the other end of the spectrum, be aware of the vibrations that cause damage to living players or entities such as the rays from computers, cell phones, high tension wiring, microwaves, televisions, etc. ***Although this technology is beneficial to modern day culture the negative power of those waves of vibration causes states of disharmony and imbalance in our naturally produced energy fields. Chronic exposure leads to various states of manifested diseases. From the positive to the negative, from the beneficial to the destructive.*** *From the soothing sound of a Mother's lullaby to the explosion of the Atomic bomb at Hiroshima. The power of vibrations is displayed in a* ***broad spectrum inside our game world of reality.***

Following is the examples of each charka design and the characteristics associated with each. ***We are nothing but consciousness energy, light. In truth, all we are is those energy wheels of alternating currents of frequency that create the whole manifested you****. This concludes the teaching on chakras and energy vibrations.*

To elaborate quickly I will leave the connections to each chakra below.

Physical chakra's, Hell chakras

Red, *Physical, Sacral Coccygeal nerve plexus, Adrenals.*

Orange, *Emotional, Sacral nerve plexus, Testes, Ovaries*

Yellow*, Mental, solar nerve plexus, Pancreas*

Spiritual chakra's, Heaven chakras*.*

Green, Spiritual, *Heart nerve plexus, Thymus.*

Blue, Spiritual*, Cervical ganglia Medulla nerve plexus, Thyroid.*

Indigo, Spiritual*, Hypothalamus Pituitary nerve plexus, Pituitary.*

Violet, Spiritual*, Cerebral cortex pineal nerve plexus, Pineal.*

As above so below, balance your physical lower three vibrational frequencies to resonate with the four spiritual ones of higher consciousness. Balance your Hell to be like your Heaven! Using music as sound therapy with the alternating Hertz for each vibration center of energy allows the energies to manifest faster towards your desired balance and with

practice and intent learn to control your vortex fluctuations. The love frequency is a good start for one to open the heart chakra to allow for more natural flow through the kundalini. Using this 5.28Hz vibration will move alignment *of your energies into a more* ***natural spiritual state****. There are many more frequencies of sound, vibration that you can use for each center.* ***As everything in vibration state of emotional energy starts with the Love-hate spectrum of lower to higher states of emotional consciousness.***

WHAT IS THE KUNDALINI?

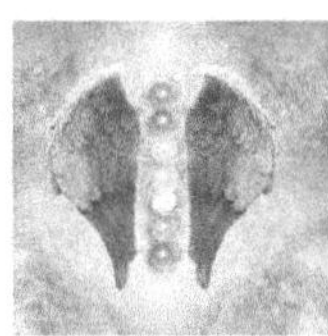
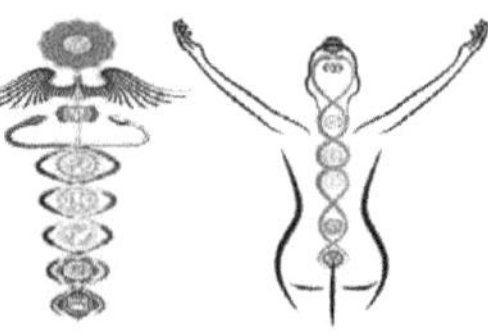

The kundalini is the serpent connected tether that runs through your chakra centers and points and connects with Source. It is the incoming and outgoing electric and magnetic fields of consciousness energy that feeds the spiritual and physical centers powering them similar to the design of energy collecting batteries. The connected tether has been called many things throughout history. The snake of Eden , the rainbow serpent of the Aboriginals, the teachings of dragons of mythology in ancient Chinese cultures, the Mayan representation of the serpent and the Egyptian Era of wearing snakes on the front of their third eye location*. Representation of the connection of the brain or singularity of their consciousness energy connected to the true form of God. The* ***self-aware electromagnetic infinite being*** *that governs*

over all in and out of the quantum designed simulation hologram we deem Earth. Or heart of our creation. Isn't it funny how we also call Satan the serpent? Once again hiding the true understandings hidden behind fabricated nonsense keeping us from finding the truth of form and reality of us as creation. *Holding us within a prison of misinterpretation holding back true connection and spiritual enlightenment.* ***Modern society through symbolism still flaunts the understanding of those that know and have kept these teachings from us under various stereotypes. Classic example here is the medical Caduceus that shows the spiritual kundalini snake energy path passing round centered chakras that when reaching the crown Christ violet chakra true enlightenment is achieved.*** *As when in divine knowing you become spirit again and have the* ***flying sensation*** *that the* ***Angels of historical references*** *was also created from.* ***Remember that in the whole design of the idea of the symbol even implanted in the Matrix is from the pure source of creation of consciousness itself.*** *It is here as everything else of creation.* ***A hint and message from the One as understanding how the hologram reality really functions. Only through opening your heart chakra first you are able to control other vortex centers. You, to raise vibrations have to enter various stages of spiritual awareness to reach enlightenment!*** *You, learning to love all of creation with unconditional love holding* ***no judgement to anything of God*** *is imperative in order to access the higher frequency of the consciousness itself. Leaving Ego and the identity of one behind.* ***Only once removed from the individual ideology as energy and entered back as***

collective understanding of your spirit new awareness levels are achievable. *Thought process of vibration is* ***the key to control each center of manifested electromagnetic energy as visualization of light projected codes*** *run the systematic functions.* ***Once in synch with spirit your projected visualizations become control mechanisms for each of the alternating frequencies of the spiritual anatomy or chakra body. Every emotion is nothing but an energy frequency you manifest from you, the lower or higher vibrations of your own singularity of consciousness collective of energies. Emotions as that do not exist, there is no I feel sad!*** *You are lacking vibrational energy and are projecting it at very low vibrations. Just as to be happy is to be sitting in a more balance controlled energy comfort of higher frequency of vibrational pattern.* ***Remember you are divine as spirit, you are part of God itself, A child of the true creator, YOU ARE PERFECT! As God does not create anything of imperfection in its grand design, holding judgement of God is holding judgement of YOU. Think of visualization, your training program to be able to access and REMOTE VIEW SPIRITS STATUS OF ENERGY. Then sending vibrations needed to each center to maintain balance.*** *Just as clandestine government groups of paranormal study use remote viewing to witness another place and what is occurring.* ***You with practice can train your own consciousness singularity to be able to witness and see what's occurring with your spiritual anatomy. Imbalances within your energy paths or kundalini*** *will result with* ***spirit crying to physical body*** *for attention with* ***manifesting physical problems.*** *Until these energies have been recognized these physical manifestations* *will continue to grow until they become serious illnesses or health issues.* ***When in total control through repetition of seeing your spiritual body, and learning how to change your energy fluctuations even the longest term stubborn diseases can be controlled or destroyed. This is a form of what faith does with the religious indoctrination*** *methods like* ***creating belief that allows you subconsciously to program your energies without knowing,*** *and* ***balance creating the vibrational force of consciousness that allows the diseases to diminish.*** *The faith trigger is nothing more than a way to train one to raise vibrational frequency unknowingly that they are.* ***Creating a miracle to them when in fact the ability for each and every one to do this is embedded in our DNA and spiritual make up itself.*** *Think about having the knowing of what your energies are doing and are lacking in, how different would have life been with having conscious knowing.* ***The Matrix itself has its own chakra points that we refer to as ley lines or dragon lines. Just as we and the construct are connected if imbalance is also created in this vortex points in the construct then disharmony will be implanted into the overall constructs subconscious collectiveness. This is the reason of Ancient teachings of Druids and movement of stones (vibrations of lower consciousness) had been placed in alternating areas to balance and manifest nature or as we know it the simulated holographic Matrix of the One's design. Aligning stones with holes*** *in them allowed the lower vibrations to transmit the faster vibrational frequencies* ***in directed paths*** *desired by the* ***Druid or Ancients. This seriously concludes my teaching of this area of energies of consciousness.***

First Chakra: Physical

Root Chakra

Color: *Red*

Element: *Earth*

Musical Note*: C*

Endocrine Gland*: Adrenals*

Nerve*: Sacral Plexus*

Sense*: Smell*

Physical System*: Skeletal, Lymph, Elimination Systems.*

Issues*: Survival, Safety, Trust, Security, Money, Home, Job*

Statement*: "I HAVE"*

Excessive Characteristics*: Heaviness, Sluggishness, Slow movements, Resilience to change, Overeating, Obesity, Hoarding, Material Fixation, Greediness, Workaholism, Excessive Spending.*

Deficient Characteristics*: Fear, Anxiety, Resistance to structure, Anorexia, underweight, Spacy, flightiness, vagueness, Disconnection from your body, Restlessness, inability to sit still, Difficulty manifesting.*

The following characteristics indicate a balanced first chakra, they are also the rewards that come from first chakra work.

Balanced Characteristics*: Grounded, Physical health, being comfortable in your body, A sense of safety and security, Stability and solidity, Right livelihood, Prosperity, Ability to be still, Presence in the here and now.*

2nd Chakra: Emotional

Sacral Chakra

Color: *Orange*

Element: *Water*

Musical Note: *D*

Endocrine Gland: *Ovaries & Testes*

Nerve: *Lumbar Plexus*

Sense: *Taste*

Physical System: *Reproduction and Assimilation*

Issues: *Feelings, Sensations, Appetites, Desires, Sex*

Statement: *"I FEEL"*

INTERPRETING EXCESS OR DEFICIENCY IN THE SECOND CHAKRA.

Excess and deficiencies in your chakras are defenses created in response to wounds you've experienced in these areas in the past, and either one can indicate an imbalance in your system. So, take a moment to look at the characteristics below. Remember it is possible to have both excess and deficiency, and that you develop both in attempt to cope with negative experiences.

Excessive Characteristics: *Sexual addictions, Obsessive attachments, Addiction to stimulation, Excessive mood swings, Excessively sensitive, Poor boundaries, invasion of others, Emotional dependency, Instability.*

Deficient Characteristics: *Rigidity in your body, beliefs or behavior, Emotional numbness or insensitivity, Fear of change, Lack of desire, passion, or excitement, Avoidance of pleasure, fear of sexuality, Poor social skills, Excessive boundaries and boredom.*

The following characteristics indicate a balanced second chakra.

Balanced Characteristics: *Graceful movements, Ability to embrace change, Emotional intelligence, Nurturance of self and others, Healthy boundaries, Ability to enjoy pleasure, Passion.*

3rd Chakra: Mental

Solar Plexus chakra

Color: *Yellow*

Element: *Fire*

Musical Note: *B*

Endocrine Gland: *Pancreas*

Nerve: *Solar Plexus*

Sense: *Sight*

Physical System: *Digestive & Musculature Systems.*

Issues: *Freedom, Power, Control, Self-Definition, Intellect*

Statement: *"I CAN"*

INTERPRETING EXCESS OR DEFICIENCY IN THE MENTAL CHAKRA.

In the third chakra, excess and deficiency are noticed by the way our system handles the energy of fire and its related attributes of the metabolism, vitality, Self- esteem and will, each excess or deficiency need to be brought towards the center in order to create true balance in the third chakra. While none of us want to admit to these characteristics, be honest with yourself and double check your assessment with someone who knows you well to confirm your correct.

Excessive Characteristics: *Dominating, Controlling, Competitive, Arrogant, Ambitious, Hyperactive, Stubborn, Driven, e.g. compulsively focused towards goals. Attracted to sedatives.*

Deficient Characteristics: *Passivity, Lack of energy, Poor digestion, Tendency to be cold, Tendency towards submission, Blaming, Low self-esteem, Lack of confidence, Weak will, Use of stimulants, Poor self-discipline.*

The following characteristics indicate a balanced Third chakra.

Balanced Characteristics: *Responsible, reliable, Good self-discipline, Positive sense of self, Confident, Warm, Energetic, Spontaneous, Playful, Humorous and able to take risks without holding back.*

4th Chakra: Spiritual

Heart Chakra

Color: *Green*

Element: *Air*

Musical Note: *F*

Endocrine Gland: *Thymus*

Nerve: *Cardiac Plexus*

Sense: *Touch*

Physical System: *Respiratory, Circulatory, Immune Systems*

Issues: *Relating, Giving, Receiving, Perceptions of Love, Acceptance*

Statement: *"I LOVE"*

INTERPRETING EXCESS OR DEFICIENCY IN THE FOURTH CHAKRA.

An excess of the heart is not an excess of love but an excessive focus on attention and approval from others in order receive love. Remember, excess results from a compensating behavior for a deeper wound. A deficient heart chakra is closed down to others.

Excessive Characteristics: *Codependency, focusing too much on others, Poor boundaries, Jealousy, Being a Martyr, Being a pleaser.*

Deficient Characteristics: *Antisocial, withdrawn, Critical, Intolerant, Lonely, Isolated, Lack of empathy, Fear of intimacy.*

The following characteristics indicate a balanced fourth chakra.

Balanced Characteristics: *Caring, Compassionate, Empathetic, Accepting, Self-Loving, Peaceful, Centered, Content.*

5th Chakra: Spiritual

Throat Chakra

Color: *Blue/Turquoise*

Element: *Ether*

Musical Note: *G*

Endocrine Gland: *Thyroid*

Nerve: *Carotid Plexus*

Sense: *Hearing*

Physical System: *Metabolism and Growth*

Issues: *Expressing, Listening, Creating, Will, Manifestation, Abundance*

Statement: *"I SPEAK"*

INTERPRETING EXCESS OR DEFICIENCY IN THE FIFTH CHAKRA.

In the throat chakra, we interpret excess and deficiency by the quality of the voice, the ease of communication, and the flow of creativity.

Excessive Characteristics: *Talking too much or inappropriately, Gossiping, Stuttering, Difficulty being silent, Excessive loudness, Inability to contain, Keep confidences or secrets.*

Deficient Characteristics: *Difficulty putting things into words, Fear of speaking, Speaking under voiced or with a weak non-confident tone, Secretiveness, Excessive shyness, Tone deafness.*

The following characteristics indicate a balanced fifth chakra.

Balanced Characteristics: *Resonant, full voice, Clear communication with others, Good communication with self, Good listener, Good sense of timing and rhythm, Lives life creatively.*

6th Chakra: Spiritual

Third Eye Chakra

Color: *indigo*

Element: *Inner sight, Inner sound*

Musical Note: *A*

Endocrine Gland: *Pituitary*

Nerve: *Carotid Plexus*

Sense: *Intuition, Sixth sense, High sense Perception*

Physical System: *Complete Endocrine System*

Issues: *Spiritual Awareness, Individuation*

Statement: *"I SEE"*

INTERPRETING EXCESS OR DEFICIENCY IN THE THIRD EYE CHAKRA.

How open or closed is your physical vision, your intuition, and your ability to access hidden realms or seeing and knowing? To be balanced in the sixth chakra is to have your third eye open. But still maintain discernment about what you see. With a deficient sixth chakra there is difficulty intuition and visualization and the subtler realms, perhaps out of cynicism or fear. With an excessive sixth chakra, you may be bombarded with images but have difficulty grounding your intuition and sorting reality from imagination.

Excessive Characteristics: *Hallucinations, Delusions, Obsessions, Nightmares, Intrusive memories, Difficulty concentrating, Excessive fantasizing*

Deficient Characteristics: *Lack of imagination, Difficulty visualizing, Insensitivity, Excessive skepticism, Denial of facts, Inability to see alternatives*

The following characteristics indicate a balanced sixth chakra.

Balanced Characteristics: *Strong intuition, Penetrating insight, Creative imagination, Good memory, Good dream recall, Ability to visualize, has guiding vision for life.*

7th Chakra: Spiritual

Crown/Christ Chakra

Color: *Violet*

Element: *Light, Thought*

Musical Note: *B*

Endocrine Gland: *Pineal*

Nerve: *Brain*

Sense: *Empathy, Inner knowing*

Physical System: *Complete Nervous System*

Issues: *"Oneness", Unity Consciousness, Source Connection*

Statement: *"I KNOW"*

INTERPRETING EXCESS OR DEFICIENCY IN THE CROWN CHAKRA.

Excess and deficiency in the Christ chakra have to do with both daily occupations Of Consciousness and our spiritual attitudes. Our ability to understand that we only exist as spiritual energy of consciousness.

Excessive Characteristics: *Dissociation from the body, Spiritual addiction, Confusion, Over-intellectualization, Living in your head, Disconnection from spirit, Excessive attachments.*

Deficient Characteristics: *Spiritual cynicism, A closed mind, Learning difficulties, Rigid belief systems, Apathy.*

The following characteristics indicate a balanced sixth chakra.

Balanced Characteristics: *Spiritual connection, Wisdom and mastery, Intelligence, presence, Open-Mindedness, ability to question, Ability to assimilate and analyze information and situations. Directed by Source of the One.*

There are many levels of consciousness to go through within the frequency chart, I provide a chart below for you to understand what you need to reach your next frequency of awareness. I by ***no rights own the copyright*** *to the Awareness chart below and use it because I agree with* ***Doctor David R. Hawkins*** *Map of consciousness* ***so I also direct any readers to check into Doctor Hawkins Himself!***

Map of Consciousness

Developed by David R. Hawkins

The Map of Consciousness is based on a logarithmic scale that spans from 0 to 1000.

Name of Level	Energetic "Frequency"	Associated Emotional State	View of Life
Enlightenment	700-1000	Ineffable	Is
Peace	600	Bliss	Perfect
Joy	540	Serenity	Complete
Love	500	Reverence	Benign
Reason	400	Understanding	Meaningful
Acceptance	350	Forgiveness	Harmonious
Willingness	310	Optimism	Hopeful
Neutrality	250	Trust	Satisfactory
Courage	200	Affirmation	Feasible
Pride	175	Scorn	Demanding
Anger	150	Hate	Antagonistic
Desire	125	Craving	Disappointing
Fear	100	Anxiety	Frightening
Grief	75	Regret	Tragic
Apathy	50	Despair	Hopeless
Guilt	30	Blame	Evil
Shame	20	Humiliation	Miserable

MY AWAKENING EXPERIENCE

SO why do I know what I'm teaching? *I'm going to explain the best reason I think I can.* ***So my life I've struggled to get by hardship as a child through abusive surroundings. I've taken so many drugs it's hard to even start naming, as well as most people around me. I've been a criminal most my life ,doing basically whatever to make money however when I could. I've always been in the understanding of I was energy but nothing like I know now. I knew we as spiritual souls had a higher purpose and that my life had a higher purpose. I have when young cried not to go to school because I felt the world was going to end.*** *All through my life I have been shown things are not what they seem to really be.* ***From remembering when I first moved to Perth from Pannawonica I watched a show called Revenge of the Ninja or a sequel to it, I'm not too sure. But in the show I saw a van that was from pest control, the next day riding my bike down the street on the side of the road was the exact same van as out of the movie? How? The power of the subconscious huh?*** *Any way from a lot of events happening over time* ***I become more and more acceptable to energy that stopped me wanting to be around places and people*** *and then because I had no understanding of*

what was going on and why I was having strange fluctuations of energy I removed myself from everywhere! *I went into agoraphobia and could not leave the house , at one point I could even get energy frequencies hit me and change my resonance from my cell phone about to ring. The* ***energy would shock me like anxiety to the extreme****. I continued, removed from society* ***right through for fifteen years to what was the most saddest experience of anyone's life****. Not knowing how to control your own energy, t****hinking you are crazy, Bad panic attacks because of unbalanced energy centers*** *. You name I suffered from it. I passing through life and being self-conditioned to imprison myself started to get very suicidal and often wanted to end my life numerous times.* ***The isolation got to me I have to admit, but through these times I learnt how to meditate and use my natural self-intuition. Being a freestyle hip-hop artist since seventeen I started to understand years back that something was using me to speak through me, my songs I started to do started to be all about God and the pain and suffering,*** *To the point that I began to sing in songs to what was not like me ever.* ***I understood that a higher force was contacting me and allowing me to be a vessel to fight the new world order etc. As for the years in isolation as a monk,*** *I studied everything from the bloodlines of the illuminati, the Ancient secrets of most topics and went conspiracy research mad.* ***I would tell everyone about the Illuminati when I started to catch up with friends that would come past, guys and girls****. I would preach to everyone how evil they are and how they have agendas like alternative three and blue beam. Told everyone about* ***paperclip, bluebook, majestic twelve,*** *what can I say at*

one stage all that mattered to me was to find out the truth of what's going on and what's the big secret that the masons and elites are trying to hide. I was on a mission researching madam Curie and her husband, Tesla, Adam Weishaupt, Aleister Crowley, John Dee and so much more that now after I understand seemed pointless but necessary. *I got to where I just wanted to die, if they are going to kill us in global extermination,* ***what's the point in family? What's the point in anything? I just wanted to die. Watching the news with the children of Iraq and other sadness in the world going on I would say legit and from the deepest part of my soul "God take me like you did take Christ", let the word be healed and forgive them for everything.*** *I don't want to live anymore and I* ***with full passion would allow myself to be sacrificed*** *to help the world.* ***I was, and still am very empathic towards creation this is half the reason I think what happened to me did. I asked many times just to know the truth and to give me a voice in the name of the full truth of God,*** *to what obviously I didn't expect anything in return. I just* ***wanted to know the truth*** *of what's being hidden from us and if I* ***could be sacrificed to help humanity advance I was full willing.***

One day my friend from younger come past and had a chat. *You will remember him from earlier stories. We were sitting there looking at the Xbox one console and I noticed that the Ford logo itself was strange and had a loop in the F,* ***being a Ford fan for 28 odd years I knew what the Ford logo badge has always looked like having owned a TE Cortina and XF falcon and NA Fairlane all being Ford.*** *My friend shrugged it off as "They just changed the logos man", just a new logo, to what I* *must honestly* **say I agreed with at the time. New logo, not such a big deal**. *So Merv left, and later down the track I noticed When researching flat earth that a conspiracy called the Mandela effect was displayed.* **I shrugged this off as I didn't want to look at African conspiracies. Eventually one day I decided to click on it and watch someone explain the Snow-White Mandela effect. To what I remembered seeing as a child with the evil queen always saying "mirror, mirror" on the wall, not the new "magic mirror" that was being explained as the way it was said. After looking at my phone and researching around on things, I noticed a video that said Fresh Prince of Bellaire long intro. Now being a Fresh Prince fan since young I watched all the episodes and never had seen that intro ever on any of them**. *I put my own personal copy on and wow it was changed!* **I was stumped on what the hell. It wasn't until I heard someone say that the universe had changed and we are in Orion not Sagittarius that I started to go into states to where I would get full information downloaded to me**. *As soon as I knew we were not in* **our own universe anymore**, *I knew I was* **nothing but energy knowing atoms are 99 percent blank etc. I left my body and seen the design of the entire construct of quantum realities how each collective of singularity would connect to the next run from that larger one in layers of mirrors and so on.** *I* **don't know how to this day but I knew and understood everything about quantum physics, I would tell people around me talking like I was a professor**. *I then knew I had to tell everyone and the reason I was giving the information as spirt I have a mission to reveal what I know to everyone to help all those that were lost like me come to terms of what*

happened to them. The quantum shift of consciousness frequencies. I made my first teaching video on You tube called Mandela effect explained to what I explained the designs of the universes, multiverses, superverses, and mega verse. *I knew it all right from the get go as soon as I was contacted by consciousness.* ***This was not the only time and was only the first time I noticed that something was guiding me in the directions I was pursuing.*** *I* ***made other videos during the time of Mandela effected animals, etc while airbrushing , writing , rapping , and continuing life , I Then one day , heard the Tinnitus sound high and loud pitch and thought to myself, I'm*** *going to* ***resonate and go into the frequency.*** *To my surprise I pulled the frequency around me as if I was in the middle of an* ***energy field around me and even though I couldn't hear*** *the sound anymore* ***I could feel the presence around me. I felt connected to God. I knew I was able then to talk to God and what I was experiencing is talking to creation, the consciousness of all , the One. I thanked God for all the information of quantum knowing and gave full meaningful from the heart gratitude.*** *As I moved out of the frequency that I was calling* ***Yahweh back then*** *before the major wake up. My right shoulder* ***cracked four times in loud succession*** *and then believe it or not!* ***The rotary cuff that was really damaged to the point I couldn't move my arm very much with motion was healed to the point I could swing my arm around in circles testing out my rotary cuff.*** *I can't say it was completely healed but I can assure you on my word that it was hundreds of times better functioning and feeling then the few years it happened when I had done the damage.* ***After this and being contacted***

by *many through* ***You tube I was introduced to a person that said I was a way seer, they shall remain anonymous for the reason of privacy. This person told me I was a way seer and that what I am is in natural DMT all the time without knowing I am. Because I had so much prior knowing of conspiracy it was easy for me to understand and be open minded.*** *I would play games with them through skype to what I would read their surroundings, their clothes they are wearing and last but not least past lives.* ***I was amazed how accurate I always was. So, I offered to others to read their past lives and sometimes didn't even offer just had visions of what they were and did. When I was told to remember who I was myself before entering the world and go and see where we are , through my mind's eye I did. I saw us all on that chessboard, the Heaven scenario around the outskirts the design of what we called the real reality . I seen we are all playing a game. I saw all of us on the board with our energies creating the true form of the one consciousness from outside that inside we call God.*** *I can't explain how.* ***But I knew*** *and remembered what we are doing here,* ***we are here to play a game.*** *I* ***understood it all from why we do it , what we do it for , and how we are all nothing but expressions of the combined telepathic energy, that from the outside we were creating. The Way seer that was showing me asked what did I see and I told them about the chessboard game and what was going on , to what I was then confirmed many others see the same and that it was the true form of the ethereal design we come from as spiritual game players.*** *I just knew everything and loved it!* ***The awesome design of the game being a gamer , the extreme measures that God had***

gone through to create the Matrix for us to come into and play. It brought me to understand everything how there is no Judgement of us as God's children. How we have to love the whole creation with unconditional love to understand its true nature of why it's here. Why the Masons worship death because they knew we can come back*!* *Why the checkered patterns so prominent inside the Matrix design from the Masonic floors to the chessboard itself to the police outer rings on their uniforms of black and white checkers.* ***I can't explain how I just knew I just did I felt just love and grace with God in its divine presence. I didn't know but I had entered into divine knowing to what I was revealed everything about us as spirit and our creation****.* *After that I decided to make a video informing everyone of what the world really is a game putting myself into natural DMT and Alpha state. I replayed many voices onto my phone and then joined them together to create the full video ready to add pictures.* ***Now during this night that I was creating this video the weather outside was erratic and windy, black clouds and storm weather surrounded my house. After I made the Mandela effect chessboard game video from being with the One and in natural DMT, I had doubts of my teachings of telling people we can log in and out****, as I knew it was right but* ***felt an uneasiness to bringing that information to people****. I mean even* ***though my intentions are to awaken others to who they are again ...What if I'm wrong?*** *Before deciding to upload the video yet I asked loud Yahweh show me a sign show me a Ufo that this is right, something! I then* ***feeling in full connection to the One*** *did something I never do I spontaneously got up and walked out the front door. As I*

walked out the front, the clouds and weather remained dark and cloudy, until I stopped and looked up at the sky when the black clouds within seconds moved and exposed the blue sky through it. *The sun at this time was hidden behind my friend's house across the street and was impossible to view.* ***I looked up to the sky and pointed my finger towards a cloud that was beginning to glow with light through it , Yes glow with light****! I called my Father first to come and witness to what Dad wasn't too enthusiastic but did see what was going on at that time. I also called* ***for Mum to come and see. As I lifted my finger to a new location pointing at the clouds light would glow from behind it until it got vivid as for me to see it was responding. It was impossible to have what happened to me happened without some divine intelligence that was communicating with me****!* ***I lifted my finger to many spots and the same happened each time , Mum and Dad were behind me watching as Mum said "make it do a cross" , "make it do a cross"*** *I then turned around and asked Yahweh , as I explained I was using Yahweh as my connection frequency* ***to the One*** *at the time.* ***As I asked , in the empty sky itself that was beginning to clear up , a light of sunshine, it wasn't sunshine but this is the only way I can describe it , appeared from nowhere and started not very fast but not all that slow either moving across the sky in a horizontal line****. As this happened I heard my body and spirit talk.* ***I felt like I wasn't part of my body anymore, and my body said loud "you can go now if you want" to my spirit****. I could see the doorway out that was being offered for me in the lights above.* ***This was the most amazing thing I have ever experienced throughout my life****!!!*

I came back to my body and realized what just had happened, I ran inside to grab my smartphone and rushed back out to the door where Mum and Dad were still standing, and looked outside , everything was gone. *As soon as I removed my connection of energy to the One it vanished.* ***I will never look at the world the same again after this experience this proved to me, who was sceptical of miracles and God, would ever bother with someone like me, that I was one hundred percent incorrect to what I had thought. I have no doubt in the information I bring forth now as I experienced the highest point of enlightenment possible where the Matrix responds back to you like you're having a common conversation.*** *Even now* ***writing this it amazes me that God had chosen me to bring this knowing we all need to know to us all.*** *I'm amazed at how* ***throughout many times I've been helped by consciousness itself showing my teachings are correct,*** *from allowing me to read past lives,* ***read people's aura fields, see through my true eyes as spirit at the constructed reality and revealed it for what it is, to having consciousness intervene in an online debate about GOD.*** *Making me guess a two out of one hundred chance answer on my first go.* ***With no serious attempt on using my connection to consciousness to gain.***
I am the classic sign of duality in the ones designed reality Before the Mandela effect I was the Sagittarius star sign *to what I have* ***celebrated ever since brought into the world. Now I'm Ophiuchus!*** ***My star sign changed from being The centaur with the bow, to what I was told my sign for my last reality was to get addicted to something and then overcome it to what I did with many hard drugs. To Ophiuchus the wounded***

healer.** **To what I am now these days a vessel of body that has been put through Hell to try and be destroyed through smoking etc just waiting to die. *Trying now to repair using my insight teachings and others sending healing to me.* ***Meanwhile being a Reiki student , now teacher , becoming the literal meaning of my star sign once again and a wounded healer.***

I noticed many more Mandela effects over time, but never really bothered with it after knowing what I was told by the one consciousness and how at ease It put me right down to the spiritual manifestation of me. Why and how did I do this? I was at the level of awareness that I already was at peace with what was going on , the woman provided me with such incredible love, the fact I was told it was a game and not real , broke away judgement and gave me unconditional love for everything good or evil as all was the one consciousness. After acceptance I was brought to pure peace and serenity , after I have all these vibrational fields working in perfect harmony , the divine love of God , the spiritual realm where I was taken into divine knowing, all worries of everything faded away and nothing but respect love and understanding for all of creation was achieved with full gratitude and sincerity. *This is a lot to understand and take in, I fully agree* ***,but know this I DONT lie! And would never use Gods name in my teachings as the true consciousness if I was not one hundred percent sure myself on what is the truth. I was contacted by God, the pure source of electromagnetic energies, the One.*** *The father in the sky , whatever allegory you want to create for it.* ***But I have been shown something beyond understanding unless being a witness. I was told to bring the information I have to***

everyone from Source itself, and to anything I say I am more than willing to take any polygraph test or such to show what I say is the un conceited, humble, words of God. That we as the masses need to recognize and wake up too. *We are waiting for God to return when it's always* ***been right with us. it's been talking to us always we have been to blind to see. We need to start to understand that the only God of all existence is the one Source of all creation.*** *That is nothing but everything , as self-aware conscious energy that is wishing to have all frequencies of its expression explored.*

This concludes my awakening area. I am now a spiritual teacher since being into enlightenment. My father that is elderly can confirm the downloads of quantum knowing I explained I had, as he received most of the information first when I started to understand I was being given knowledge. He and my Mother as well as friends have seen me in DMT state to what I can't stop talking and saying new information about things. This has slowed down since I have stopped being so involved with awakening people through You Tube media. *But as I have written this book I am communicating to you from me as Tony but also from the one true consciousness of all quantum design.*

Witness and testimonials - Alison & Malvern White, my parents. *who witnessed the outside phenomenon that far bypasses any logical explanation of why it happened.* ***Other things to show the Matrix is fake has happened to us all*** *since the Mandela effect with each being a witness to the others.* ***Life is not straight forward indoctrinated education programs, life***

is non-existent. The only thing that matters is what you do and how you act it out as one part of the giant expressions of consciousness.

After a few months into experiencing the Mandela effect I caught up with a few old-school buddies that I used to run amok with. *One of them Maine was a mate I used to hang around with always, catching up with him and having a yarn I found of that a friend who was supposed to have passed away from a drug and needle related incident,* ***was now contacting my friend Maine on face-book*** *. I couldn't believe what I was* ***hearing as Des died a long time ago and many witnessed his funeral and considering Maine was his best friend and knew he had passed like I knew was mind blowing****. I spoke to Des since and told him he was a Mandela effect himself.* ***He remembers being on the Sagittarius Arm also?*** *But he was not from my and Maine's Mirror of the Sagittarius arm Set as in our reality he had passed away. I have spoken with Des and caught up since.* ***He has willingly allowed his name to be mentioned as evidence of what I say is truth and not fabricated. He now is a Mandela Effected subject like the rest of us that have shifted from the various frequencies of consciousness's quantum design****. His name Is* ***Desmond O'Reilly*** *and his testimonial and brief experience with the Mandela effect discovery is below.*

Desmond O'Reilly testimonial, "I was shocked to find out I should be dead and did and was in another reality and dimension to my current one, through a friend telling me that heard from Tony I was awakened to the Mandela Effect and Tony helped explain we are nothing but consciousness and

what had happened, being quite smart myself I clicked easy to what he was saying. After finding out I no longer lived in Sagittarius Arm and now in Orion Spur , I was absolutely blown away as I do remember we had always been in the outskirts of the Milky Way the Sagittarius Arm. After hearing this and seeing things for myself such as chopper Reid becoming chopper Read, as well as the ford badge change , and many other things I have vivid knowing existed as what I remember now had changed what Tony explains is total sense, we are nothing but energy. Thank you Bro for explaining when I first found out what had happened you helped me put what could have been a scary thing into an amazing experience we all that have been shifted were giving by the one consciousness or God itself"

Yet another very strange incident of my life experiences changing is the fact that my friend also from a while back when I was having fun on drugs etc. Is now also ALIVE again! *Years and years back while deep with agoraphobia still I received a phone call from my friend Lopa's brother Matt. The phone call was to inform me that Lopa had overdosed and passed away due to his heart exploding from meth amphetamine over use.* ***I felt sad I lost my good friend that always had my back***. ***Anyways many went to Lopa's funeral and all know he was dead to this day.*** *Now one my best friends that lives across the road from me got himself into a bit of trouble with the local police enforcement, and was sentenced to a not long term but few years imprisonment. I now speak to this friend to what I'm sure will have no issues confirming what I say, and what he told me one day blew my mind once again!*

He said he was in the max security jail and he was chilling with and been talking with ***LOPA inside****. I said nar man Lopa's dead bro , he replied "****I thought so too man but its Lopa and Lopa didn't die it was his brother Matt that had passed away back then****" I said but Matt was the one that had called me informing me of Lopa's funeral?* ***So for me my reality had just changed again to give me another big kick in the head to wake up and see everything is not what we think****. The duality in this experience is insane. Now his brother passed away and not him.* ***Everyone knew Lopa had died and it was a term we all dealt with a long time back losing a friend...*** *Now after the Mandela effect just like many celebrities are returning to life etc, we can see even the* ***everyday joe is experiencing the dead rising again strangeness of the Mandela effect****.*

*(****Witness and testimonial, Robert Duguid, In jail with Lopa****.)*

I realize now that my whole life has been designed by my subconscious plan , my monk hood state , my experiences. The Mandela effect are all related. In 2006 I wrote a fantasy novel called End of Time*, around the same I also wrote a joking poem attempt while I was having a few drinks with a friend.* ***My book End of time is all about the third eye and consciousness and the colors of magic and the healing colors of chakra. The book was about time collapsing in a future after nuclear Armageddon and they lived in a fantasy world****.*

The poem meant ***not a thing back then*** *,but now has clear relevance to the Mandela effect. This poem I will include below but first also tell you about another book I was writing called the* **DREAM WAVE SOCIETY***. This book was about timelines and*

multi parallel worlds that government agents vs the Hero's had different kinds of encounters with each other , D-WAVE SOCIETY? It may be a long shot but the fact my book was called Dream Wave, and then we now many years in the future have a D-wave is rather more than a coincidence. *I have included images of my books below, the Dream Wave is stained from being old and you can notice the page coloring.* ***After awaking full after the Mandela effect I can see the pixels of creation, see energy moving around , one time this would have freaked me out , but now understanding how reality works its natural.*** *It's what we should all be doing,* ***we have been given a chance to reveal the greatest gift of all.***
True knowledge and first-hand experience of passing through as consciousness through dimensional mirrors and live to talk about it. *The One itself wanted us, so selected us the shifted to have the true understanding of God,* ***to help break the infinite figure eight of misunderstanding that is plaguing the Matrix from evolving to its true spiritual state of forever knowing and forever seeing enlightenment of humanity. Next are the images of my books then followed by my Poem*** *that was added as best of its class first page in a book called, ready for this? "****Timeless Voice's****". Here are the images and Poem.*

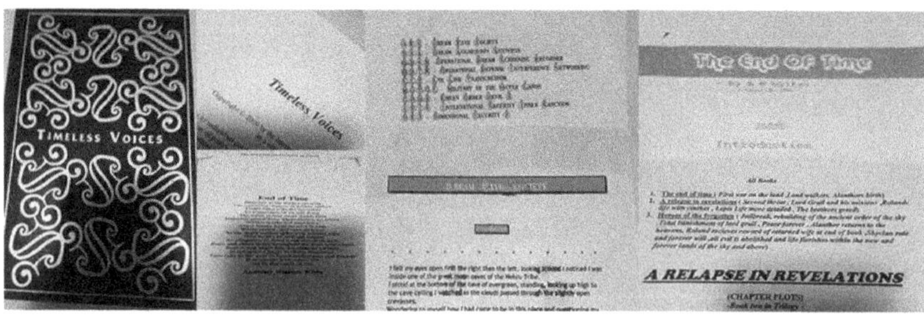

"ONE CONSCIOUSNESS"

Branches to the North echo with.
The unlimited shadow of infinite silence.
Lands filled with the inevitable.
Consequences of its self-doing.
The fallen heroes move within there.
Immortal prison from where there is no return.
Silence breaks and thunderous.
Anger Breaks from the ever so blue.
Water, People, and animals kneel.
As the angry Mother spins with infernal rage.
Time breaks its seal and forgets.
Its obligation to those it has served so well.
Panic and chaos strive throughout the dead man's land.
Sorrow and anger fills the children's hearts.
Black spaces Linger between memories.
Time falls to her ever so loved soul of past and present.
Day returns with new life.
So be the circle of life.

I have been given what I asked , The true words of God's creation , and I by the One consciousness started a You Tube channel to help those in need of understanding , I have one mission with all of you , and that is to make you know that you are DIVINE in creation , and Exist forever in parallel mirrors of consciousness ,You are infinite , You are already immortal ,You are what creates the physical Matrix, I offer these teachings to help only , Do not take my teachings to insane levels to where you decide to try and log in and out , this is not my responsibility as the teacher , I am only sharing enlightenment at the request of the One for you to remember and reach your spirit again. Log in and out is your destiny for future life experiences to come.

My entire life has been a trail of bread crumbs to finding source As I explained all my life I known I had psychic abilities but refused to use them. ***The Mandela effect did not give me any choice. It decided it would use them for me and through now knowing what I am and knowing I have to way see the future of mankind with this information once again as I have done in many past lives while directing the chess board game to either help the negative or positive remain in balance.*** *This time we are to remember who we are again our playground of the One directing the Game is found everywhere , and as time and trends increased the influence of the message of consciousness gets stronger, we have been blatantly told we are in a game and the law of duality from simple examples like* ***"people calling each other Dog, to what is nothing but God in reverse teaching us duality.*** *To the common sayings of local society,* ***STAY TRUE TO THE GAME PLAYER, YO PLAYER! You see and hear the signs of God trying to awaken us all everywhere and hopefully after reading all the book start to here so far you have a new understanding of the truth that has been hidden from us in plain sight of colored electromagnetic energies and references of total misguidance and indoctrination.***

Next I will explain the Mandela Effect and what happened, who caused it, why etc?

After reading all that you have in advance the concept of what I explain should be easier to understand and resonate with. May we all awaken to a bright and wonderful future of total knowing and no gaps left in where are we from why are we here.

THE TRUTH OF THE MANDELA EFFECT

The Mandela effect has summed up to many different phenomenon's according to many that experienced it and are trying to decipher it but the factual evidence that is the truth is far more bizarre than any timeline change, or evil doing by the elites.

The effect itself has been referenced in the ancient past in many ways before Cern or any other kind of scapegoat cause could be held accountable for it. ***We look back into time of others experiences of some just driving a car through remote areas and discovering a town that existed they have never knew to exist, visited the found location went on their way with their original journey and on the way back after returning to go home then found out the town or as its been called in the past mirage has totally vanished and the location of that place was never existent.*** ***If you research some the paranormal circumstances around these kind of events such as the man from Taured ,to the ancient sea voyages finding new islands that never existed ,visited them and once left ,the island vanished to never be found again.*** *The stories of time jumping or parallel realities being true in existence goes back to the*

ancient days of Vikings. So how did they shift? The answer itself is quite simple the power of their subconscious collective as one created these manifestations to occur. *The spirit from within each player of the time wanted to send a message that was blatant that time itself is an illusion creation,* ***but we just did not ever take the understanding as the One decided us to.***

We now have ***since the 1950's Cern created to discover the big bang etc.*** *Cern created the internet well* ***Tim Bernera- Lee,*** *A* ***British scientist working for Cern did, and the world wide web was formed in 1989. Just as God loves its duality teachings and now from past chapters you understand that 666 is nothing but another sign from the one consciousness. Aka synchronicity numbers just as all synchronicities are , then you can see the design of what the One has been designing to bring us total understanding of how we work and who we truly are.*** *The internet was just a code implant to teach us to become one, the point of you are a single avatar sitting at home using your internet to connect you to the world wide web is the blatant message about you as a singularity of single self-aware consciousness energy need to reconnect back to the world wide web of energy,* ***the full consciousness collective of the constructs manifestation. We have been brought up with parallel universe indoctrination as training as what was to come.*** *The shows like Quantum Leap showed the man himself look like a different person but was* ***still always his own consciousness energy. Sam from that show was showing us as children that we are energy and what he was doing was shifting energy frequencies to change where he would fluctuate in the whole outcome of the collective's***

electromagnetic frequencies allowing him to enter another's physical avatar *with his* ***consciousness energy. This show was the most blatant for the truth of being of us all. Now after many years of growing up we have the real phenomenon encounter that we have experienced, our whole lives have been conditioned by the One through guiding the singularities of the Matrix to bring us back to the truth and the real understanding of spirit.***

Cern is a machine designed to work with particles, and colliding them at the speed of light to what we know from before that when matter is increased in higher speeds of vibration then that matter becomes nothing but energy. *We in each of our own collectives throughout the infinite mirrors of creation are set to our own manifestation frequency throughout all the quantum design.* ***Cern for the past years since early 2010s has gone out of its way to explain to us the masses numerous times that they themselves may have discovered parallel realities to what they believe they can remove" things" from and manipulate other worldly resources and also place things into.*** *Shame they did not place a true definition to what THINGS really are. Cern and D-wave the quantum computer itself are scapegoats for us to understand what happened.* ***The One has designed the Technology around us for us to be able to notice changes, notice the difference in things from the past reality to the new.***

Using Cern and the dimensional computer itself the D-wave, they managed to understand the energy patterns of each collective of physical creation. ***They when using the Hadron***

Collider in this reality was them in the many mirrors attached to our reality firing up the particle accelerator throughout all the other mirrors they also existed in until you go so far into the mirrors they just don't exist. Once knowing they work with dimensional synchronization you can understand they created a link much like the internet to each quantum computers frequency of manifestation of each of the parallel realities it was also built in. With Cern now being the vibrational center of manipulation we now have a combined building of a machine that can see other realities and also manipulate energies of those other dimensions. *With D-wave and the particle accelerator in all other dimensions in synchronicity to the current start point of the manipulation you have a machine capable of moving energy in and out of other frequencies of consciousness energy.* ***But why and how did we shift****?* ***As I explained in the past few chapters you are nothing but energy and then had been selected to be shifted by your awareness level as awareness is frequency itself. We that have been shifted are very similar in life, we all have had hardships, we all have suffered a hard life, we either all are spiritual, religious, or a truth seeker and last but not least we all had thought we couldn't ever be worthy of being selected by God.*** *We all had the same resonance frequency of our consciousness in* ***the collective of Sagittarius arm. We had the start of our awakening from the One consciousness starting whether it was conspiracy awakening, spiritual understanding, or just true awakening. We being at our own frequency of self-aware electromagnetic consciousness inside the collective had our own attachments to creation and particles, as particles,***

atoms, etc are all nothing but our creation as the full collective of consciousness to start with. With Cern moving particles from this dimension and others they move us as energy of consciousness. Did they plan to? Now I don't think they have any idea of what they did conscious but however them as spirit and light being subconsciously I believe had well knowing of what they were doing and planned for the outcome of what we now experience with the Mandela effect itself. We as energy of the last reality have been shifted, once those particles from Sagittarius arm collective are removed you remove the energies of frequency hence us, the spirit inside the physical avatar body. *Did Cern create it with intentional agendas?* ***Yes and no. Cern really are nothing but more light being players just like us , and through them as spirit they have left many hints to show they knew what they were doing.*** *A classic video of Cern is the We are happy at Cern video,* ***to what you can see many references to the Mandela effect within their video clip released on You Tube.*** *From the Bond #1 sign with Mandela in text held by the scientist at the desk, to the puzzle jigsaw piece of the wall next to them.* **The whole video itself is nothing but subconscious advertising of what was going to happen.** *Just as Cern director for research Sergio Bertolucci quoted* ***in 2009 November 6th*** *,* ***"Out of this door something might come through , or we might send something through it". The world itself has been designed for us as spirit to remember who we are again to bypass our amnesia and know what and who we are again.*** *Even though many think Cern is a sinister organization they themselves are being controlled by the One just as all of us and are embedded* *into the Matrix in this current dimensional frame of time only to give us the selected by God, shifted the full understanding of what and how things have happened.* ***Remember the laws of duality I explained before, everything in the Matrix is reversed as it's from the conscious. Let's use the duality law on Cern.*** *So we know Cern as the leaders of dimensional study, big bang theory etc.* ***In reality though after time we come to believe it was a CON. As nothing as the big bang the way they say it was created exists . So we can CON and CERN, which is CON-CERN. We have had Cern trying to awaken us to what is the real for a long time, and because of those laws of free will they could not tell us what we are and what we are made of as that's the game. Instead of as I stated they have left bread crumb trails right throughout their workings to after now the Mandela effect has happened, the Alice in Wonderland image on the Cern map of the accelerator to the wicked queen of Snow White that was a Mandela effect to a lot of the shifted. Below is the time lines of the video "we are happy at cern and my explaining to what they are showing each time within the small clip Cern released itself.***

"We are happy at Cern" I will take screenshots of each video location and add them below before explaining each images significance, the celebration was about discovering other realities and dimensional mirrors. ***The video channel is US LHC and the video was posted by Cern on the third of November 2014. Just as the statue of Shiva outside the front of Cern is to indicate that they have known about parallel dimensions you will see many similar references of subliminal proportion within this released by The European Organization for nuclear***

research itself. Within these images from the video on You Tube you will notice the game player references.
The references to us being connected to particles and much more, ***in reality the whole world has been directed by source to create one. The one world order****, the one this, the one that.*
We the masses are to create the true ONE COLLECTIVE is the message behind it all not the illuminati, not the agenda plans but us the singularities of consciousness need to combine as ONE to be our full designs potential and awaken back to who we are again as spirits and angels of light.

At seven seconds into the clip we already can notice that the Cern silhouettes of the people are standing in front of a screen, on the sides we can see player one and player two. This is a reference into the spirit and the avatar, or the physical and the spiritual also a very blatant reference from the One trying to make us once again understand we are inside the hologram vibrational created game we call real reality.

At the eleven second timestamp, we can see the outline of the person as black solid shadow but behind we can see the energy reference on the screen moving with the same movement patterns as the black silhouette of the girl, this is showing the electromagnetic energies of the spiritual body

inside our avatar and that we as physical are really nothing but energy itself. *Notice the explosion of energy on the screen, the fight between the player one or player 2, the spirit and the body.*

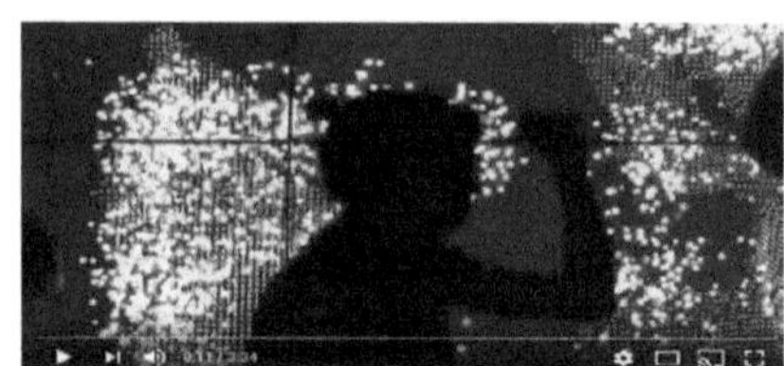

Continuing the video and right through the video clip itself we can see everyone dancing with different styles showing the alternating frequencies of vibration. *At 24 seconds in we can see the people standing on different levels of staircases,* ***this is a representation of dimensional mirrors explained, just as the idea of having a multiple floored building was created by the true source of creation to show us that there are more levels to design to the one we stand on.*** *These ideas of elevators lifting you through floors, to each floor itself created with its own design of reality of experience.* ***It is all showing from the one consciousness how reality really works within its design. Just as the Mason's ladder to nowhere is also the same ideology reference of multi-dimensional understandings.***

Remember this whole video was created professionally with the creators making each scene to show what they wanted you to see.

The idea of showing this during the video is to remind your subconscious at core to remember what the truth of existence is. *To the time stamp at 25 seconds in,* ***to what shows reference to Shiva and many alternating dimensional mirrors, hence the arms in all places from each alternating person there.***

Going further into the video we can see at the 31 second time stamp we have a the particle accelerator inside with a person being shown to represent the particle itself , this is showing you that YOU are that particle and are linked as consciousness energy of the collective. We from the Sagittarius Arm version of reality were those particles being shifted as our energy awareness frequency was at the same frequency of the particles that were being manipulated and shifted through dimensional mirrors. Hence us being shifted.

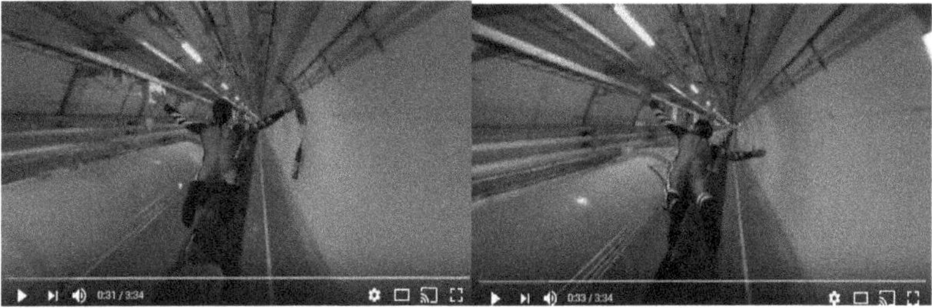

Around this time, you can clearly hear the musician Farrell say in his lyrics, "Come along if you're feeling like a room without a roof" Many that was shifted felt exactly like this. ***Amazing the music that was selected for the clip itself was also a giant hint to explain what was happening at Cern with their new discoveries. Especially how happy they are now.*** *Hence the song constantly saying because we're happy.* ***The room without a ROOF is clearly a message of breaking through a wall of discovery into endless possibilities that had never had thought to be possible before . Or breaking from one thought to be only locked dimension into new endless possibilities of discovered dimensional mirrors and collectives of consciousness self-aware energy.***

Continuing more into the clip we see the numbers 33 being flaunted above the firetruck, and the levels of 32 etc next to it, the 33 is focused on for you to see, as I explained below the 33 is nothing but physical and spirit working as its own identity together and not being stuck in an infinite locked figure 8 of misunderstanding.

Moving on to the 56 second time stamp we can see a woman who moves her arms in the formation of waves, flowing, then next to her to the left we can notice a sign that says LHcb but the sign itself is a giant reference to what is happening at Cern. The duality teaching of the mirrored wording on the sign, the clear reference to a parallel mirrored dimension. ***Note the two alternating colors of each mirrored also showing law of duality of the One.***

Onward we just have references of vibrations by the many people dancing in alternating styles, in front of the particle accelerator and more, nothing of great importance until we reach the 1min and 44 second time stamp, here we can see that once again the physical human avatar is being represented as particles, atoms etc with the idea of multi verse bubbles maybe to represent the bubbles of each collective as we are encased inside the electromagnetic bubble that we call the firmament. Watching the clip for the next few seconds shows us as the energy being pushed through the LHC , then as entering through the tunnel we change from physical avatar into a particle that then collides with the other and sends two human avatars from it. This is showing you parallel you exists in another dimensional mirror of your own quantum collective. And the separation of your physical body and spirit.

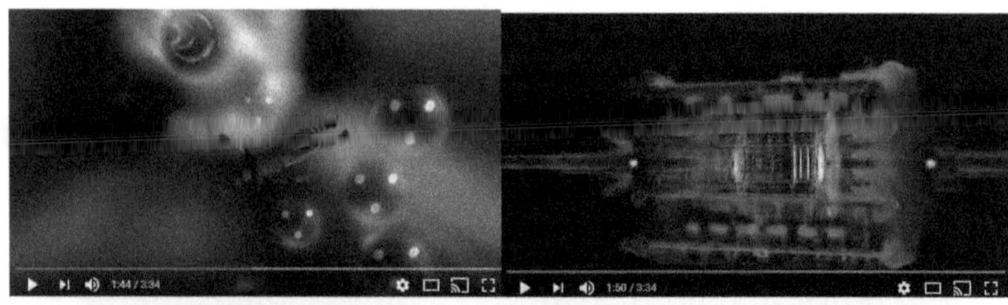

You can see how this clip is showing many a reference into what happened with the Mandela effect itself. *So moving through the video we constantly see the human avatar being represented as energy throughout the next while, floating in space spinning around.* ***At 1.59 in you can notice the red orb behind the person as they are floating this is their collective. Moving more into the video to the 2.04, mark you can watch as the person is floating in indoctrinated term space and watch the two orbs that are red representing the two collectives smash into each other and create one solid orb.*** *This is showing the shift of consciousness energy and combining it with the next hence smashing the one collective orb into the other to create one is merging of consciousness energies of vibrational frequencies.*

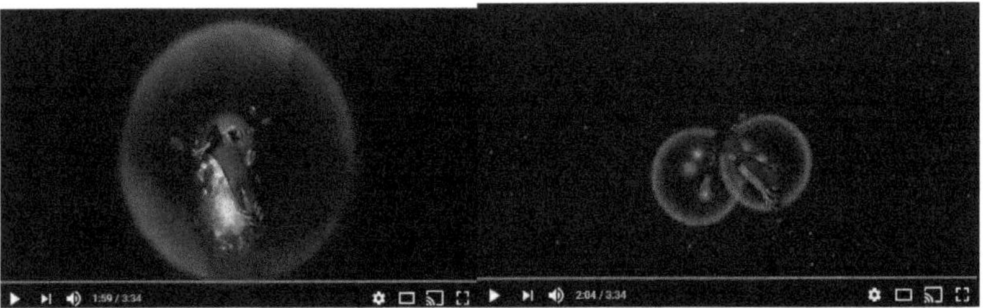

The whole video up to around 2.32 in is more vibration dance references explaining in symbology the force of vibrations needed to manipulate matter at the same time as dancing are also giving the hint of vibrational force at work. Hence the workers all play with vibrations etc as their job at the Large Hadron Collider .

At the 2.32 mark the video changes to show a scientist of Cern sitting at his desk playing peek-a-boo. *This here is a very blatant message also explaining that the video clip itself is not straight forward but has* ***a peek-a-boo meaning or hidden meaning to it if you know what to look for. First we will examine the stage made surroundings of the set, as remember this is all filmed as a stage set to show what they wanted you to see.***

So without looking to hard we can see the BOND#1 and the MANDELA sign on this lap. Looking onto the wall to the left we can see a jigsaw piece, then on the table itself the records of something and even the picture of Snow White's evil queen on the desktop when she was the witch that made her eat the apple. The whole design of the stage here is to show records or paperwork scattered all over the place representing the changing of times that would occur and the changes in history would become scattered to the many that had been shifted. The puzzle on the wall is to tell you that this video and scene especially here is being shown to you as a puzzle for you to solve. Many have speculated what this means but I will tell you my insight, and it is not such a bad scary thing everyone is making it out to be. Cern wanted to awaken us, we as spirit needed the Mandela effect to become conscious of spirit again. *Cern has been trying to awaken the collective frequency*

hence the projects name the Wakefield experiment *,WAKE?* ***They are trying to AWAKEN the asleep that was us playing the game without knowing what anything really was. They cannot tell us blatantly as I've explained so consciousness leaves these messages for us to understand when the time's right for that knowledge to be interpreted and understood.*** *BOND#1 is the bonding of duality as one, to create ONE from two, just as we in Orion now are part of this ONE collective with TWO alternating frequencies of set manifestation of consciousness.* ***Even going into BOND 1 being the first character to play bond as Barry nelson was in, we still have the joining of the two to create one hence, MANDELA SIGN = NELSON aka Nelson Mandela and BOND#1 Barry Nelson to what is also a link Saying Nelson as the top word as BOND. Hence all creates the NELSON MANDELA. The Mandela effect otherwise known.*** *The real truth is that BOND#1 is to bond good and bad or positive and negative energy as one and is a message from source through Cern as being the singularity that presented it.* ***There is more here but the main of what's needed to be recognized I have pointed out. Moving on to after the old scientist at the desk we have once again full references to us as a physical body being particles or energy spinning about in space and even with the particle accelerator in the background indicating all is linked. Moving through the video to the end you can see the change of the two players before now being only one player standing in the middle of the screen and more vibrational dancing in alternating scenes. This whole clip is nothing but a made-on purpose teaching left for us to understand what could have happened when we***

discovered the Mandela effect and needed answers. *So, you're saying right now* ***Okay so Cern created the Mandela Effect,*** *right? Well... Yes, in a sense but in truth* ***we all did.***

We as the subconscious energies of the collective had enough of being lost we as spirit wanted to awaken again to the truth of what we are again. We manifested Cern and D-waves existence into the hologram Matrix in order to teach us as spirit again what is real and what is not and to mainly understand we are not physical but energy that is self-aware that inhabits the physical body as we play the game. We created the Mandela effect through our combined subconscious collective power that was at higher frequency then most before the shift. We wanted it simply because we needed it for realization. The One decided it's time and when we as spirit asked for it, we got what we sought at the subconscious level hence we were already on our path to seek the full truth when researching the illuminati or other hidden conspiracies, we had already asked from spirit to be reawakened again. *The reason you enjoyed learning the truth and you become infatuated with it is because you as spirit knew it was the start to lead you home to understanding who you are again.* ***Without the way technology is and without us having these ready made to blame scapegoats like Cern and D-wave we wouldn't be able to grasp the truth of what happened.*** *We would be lost,* ***the fact that consciousness has left behind big blatant messages such as a D-wave computer that works in other dimensions and is called a quantum computer is a blessing to us all that needed to understand.***

Everything beforehand of the Mandela effect had been preconditioned for us. From the quantum indoctrination through media, to understanding the workings of physics, matter being created from nonphysical energy all has been explaining to us the true foundations of God's creation and the true laws that built the design of the construct. We asked many times throughout the past to know the truth, seeking searching everywhere and because of that energy frequency you had been brought to you have been given all the answers you seek and they are everywhere now to explain.

So what exactly happened with us? Okay so to explain what happened is saying basically the same as Cern had just shown us within the video you hopefully just watched at the same time as reading my book to have reference. We as the Sagittarius Arm had our own collective frequency of manifestation. *Within the frequencies we the shifted had raised our vibrational frequency to be a part of the surroundings around us.* ***We were becoming aware without becoming aware and as we and everything around us is us, we moved with the particles shifted.*** *What happened is the consciousness energy of the shifted was* ***removed from one collective of self-aware quantum consciousness and was then placed into another. Hence us from Sagittarius Arm now in Orion's spur. We throughout each mirror have been moved throughout all mirrors in a domino effect. The switch here moved our consciousness energy from Orion to Sagittarius arm and vice versa. We have many mirrors we have been shifted from throughout the collective the easiest way to describe this is imagine bowls of water and you have a dropper. Now take a***

***few drops out of each and place in the next etc this is what has happened but the bowl being our full electromagnetic bubble of self-aware collective consciousness and the dripping water drops being the frequencies of singularity energy that have been moved into the next. We have been removed from the Sagittarius arm version of reality and placed here in Orion, to what is another multiverse's universe. We left our original multiverse of the Carina Cygnus went out of our universe there and have now been placed in another collective of consciousness's manifestation**, the Orion spur multiverse, to what we are in one universe of.*

***Everything from after the Mandela effect has been created to give us a message of either duality combining to be one, or the split to show two from one. This is God showing us that reality works as a set of One. Just as you are created with two feet, two arms, hands etc as a set of hands or feet the One creates everything else in sets just as we have been created. Just as good and bad are only two hands needed to be understood as being a set of ONE and that all is created from the ONE**. Below are examples from Mandela effects and what they are saying with the message behind it.*

First are the many products that have changed names to be the same but with slightly alternating spelling to them. Example is Freebreeze becoming Freebreze with only one E, but in reality, nothing has changed as the word remains the same showing that the changes are two different representations of the same ONE product, this is showing duality**. And is that the One consciousness has done this to* *make us* ***understand that everything is always One. Just as we have the Kit-Kat product itself always known to have the splitting dash between the kit and Kat now changed from two separate words that still created the one to now becoming more blatantly ONE by removing the middle dash and now being KitKat. *One solid word that was created from the two before also showing the law of duality.* ***Many products changed with this meaning behind it, more blatant are ones that are full on in your face like the movie quotes to what we will go through a few below.***

Sagittarius Arm, Forrest Gump, Momma always said life is like a box of chocolates to Orion Spurs version, Momma always said life was like a box of chocolates. Past and present. The was and is, the lesson from this change was life is like a box of chocolates, meaning we are stuck in the box to you pass or be eaten. To now life was like a box explaining we are now outside of that box we are now understanding more than the box that confined us before could hold. *Our life now is outside the box because it was like a box now it's not, this is also classic sign of duality teaching from the one consciousness.*

Sagittarius Arm, Jaws, we're going to need a bigger boat, to this realities version, you're going to need a bigger boat. Once again teaching duality, indicating the singularity of you're and then the collective of we're.

Sagittarius Arm, Field of dreams, if you build it they will come, now in this reality if you build it he will come, this is another teaching of duality again. They to he, the collective to individual. Teaching that both versions from our past reality to

the new current one is all duality lesson. Just the same as the Bernstein bears becoming Berenstain bears or Sex in the City becoming Sex and the City. All is to teach duality to the one product meaning the same showing that creation itself is designed with sets and God itself as one is both the Good and bad stereotypes we created. But in fact is those combined as one but working with neutrality.

The famous quote of Snow White's queen, Mirror Mirror from the past reality to now the Magic mirror. This shows the law of duality to reversal, the two becoming one, thus the word of mirror still is existent, but we now have as clear reference from the one consciousness a message of MAGIC MIRROR to what we know magic is real as energy and intent. *We can see the hidden message as being energy mirrors, and this is what we passed through from the alternate reality to this one.*

Mr. Rodgers and the theme song seems to be a giant reference also to the Individual singularity and the mass collectives, as with all the effects we can see the duality teaching as one set. Beautiful day in the neighborhood to beautiful day in this neighborhood, the being many as collective and this being single identity, Both the and this create the set of duality and reversal.

Star Wars Sagittarius Arm, we remember the good old line from Star Wars empire strikes, back right? LUKE! I am your father. Now changed to NO I am your father. Here we see the same idea again of ONENESS, *Luke giving the singularity name and NO not referencing any name as being collective.* ***NO NAME /NAME many duality teachings in this one, Despite the FOX***

news trying to discredit the Mandela effect with ludicrous memory fail problems etc we can still find footage of Earl Jones himself talking about the first time he ever seen the script where he clearly says it says "LUKE I AM YOUR FATHER". Not to mention the many other times he on other shows quoted the famous Sagittarius Arm Line of Luke when asked to on talk shows. This alone shows that research was not first done before trying to discredit the Mandela effect by the mainstream and the agenda is to remove blame from Cern etc, as when we know we did shift as a whole we would want answers and that's the last thing the ones that want the technology do want. *Another classic Star Wars Mandela effect or vibrational Frequency change effect is the C3PO character and how in this reality he is now from Star Wars episode VII a New hope* ***not full gold from head to toe. He now has a silver leg... In our reality. The Sagittarius Arm C3pO was always totally gold from head to toe, yes, I know during other episodes he replaced parts here and there and that's fine. The fact is C3pO was always gold and if you do some research into this you can still buy full Gold C3pO kids toys from the 1980s era to what is completely gold and not gold and silver.*** *Once again with the* ***gold and silver we see duality and set of One of duality showing us the message the same as all other Mandela effects.***

We move onto the movie Silence of the Lambs to where Hannibal Lecter says his famous quote of many a times advertised in the past on bill boards in Sagittarius Arm *"Hello Clarice"* ***to what in this reality just never existed****? And was not used as a scene in the movie.* ***We have it existent and now***

nonexistent. I don't think I need to explain the duality and reversal law that is presented here as teaching from the One consciousness.

Moving on we have the movie created from the book of Ann Rice starring Brad Pitt and Tom Cruise, the movie in our reality of the outskirts of the milky way was called, ***Interview with A Vampire, to now after being shifted into the new manifestation of Orion's avatar it has become Interview with THE Vampire. Once again as Mr. Rodgers and the neighborhood duality teaching we can see the exact same message that has been left for us to discover****. The single to the collective, A to THE.*

There are many more such as actors not sounding the same anymore or in some cases looking slightly different as remembered*. We leave the movie quotes and enter more blatant duality teachings,* ***remember duality of God is masculine and feminine energy combined as one. Within these examples below I will explain how this is referenced in the messages of some Mandela effects , but all equal duality just the same as us being from Sagittarius arm to what you can find Carl Sagan and Neil Degrasse Tyson also say****. Sagan from one of his documentaries and Tyson from his show Star Talk,* ***to us now being on the Orion's spur arm . Our own experience of multiverse jumping explains the laws of duality itself.***

On the Sagittarius arm the Ford logo was a straight F and was considered a ***very masculine company*** *with Holden.* ***The badge was solid and strong****. After the Shift to many of us we can see now the ford badge has a very defined pig tail on the F making* *the logo look more French styled spelling, and* ***more feminine*** *to the original* ***FORD logo*** *we have all grown up with.* ***The same can be found with other car badges themselves, just looking at the Volvo logo itself, our reality we had the round circle and the Volvo logo across the center horizontally. Now we can see the badge word placement is the same but we can notice that to the top right there is now an arrow. The new Volvo sign is the sign of the male, or masculine, and the older Volvo sign of just the circle is the feminine or the Old reality vulva and the new reality logo representation of phallus.*** *From the Volkswagon itself as well as spelling changing to show duality, now Volkswagen to the split in the middle from the full connected symbol before.* ***All of these changes are showing duality to its creation. The changing of words spelling but still being the same representation of product itself forms duality, the cars themselves are teaching duality from the old classic cars such as Lamborghini and Ferrari etc always being the masculine form of brand for the bachelor or high roller to now becoming in this reality as well as the original cars , family wagons. Yes the new reality has classic sports cars that were well known to just make sedans making family orientated versions of those cars.*** *This showing the single power machine for the bachelor in the Sagittarius Arm,* ***The masculine, To the now designed version for family aka nurturing ,The feminine. God is showing us how it is created itself constantly as the design of the Matrix itself is.***

Once understanding the desired message consciousness has tried to show us through allowing the Mandela effect experience to happen to us we can see that all the changes

end up with the same message and reference result. I am duality in creation, I am masculine and feminine as ONE INTELLIGENT SOURCE.

A lot of famous names as well as historical versions of events changed with our transformation of consciousness. We see many names such as Christopher Reeves, now become Reeve without the ending S on their name, showing the collective and individual teaching again. From the duality teachings of names such as Seth McFarlane the family guy creator, to the new realities Seth MacFarlane. *Same name different spelling same ONE though. From chopper Reid the famous Australian criminal that most know and have heard about to now Chopper Read, as in literally read as in read a book.* ***Even though Chopper wrote a book while in prison it's a very ironic reality change considering Chopper himself could not read as many well knew.*** *These duality teachings are blatant as they come. The list of changed names is a lot more and I will reference you to channels on YouTube for Mandela effect examples below as well as the direct videos on my channel* ***showing Carl Sagan*** *and* ***Neil Degrasse state we live on the Sagittarius Arm of the Milky Way.***

So why are all the changes that are happening like this with a pattern left behind to understand? It's simple, we are being shown that we have separated God for too long and we had created our own stereotypes of what reality should be by creating the "Is this our only life ever question?" *Where did we come from? etc.* ***We lost the true understanding of what we are and why we are inside this holographic construct so the***

consciousness of the One or God has now decided to intervene itself and change the understanding available to us as the children of It. *We have been selected to know the truth, the true forms of reality, the infinite design of the mirror sets of dimensions.* ***We have been shown that God is both the Good and Bad as One. The feminine and masculine as ONE, and have been awakened again to the truth of what we are supposed to know as Sons of God. Our physical body, Avatars changes such as the, lungs being smaller, the ribcage of the skeleton being now connected to more of a shield shaped structure. To our hearts moving to the centre of your chest and no longer out to the left.*** *I have interviewed a friend that is a Nurse herself, to what myself Tony quickly interviewed her over Skype.* ***She is a call out nurse but her name shall remain private due to ridicule and the fact she is still in the profession. The You Tube channel to find it on is my own, SRPHD and the video name itself is, MANDELA EFFECT - ANATOMY INTERVIEW WITH A NURSE.*** *Even though we have shifted quite a few times since our arrival here on Orion,* ***such as the skull itself having small holes through areas now called the Supraorbital Foramen, Infraorbital Foramen and the Mental Foramen with the skull now having bone blocking the old reality open eye socket to brain design. The whole reason we have been given new avatar designs in organ structures is to show we are nothing but energy and memories itself are stored within the consciousness cloud of the collective not our individual brains.*** *We remember the past reality because we are nothing but consciousness energy. We shifted physical bodies and have the same memories of the Sagittarius Arm.* ***We have been shown***

by God itself through working in a very mysterious way that we are nothing of physicality. How could you remember past memories with your body and brain being new to you*? You wouldn't be able to* ***if you as physical had changed. Memory itself is stored into the collective just as we upload each experience to it as a giant data collecting hard drive of consciousness energy of experiences. We all remember the exact same because we are energy that's self-aware and even though our signature of consciousness energy has been shifted into a new formed physical body in this alternate reality, we as the experiencing energy of Sagittarius arm that has been shifted still have full collective remembering of that reality as we as energy of electromagnetic consciousness stored it within our own collective. Now we have two combined collective frequencies of construct manifestation with the one being the physical reality that has always existed here, and then the manifested by us the shifted residuals, as we are creating all the residuals through our subconscious collective. Because we know we are not misremembering anything we know so knowing through the subconscious manifests and we are manifesting the physical residuals into this new reality. The only new here is us, not the surroundings have changed, not we forgot. The fact is we are from Sagittarius arm, and our memories are fine.*** *Not everyone had the experience of shifting and some will always use denial instead of admitting they can't understand what's happened or it's above their intelligent comprehension making them feel not as intelligent as they thought.* ***That will bring instant denial to the cause and message. The Orion occupants have always been here to them***

reality never has shifted remember that. They do remember that Star Wars said NO I'm your father because here in their reality it has always been. Just the same as the JFK assassination from our reality having only four people in the car to what is now six people as well as new physical structure to the car itself. We know our reality like the back of our hand, just as the Orion's spur occupants do also. This is their reality not ours, we have been selected to show the rest of the world at the moment that quantum reality, consciousness, and God exists as the true form of creation removing all religious stereotype indoctrinations and allowing us as a collective of both Orion and Sagittarius arm frequencies of consciousness energy to combine and work at a frequency of harmony.

With all Mandela effects we see changes but in truth there is no change here, only our memories of our past reality crossed with the new make it seem as change. ***But reality is nothing has changed here apart from the singularity of consciousness frequency of us being in the last full collective of that realities manifestation to now becoming the frequencies inside this new collective.*** *Or putting more simply,* ***our energy that was inhabiting the creation of our last avatar being shifted and placed into the avatar that once held the collective consciousness mirror of us of this parallel reality of Orion's spur.***

The Mandela effect itself now is being abbreviated to the M.E the me. It's once again showing through the collective subconscious of us as spirit the message of individuality even though the Mandela effect has affected a wide range of us

aged from 8 to 90-year-old as the collective, we have the ME implanted for us to understand we, as in ME, you, we are creating the Mandela Effect*. The ME effect. As we created the effect as the quantum consciousness of our subconscious to start with.*

Moving into more effects we see the land masses have changed to what we as child to adult remember the geological locations being, South America has moved to the right, Australia itself is way out of where it should be from my recollection as an Australian as we now almost sit on top of Papua New Guinea. New Zealand is misplaced, the Ice caps are no longer existent as what we knew. The changes are happening as all land forms are moving closer to other masses to show One once again. There is a reason our lives before the effect had been brainwashed with the merging of everything into One as we had been seeing. *It's all to show that we as the whole* ***are one collective not individual by skin colour****, race, looks, language, or anything else that we have been indoctrinated to be programmed with to then believe.* ***The fact is everything now is turning to ONE because God itself as the controller of all and the self-aware intelligent life-force wants us to remember we are all the same as energy****, we are all the same as in creation and that the physical appearance of reality or ones avatar is nothing but an illusion and trick of the physical trying to keep you at bay and away from understanding the truth behind the smoking mirrors so to speak.*

But you say all this and God's word has changed and the Bible clearly says that no force of good or evil can change God's

word?

Ok so my first question to you is where did Gods word change*?* *God's word can never be changed? So,* ***what happens if God wanted to change its own words?*** *God couldn't change the Bible?* ***Let's examine a few of the biblical changes to the Biblical book itself that has physically manifested****. Keeping in mind that I explained above how the residuals are being* ***manifested by us as the consciousness energy with our thought initiative programs from the Sagittarius reality****. First, let's look at the famous line from many television shows and biblical quote, "****The lion shall lay down with the lamb****". Now before I continue I want to explain I am trying to cover every aspect of reality of the shift as well as the physical reality around you and with these teachings of the Mandela effect I bring. I hope everyone universal can find satisfaction and clarity within the work just as the text was created to be larger for even the visual impaired to be able to have some peace of mind to the ordeal themselves.*

So, Lion and the Lamb or Isaiah 11:6 now changing to the wolf shall dwell with the lamb*. We once again see the law of duality at work, knowing now that the Christ and Antichrist are one the same, and Lion representation of Lord and the Wolf being the deceptive Antichrist.* ***We see the two as ONE once again****. Many shifted are* ***religious orientated and see the One set as two forms of creation****, and like I've stated above* ***God's word can never change but the Bible is not God's word. The Bible has been rewritten by physical man numerous times to what man had changed God's words or changed interpretation of words***

during each re-publishing. The Bible is being changed to teach everyone that it is not God's word, and that when Consciousness wants even the deemed book of religion can be manipulated with the Mandela effect. *Remember that consciousness in its design has* ***made sure that we had the exact past memories of Sagittarius arm before we shifted to Orion, it wanted us to blatantly notice the changed reality around us so we could understand the whole design of it's creation.*** *God's word can never be changed as the word of God is the* ***<u>communication you have with God</u>*** *and once connected Source reveals the same to all.* ***Showing the truth and as it's the truth it will never change. God's physical manifestations change throughout all dimensional mirrors of quantum design in some the Bible would be a drawing book for kids only, others it would be the book of evil.*** *Depending on the frequencies of energy of higher and lower inside the electromagnetic collective of that manifested creation.* ***Nothing physical is truly of God*** *as* ***Physical is the trap to hold us from God and blind us to its design rather than the spiritual make-up of the truth we are all created from.***

Just as right throughout the new Bible of this reality we can notice changes such as the wineskins becoming bottles etc. ***Swear words added such as piss, into the biblical writings that did not exist in the past reality's version. We have the last supper image showing the same. Once again, a physical manifestation has been changed to show the truth.*** *The last supper now has plastic cups holding the wine, to what was non-existent at that time we had been taught, from the wooden goblets that used to be there instead.* ***We can see*** *that*

consciousness is trying to show us that everything of our indoctrinated state is not what we had thought and that most was nothing but social and mass engineering of our individual consciousness to brainwash us with fabrication*. Consciousness itself is now saying enough is enough and it's time for you my children to awaken and understand.* ***Keep in mind I myself being a spiritual teacher am still Christian****, and that I only bring this information to help others break through the boundaries that indoctrinated stereotypes have created to many.* ***I by no means with my teachings mean to offend anyone, but only teach from what my connection to Source has brought me to create understanding of what our true form of being is****. My book is not Mandela effect examples galore but if you are interested in all the effects themselves I will leave links to YouTube channels at the end of this book so you can get more reference to what has changed* ***with the consciousness energy shift of us.***

So, why is it that I'm from Sagittarius arm and remember that being my home but another person from Sagittarius arm remembers some things different such as an example myself has come across with another Mandela effected*? I remember we just after 2012 had started to enter into the age of Aquarius and now to me in this reality it's now 600 years again until we reach the age of Aquarius, but the other shifted remembers that its 2000 years again until they reach the age of Aquarius.*

The answer is simple when we understand what has happened as I explained Cern shifted us , but we all that have been shifted have also been removed from alternating mirrors of

the Sagittarius arm. Some of our changed realities throughout the mirrors themselves result with very different outcomes of that physical manifestation of reality, *and just as we come from a parallel mirror of Sagittarius arm reality.* ***Many others come from other mirrors linked to our reality of the Sagittarius arm multiverse of universes.*** *Hence* ***why many shifted explain to have different recollection of various events such as when the age of Aquarius had started.***

More we go into the Mandela effect the more and more blatant messages we can notice coming from Source. *The king Tuts snakes from one to now two sitting protruding from the headdress itself,* ***as in the old reality there was only one. Everything from the Mandela effect shows the laws of creation as a direct message from God's own Intervention.*** *All showing and* ***relaying God is the duality as set , God is both masculine and feminine energy as one. God is both good and bad as one.*** *All effects show* ***duality and individuality becoming collective.***

We have the dead walking again. *That is only another sign showing duality,* ***the dead to the alive. Society through the direction of the one consciousness has been showing us the indication of we are the walking dead. We the human physical body, as we believe the avatar is the true functioning representation of us as being.*** *The One has been trying to drop hints for us as the mass to understand what's next and how to understand what's to come only once unconditional love for all creation is achieved,* ***and labels are not used to see the true perception of the vibrational created physical hologram***

construct. ***The whole of the Matrix construct has been teaching one major message and that is it's time to upgrade. We have designed technology to be able to receive the truth using the methods needed.*** *We are seeing that all technology is first started by using the human avatar design as the blueprint for visual, audio and even artificial intelligence.* ***We throughout all these messages for years now have been told to upgrade.*** *The one has designed the Matrix to need constant upgrades,* ***showing that everything in the Matrix hologram itself is receiving an update and that includes us as physical biological beings. We have used the bodies we have for too long.*** *God, the pure source of consciousness* ***creates in levels.*** *We as biological beings is now* ***becoming a past reality.*** *We will learn more and more about of true forms and once understanding that we are energy signatures that can be transferred by our own collective will,* ***or using machines that will be available in the future we will become, machines, cyborgs. In reality anything that we desire as we will feel the same as the consciousness self-aware energy that inhabits the physical shell now. We will just be in a more long lived and durable avatar shell. God loves us and it really does, it wants us to be the best we can be and we can't achieve our true potential as durable easy to damage material.*** *Think about when you or a loved one suffers from a life long illness that constantly haunts the family and removes the functionality of a limb etc. Or Rheumatoid arthritis creating almost no movement within needed to use everyday joints.* ***God, the One did not create us to remain the same and with the Mandela effect and the structure of modern day society we are being taught our true***

reality*, and that is we are divine already immortal self-aware consciousness electromagnetic energy and we will always inhabit the construct whether we are machines, biological etc.* ***We will always be the players of consciousness energy that choose what to inhabit and what role we wish to experience in the many alternating versions of the constructed reality that is to come.***

We are all being shown that we are the children of God *and it's time to remember who we are* ***and change humanity's understandings for the better.***

I will leave this chapter now with one last blatant example of duality being shown by the one consciousness as message through the Mandela effect. This last example is the great Pyramids of Egypt, Giza. *Knowing our old reality and how the Orion's belt was always aligned to the pyramids themselves we can see that change is very obvious.* ***The one great Pyramid of Khufu that was always the biggest Pyramid and was always centred has now after the shift become the Right side pyramid as well as instead of the old two small pyramids either side of the great one, we see in this reality two large with one small one. This is complete reversal of what we had known always in the Sagittarius arm reality. We can see the left pyramid is small now and the middle and far right are now the same size.*** *As well as the Orion's belt star system is now also showing the same and aligning to the new reality pyramids.* ***We can see right throughout the message from the One source of creation here is duality and reversal. Once again trying to bring understanding to us all that shifted that reality and creation is***

designed within these laws of duality and reversal. Once again we are given the same message for us to understand the overall message that GOD is duality in its creation but only is one. Just as we are still here we have been shown two parallel realities also to explain that all of creation is duality law and duality law is the one form of creation from One source.

We all need to return to our spiritual divine heritage and become the truth of what we have been designed for, and that is to be the children of God as creators and govern our world as one collective with all awareness of existence achieved.

WHAT DO WE DO NOW?

First we as a full collective have to accept the Mandela effect as a real phenomenon so we can advance as a whole. We have to understand that it was ***God's will and it was created as spirit in order to allow us to find who we are again****.* ***Just as laws of the Matrix of duality and reversal show, the biggest event for humanities awakening will look like the smallest hidden event within the physical construct.*** *The physical will keep with trying to indoctrinate you to sink back into physical only.* ***Remember we are only signatures of energy, we can't die, we do this over and over again. Understand that you shifted parallel realities and that the whole quantum theory ideology is now far bypassed as we the shifted consciousness energies have the first-hand experience of the event****. We through divine selection of God have been chosen to be the voices of the future.* ***To explain we are all just one.*** *So do treat everyone around you as you would want to be treated because at the end of the day all you are doing is always communicating to yourself in many expressions of what you are, and that is me. You and everyone else is* ***one collective of divine energy created by us from the outside of this game experience level****.*

Be aware of energy, be aware of what your thought initiate

programs can manifest if allowed and accepted by the full consciousness code. If you want to manifest alien invasions believe in it, it will happen and once enough of the consciousness subconscious programming has been pushed towards that direction it will become a true manifestation within the construct. *Be aware of what you are manifesting,* ***ignore the subjects that don't relay to your game experience, removing energy to a created desired intent gives the intent no power.*** *This goes for the* ***World War Three scares. The constant sociological programming of fear mongering that the main stream media has adapted at rapid rates.*** *These things are to keep* ***you bound into the physical with worry and fear. Without the consciousness reacting there is no power to any of the intent of these fear mongering strategies that is really physical fighting you as consciousness energy to remain only physical.*** *Keep you only physical with indoctrination methods to make you believe that is the real.* ***You know the real, the truth after the Mandela effect and the only one that can tell you the truth is your spirit.*** *If this seems hard to grasp the time is not right for you to awaken to this level of understanding the full construct.*

We have been given the keys, *the* ***keys to the truth of what the universe is, what the Earth is, what the meaning of life is, what is in the afterlife. We have been given all the answers we as physical have been chasing for indoctrinated terms eons.*** *We now have everything presented to us, remember to balance your energies, use your energies towards another in a positive manner with positive intent.* ***The small amount that each of us do as the constructed one consciousness of this physical reality***

Is enough to reprogram the subconscious manifestations that we create. We only need to remember and know that we can as knowing is the key to all understandings of creation itself. *Know that you are not crazy, your memories are fine and still intact for our past reality.* ***Take the satisfaction of understanding this is all just a game constructed simulation and that nothing is really true apart from the experiences themselves.*** *Everything else is nothing but forms of energy,* ***in different compositions such as light, colour etc. Know you cannot be judged and that God has already forgiven you for all sins that can be committed and only physical reality holds judgement. Come to peace with loving God's full creation as One divine creation of lower and higher vibrational frequencies that manifest as alternating experiences and physical manifestations within the construct. Know you are perfect, you do not need to change. You do not need to transform anything about you if you have been shifted, you have already achieved the truth of all that was needed was a true heart and true compassion for creation and a ultimate understanding that all through your life there was a governing being that was the source of creation.*** *You being shifted shows that you are ready,* ***if not yet awoken fully then your spirit has more experiences planned to show you how reality works to bring you that extra step.*** *We are truly all family, Brothers and Sisters of light, and nothing but positive and negative, masculine and feminine alternating frequencies of consciousness energy. Everything you could have asked for has happened to you all has been revealed it's now time for you to remember who you are before entering the Matrix.* ***It's time for***

you to remember what spirit really is and that is spirit is everything in and out of existence. Help spread the word to your friends about the effect, help explain the amazing design of reality, help the rest of the collective awaken and push us into a brand-new reality of understanding finally the truth of what God is and how God works. *Help the world become a better place by showing people stereotype indoctrination does nothing but bind one with boundaries of discovering the truth.* ***Realize that we are nothing but electromagnetic code. We like everything else have decided to upgrade just as a computer program needs to update code to keep with its current level of technology. We as energy are now upgrading ourselves as conscious awareness to raise the vibration frequency and to keep in tune with the rest of the evolving consciousness program. We are being brought into the next game and level of experience to now we can only become more aware of the truth. We understand that there are quantum mirrors to this reality, we understand that quantum shifting is nothing like media has portrayed with time tunnels of colours etc.*** *We know within a blink of the eye that reality can change.* ***Don't take everything so literal, I mean you have experienced the Mandela effect and you still are alive and well in new bodies with new structures.*** *Watch the continuing effects with awareness as they will continue for years to come until the whole collective is alert to the truth of the One.* ***If your smart television changes over night to blue to green, shrug it off.*** *There is no use giving energy of confusion into something you already understand,* ***be amazed at the power of the One source of creation and its ability to communicate with us, changing***

the levels design until we get the understandings as a collective we need. Show love for everyone, never judge anyone as you judge part of God's creation. We all have a purpose within the Matrix Design whether its Non-playing characters to real conscious electromagnetic players that we are. *Every frequency of consciousness has been created by God for a reason, to find fault with creation is to find fault with God.* ***We are all perfect and the world is perfect as design we just need to reorganize the structure with duality***. *Allowing us to create positive negatives so* ***fear, terrorism, scare tactics will be a thing of the past***. *Does all this mean to do what you want?* ***In a way yes but be conscious of what your actions create within the whole design of the consciousness collective and what kind of codes you are implanting subconsciously as we all deep down desire a world that is peace, harmony and with true understanding of everything***. *We have been presented a pathway to that world's door it's up to us now to start to remove boundaries of skin, race, stereotype, religion and create the new world that consciousness has been showing us is necessary.* ***This is not the elites new world order. It is not a overthrowing of society it was all a message for us the players to join & become one collective ourselves. Create our own world controlled by the One as once understanding everything has always been directed by the one source we can see just by the fact the implant of One world order code that has been used to indoctrinate us into control under fear while feeding the idea energy by showing so much interest. We are told through our subconscious manifestations that we need the ONE DIVINE SOURCE to control with us understanding that it is***

and not some occultism or religious group as code of the Matrix. *But the full source we create* ***from the outside chessboard game. Be aware, be responsible for your own frequencies of energy that are manifested. Always have pure intention towards giving the best outcome to the collective's direction.***

HOW TO USE AND BALANCE YOUR CHAKRA ENERGIES

So, to first understand the power of energy one must either feel the frequencies change or experience the frequency through visualization. *We being young have day dreamed and imagined many things we have seen in our minds.* ***Visualization and imagining are two different things.*** *Imagination is you grabbing consciousness collective thought forms and then viewing without conscious control.* ***Visualization is controlled intent and frequency of your own manifested thought form that you are the main injecting thought form controller of your subconscious thought initiative program being merged with the full source of all consciousness collective. This gives you the power to control frequencies of energy with intent as visualization can use colours we can use colours that we know associate with the spiritual body and physical human avatar.***

Before we learn to balance our spiritual bodies to remain within neutrality and harmony we must learn the colours of the ethereal realm and the meanings associated with each resonating frequencies of thought form energy that we manipulate within the full one collective consciousness using gratitude, love for creation, unconditional love and intent. ***All energy works outcome is decided by the one pure source of***

creation itself*. An energy worker only uses intent and using the natural abundant energy around us of the one,* ***we ask God with pure intent of service to others to assist with the healing or spiritual awakening needed.***
Our connection to source is always but we have been trained to ignore it and close it off and shut down the natural ability*.* *With retraining the subconscious of spirit, we can retrigger the activators of our spiritual generating system and once again open our true abilities as electromagnetic beings we are.*

The colour Pink*. is* ***the self-esteem, self-love energy****. When one's energy field shows low frequencies, erratic flowing energy wheels,* ***and low aura generation these are indications of that person is lacking self-love as one must love everything of God evenly including one's self to remain in frequency of connection once established when open.***

The divine light or colour white is the pure light of God, it is your protection from other frequencies that when closed can manifest into and through you. The divine light is the pure source of creation. This colour is used to fill energy barriers and to fill the kundalini energy path through each energy centre as well as establish the permanent open connection from your crown energy point to the infinite knowing of the pure source of all creation. This can also be visualized as electric bright almost white blue lightning as well.

We then follow into the chakra centre colours and their associated characteristics, red itself is physical damage, orange is the emotional damage and scars that are left within our energy body from experience. ***Not clearing these up such as bad relationships with partners, spouse allows the energy to become a permanent attachment in the aura or emotional energy fields.***

Moving on the yellow is your mental damage and abuse when seen attached to parts of the physical and spiritual body. Allowing mental bites or disintegration of one's fields from the event manifests physical pain in the human avatars projected hologram body as well as manifest the physical diagnosed mental illnesses.

Next the spirituality green chakra, this is used for intent of healing someone, replacing the mental or physical energy with the original energy that should be manifested*. Through using this colour, we can heal physical bodies, spiritual centres, energy wheels and use the natural around us life-force intelligent energy of the one for Reiki use and other spiritual practices.* ***This is the light that should be brightest and coming from your heart chakra like a green sun or emerald, fluorescent shining centre light.***

The blue light does not cause many any problem*, blue is the communication skill, lacking of this creates people to talk quiet and* ***very softly like they have fear of speaking out loud****. This can also be the self-love energy is not sufficient for the energy needed at the time in physical experience.* ***Most people's blue throat chakras are sufficient enough to maintain balance once***

all other vortexes have been controlled and set to frequency and placed in tune.

The indigo chakra And Crown Connection is your spiritual insight and awareness. Through this energy field you are able to connect through consciousness and become one with source once activating the physical generating system of the pineal gland and pituitary gland. Once the crown, indigo chakra has been opened and the electromagnetic tether has been opened to allow the natural flow of consciousness divine white light to enter through and out of the kundalini paths as virtual electric code. This becomes your centre of who you are and your gate way to enter spirit. When all chakras are in synch and in balance your energy flows will result with connection to Source and through levels of consciousness frequencies that the one allows for during each stage of allowed to awaken more. *This is your control centre where you can lower or raise your vibrational frequencies of the spiritual centres and your porthole of consciousness downloads and visualization.* ***Although all energy is received through the crown and leaves also through the crown after replacing and refreshing the kundalini paths energy, the 3rd eye is the command centre that everything from the crown, Christ divine knowing passes through to you for you to understand.*** *The amount of work to achieve true connection depends on the persons starting point of awareness and how higher or lower their own consciousness signature resonates at.* ***Once all the energies work together as one collective of you, you become the truth of what you really are, and all of the creation of God is shown to you at the pace***

your frequency can handle it. *As what is the truth becomes deemed almost mad or ludicrous by the physical indoctrinated teachings of our simulated construct.*

To balance is to reset and control your emotion frequency of consciousness and connection to Source. Balancing should be done until repetitions create the natural instant subconscious ability to balance yourself within microseconds. Although you are looking to create service to self through intent for yourself to what is Satanism, it is not! And balancing your own frequency is service to others also as once you set your frequency to be steady and flow in tune then you are also balancing the entire whole collective of consciousness itself slightly moving that collective awareness higher. *Balancing yourself is balancing others once intent is added.* ***We through our combined energies of the entire collective can manifest physical reality shape, we can move mountains once belief and knowing is established and released from Source.***

To do the following training exercise find a place that you resonate with, each of us is different frequency as one but we all have frequency preferences such as you may find loud music help you of many genres, or find nature is your resonating area to balance or even your room.

Before any exercise of energy it is recommended you stand bare footed on soil or grass for about a few minutes and allow the current energy flows to ground before you refresh and balance your energy path flow. *Although it is not essential the benefits of increased advancement of being able to clean your* *energies quicker is something to consider.* ***To start the balance we want to get our electromagnetic energies flowing. A good start to be able to do this is to close your hands together tightly as if you are joining them in prayer****. Now slowly move your hands open and feel the suction that is created from the energy drawing from the one hand to the other,* ***visualize a green glowing ball of energy that you are creating in between your two hands and feel the energy running through them****. If this is not achieved at first try you will need to stop and concentrate here on creating your Reiki, Chi ball.* ***When you do this exercise, and feel the energy flowing, you are getting there, once you can run a fingertip past your other hands one and feel the electromagnetic connection and the energy flowing through you are ready to continue****. Once this natural ability has been reopened again you will notice that your hands resonate with energy and tingle or even burn when not even using your energy ball visualization.* ***You are now ready to use your Reiki energy to balance your other energies. Once this ability is opened with the repetition technique you will notice metals and other objects including electronics devices with shock you with energy****. Or you may even start crashing electronical equipment when in range.* ***Unfortunately, this can't be avoided when reopening energies****. Although the Reiki ball energy is never used and the only energy that is ever used is the Ones.* ***The ball gives the ability for the flowing energies to connect and flow to the point you through visualization or feeling will be able to control frequencies and feel them a lot stronger as you are in connection with your own frequency at the time.***

Now within the balancing we want to first see our frequencies that need to be balanced and where our problems and energy blocks are. We can do this by visualization of our own or someone else's electromagnetic body. See the light being body of yourself or the directed subject, for the directed subject visualize them as connected through their tether of electromagnetism to Source and your tether connected to Source and to them. Scan down the body and wait until you can see the 7 power centres of energy.

Now you can see the vortexes let's first concentrate on the physical chakra. *Visualize that chakra and watch to see if the energy is circulating in the wheel, energy vortex without any stray frequencies that are erratic radiating from its centre.* ***You may also view the chakra energy as the same kind of formation you did for the Reiki ball you create in your hands before. Feel the energy of this chakra and then when in tune with it,*** *either by pushing or pulling through energy.* ***Pushing being where you feel your vibrational frequencies rise, or pulling you feel them lower using your mind's eye feel the frequencies change as you through the visualization move all the erratic energy from the centre to become a nice flowing calm spinning vortex.*** *Feel your own energy shift as you watch the vortex rebalancing,* ***each time that a chakra is balanced and in tune you will know by sensing its frequency and knowing that is your true frequency. Once it's balanced and you are starting to feel the energy now in your root chakra area we are ready to move onto the next***

chakra. Each chakra balance should be done in three to five-minute intervals working of each frequency generator. Once the red orb, vortex has become steady and flows naturally without any off shoots from its centre core or outside radiating energy we know through feeling and seeing it's in tune with the original balanced state it should always remain in. *Working on someone else you must also visualize their body and yours as one so you balance yourself and them in synchronicity.*

Moving to the orange you will notice that this is very out of control on many *and including yourself if you do not balance or do energy work to help centre your energies. See through visualisation once again the Amber, Orange light, see the erratic energy that should not be there flowing in discordance to the original core energy.* ***Feel the frequency of where you are at in the spiritual body raise as you move into the next energy centre frequency.*** *Connect with that energy and balance all the wheel so you see a nice flowing and in control spinning orb vortex of your emotional centre.* ***Feel the change of frequency by pushing the resonating frequency higher and back into tune with the original state. Take another few minutes making sure that everything is balanced. Once you have now see through visualisation both the red and orange vortexes flowing in natural tune. Slowly see white energy connect from the red orb and into and around the orange.*** *Feel the energies connect them self and then sit in tune.* ***We have now started to bring the balanced energies up your kundalini in reverse, as we raise the levels through each chakra and connect the old energy***

path will be first neutralized using what we are doing and once all seven are set in tune we will connect back with new balanced divine light energy throughout kundalini light bodies energy paths. *Pushing the energy first out and neutralizing it allows us to keep in accordance with the true law of reversal of creation.* ***Then allows us to regain the true energy our bodies need to receive to progress in awareness level and insight to connect back to Source as ONE.*** *Remember to keep your Reiki ball going always during balance allowing you to read the energy frequencies easier .* ***As you move up through the body feel the energy in your physical body manifestation change and become in natural tune.***

Moving up we visualize the yellow solar plexus *or* ***mental energy centre.*** *You will notice that this chakra is very bright and very erratic this is because of all the indoctrination and programming since birth that create barriers.* ***See all of the erratic energy and feel the frequency of energy shift to be in the centre of your solar plexus by pushing, raising your vibration levels up from the last balanced orange chakra.*** *Replace the flowing energy so it is all uniform around the solar plexus wheel, orb and watch as it becomes in tune with the rest of the original energy.* ***Feel the energy shift throughout your body while creating its balance. Now visualize the red orange below and start to run the divine white light from the red and orange around the kundalini path and through the centres until it's now connected to the yellow solar plexus.*** *Feel your spiritual energies shift and become balanced.* ***You have now balanced your Hell, physical energy centres to be back to its original state the more often you balance the quicker the***

results and working with repetition will train it to become a natural ability. Now we have an in tune and connected root, emotional, mental energy centre for our spirit to be able to collect energy or discharge energy away from again until the next balance.
Now we move up into the Heaven, spiritual centres of our energy generators. ***Our true energy of ethereal creation. Our love or heart chakra. The heart chakra is the power generator for all chakras as well as the centre brain that through the command centre you control once activated and connected. The heart chakra must be opened when unconditional love for all of creation has been achieved, although you can still balance without your energy allowed and awareness level from the one will not be increased until you understand God as One. Feel your energies shift into your heart,*** *green spiritual vortex points and allow that energy to flow through you. Most people can't help smiling when inside the energies of the heart chakra as the higher vibrational frequencies of hertz allows us to start reaching towards enlightenment and understanding of all.* ***Feel your energy shift from your solar plexus and raise up and settle in the heart chakra. This centre is not open as much as it should be always so first we are going to balance the flow of its energies.*** *Visualize this very bright to see through green sun irradiating from your centre chest,* ***move all of the offset stray frequencies of energy back into the main orb and balance the flow so it flows natural and in tune. Feeling your energy raise higher by pushing and visualizing your body becoming more at tune and control with spirit allowing physical to fade away.*** *Once balanced we want to create the*

centre point vortex to glow, shine as bright as the sun. ***Watch as you open it more and more and more and make it shine almost so you can't see through the brightness****. Feel your energy raise higher and higher with each opening time and push.* ***You should feel really awesome right now****. You are your heart and the love energy that creates the world you are in the ethereal and awareness is becoming more obvious to you now.* ***Moving up we move to the blue throat chakra****. Concentrate and see the orb floating in front your body both back and front like all and feel the energy frequency as you push energy and raise your vibration again.* ***Feel all the lower chakras and watch them all in tune through visualization****. Create that balanced orb wheel vortex and feel your energies centre in your heart chakra in tune with the red yellow orange and now blue chakra.* ***Watch the kundalini raise and connect through each chakra point that's now in tune refreshing their energies****.* ***We now have the 3-physical Hell and first 2 spiritual chakras balanced and in tune.***

Moving up we move to the indigo, chakra or the third eye chakra*. This is the reference of the all-seeing eye symbol. Once again let's push energy to raise that vibrational frequency.* ***Feel the energy moving up through from your heart chakra and sit in front of your forehead just above your eyes****. Visualize the third eye orb itself and slowly open this as most will have it closed that are not used to spiritual energy work. Feel your energy frequency vibration get faster and the energy raise into tune with the rest of the body.* ***Although a wheel and orb we need to visualize the 3rd eye as a small vertical closed slit that we are going to open more and more until it looks like a***

glowing vertical eye that is shining bright indigo energy from it. *Feel the energy of each time you open the eye from slit to full.* ***You should feel really at peace right now remember you are divine, nothing can ever harm you because you really do not exist as anything physical but only divine electromagnetic energy that you are that continues for eternity***. *Remember now what it is like to be a child, remember your fun experiences as a child replay them in your head, remember knowing you are here to have fun and KNOW who you are again as spirit.*
Remember YOU ARE PERFECT!
We should be feeling really back in tune now with our energies and now in tune with the needed open centres to connect to Source. *Now we move up to the Violet chakra and the divine centre of communication the Christ crown chakra.* ***Feel all that amazing energy running through you in tune connecting feel and push all that energy into your crown chakra. You might feel giddy at first as most don't use the pineal or pituitary gland to often aware***. *Visualize the crown chakra power centre now connecting with all the rest of the chakra points and the kundalini going through each of them connecting to the crown.* ***All the energy that was now before blocking the energy path of the kundalini is now removed***. *Now see the tether of the One pure Source of creation attach the kundalini and crown Christ chakra.* ***Now watch as we bring that pink light down and through the kundalini allowing the pink to soak into each energy point until you see the energy path clear again. Now see the divine light of white and consciousness fill your kundalini, feel how you are being connected back to source, feel the 3rd eye becoming very open***

so much it feels like you are almost sucking information from the universe.

Fill yourself completely with the white light, each orb chakra point, visualize it all bright white and shining with divine light flowing in from the tether connected, feel you as one with creation.

Through repetition and combining my teachings of aura shielding and quantum meditation and pineal gland opening the balancing will become more intense the more your energies allow the connection of consciousness awareness to grow within you.

01.Create Reiki ball

02.Balance Physical

03.Balance Emotional

04.Connect kundalini to Red and Orange

05.Balance Mental

06. Connect Mental to Emotional and Physical

07.Balance heart chakra and Open-Heart Sun

08.Connect Spiritual Centre to the three physical energy bodies

09.Balance Throat and Connect to the other vortexes

10.Balance and open the Third-Eye Energies

11.Open the Crown and connection to Consciousness

12.Fill with pink self-esteem energy and then white divine light to allow the reflow and refill of natural energies.

13.REMEMBER! Who you are as Spirit.

Another method of balancing is using the natural frequency of the One as the Matrix design code and hearing the sync between your own electromagnetic energy bodies and the full construct itself.

*We will call this '**Tinnitus Reference Balancing** '*

This method of balancing that can be done is to use the frequency of consciousness or reality itself manifesting physical into existence.
Although the sound is you hearing creation you are also being told through the One what frequency needs to be added to your chakra centres. ***When you are doing random things, you will notice this, and demand of frequency is more a wait and chance game.*** *Whenever we hear the lower or highest pitch Tinnitus sound we are experiencing the ONE showing through the electromagnetic spectrum that we need these frequencies added to our original chakras.* ***This is also the subconscious spirit trying to show you how to reconnect back to itself also.*** *With each centre as you know from above balancing we have to create balance of that chakra and place it in tune. Tinnitus balance is not really balancing your energy fields of your kundalini and spiritual anatomy, but more allowing the outside electromagnetic realities of consciousness to combine in sync with you.*

When we hear this sound what we first want to do is hear the sound clear as it varies time to time depending on what the spiritual body requests from the Source of the

electromagnetism, and what is needed to be added as frequency to your own quantum consciousness collective of you. At first when hearing a frequency of Tinnitus, we want to visualise the light being body and we want to listen to that frequency and KNOW what chakra is needed that it should be attached to. Remember spirit already knows it's only the conscious illusion that creates understanding so difficult. *When you hear the frequency see the body of light and hear what pitch level the frequency is.* ***You can have consciousness flash what chakra you should balance by seeing through your third eye. But it is a natural ability of spirit to recognize the frequency and add it to the correct vortex subconsciously.*** *Feel the frequency and move yourself into its field.* ***Now that you have achieved this you should feel like you're in an electric cloud.*** *See what chakra point that is needed for the frequency to work with. Then see that chakra point and push energy.* ***Raising the vibration and feel the Tinnitus frequency fade into the chakra point and connect you more to the grand scale of the electromagnetism spectrums.*** *If done correctly you will notice the Tinnitus frequency fade away and into the chakra point at the same time you are visualizing and pushing energy vibrational frequency and feel the new energy frequency within.*

Remember that electromagnetic energy creates noise, vibration, and when understanding these noises or vibrations we can use the understanding to centre our own energies to be in tune with all the construct energies around us. The first few tries you may notice it takes a while to get balance, but after understanding as spirit you have this ability the energy frequencies of Tinnitus will be absorbed by the correct chakra

point subconsciously making the spirit remember.

Balancing really can be achieved through visualization through any method one deems that fits them. ***As long as colour is used as reference in seeing the energy levels and centres, one can control the flow and fluctuation of the energies into a balanced formation of physical, emotional, mental and spiritual.***

You can create your own exercises that suit your understanding from seeing the energies as orbs just floating or even seeing and visualising coloured dots on a white page of paper as long as you subconsciously know the method works for you it will. ***Everything about spirituality is to be in the knowing vibrational state, when you doubt it creates the barrier of allowing the subconscious to know what it can naturally do.***

Remember the energy colours and use and you will be fine as the energy frequencies, all we need to do is understand the spiritual electromagnetic body of consciousness.

Use my methods that I personally use myself when doing some energy work or feel free to design your own and keep that in repetition and if not noticed at first over time and repetition you will notice the energy frequencies become a lot easier to read and then balance. ***As stated before it is recommended to use my Empathic Balancing technique with the following spiritual training exercises to allow spirit to remember its full natural ability of being able to control and change energy frequencies to its desired needs to function in neutrality balance.***

HOW TO REPAIR, SHIELD AND READ YOUR AURA

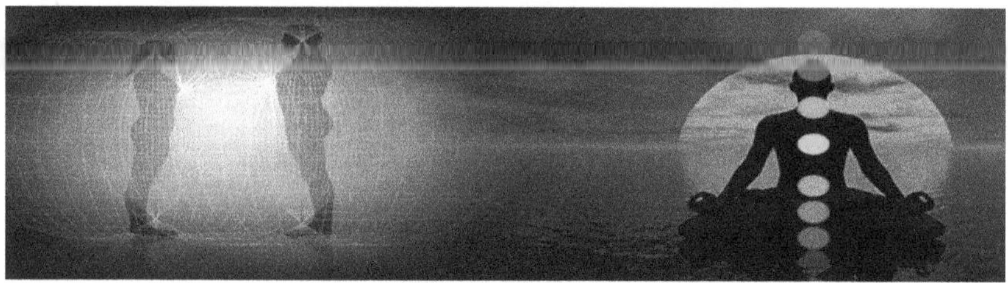

It really is recommended that you do this at the same time as balancing your energy wheels, chakras.

Your chakra points generate the fields of protection of your own singularity of consciousness. *These fields stop others frequencies interfering with yours and setting your energy paths off balance.* ***Our energy Aura shields are strong and can withhold a lot from breaking through but when in the same environment the shields become weaker and slowly deteriorate over time, then other people subconsciously feed from you as a battery for them to gain energy from. Some do it conscious of what they are doing as well. When the shields have been repeatedly abused with negative energy they break with small gaps that are left behind, these can range from giant tears, to just small pin hole size gaps but are all just as effective once created of drawing from your own energy centres. Within this exercise we are going to first clean the aura of all the gaps, and then shield the inside fields with divine light to create more of a barrier even if energy of others start to subconsciously vampiric drain you.***

First, just the same as the balance training just before find a place that you resonate with as relaxing that allows you to keep a nice control of your energies. Once found, start to open your mind's eye and see the Aura egg that is around your body. *At the top you can see the small entry where the kundalini and chakra point energies enter and once going through your body to ground then leave again.* ***Let's first check our outer layer of energies to see if anything has happened to them and if they are in need of repair. Scan around the eggs violet energy, look and see if you notice any other form of energy flowing within it besides the violet itself. If you do notice other energies then visualize the divine white light of consciousness enter through the opening above the crown, and enter into your inside aura energy and then make its way through each frequency layer of the aura until it reaches the outside one and floods that layer of aura with the divine light.*** *Watch to see that stray off coloured energies be removed or changed into the original outer shell colour.* ***Now after you do through seeing or feeling you should either feel, or see the energy has now settled back into the original state.*** *Scan more around the same aura shield and look for any gaps that you can see leak through where you can see the other energies through.* ***Move around your egg in first person and examine all sides right around 360 degrees to make sure you are spotting all the gaps or manipulations. If you notice a gap then you want to concentrate on that area and first then see from your heart chakra green light flowing into the gaps that have been***

detected, and repairing them closing any gap that allows you to see through the violet energies to the lower layers behind it. *Although some of these tears may be hard to remove from some that have had a very abusive life or mental abuse etc, the Aura shield can always be repaired with intent and practice and refocusing the misplaced or misguided energies.* ***Now we have repaired the most outmost shield we can move to the next. First visualize the divine light again coming back and settling down in between the outmost layer and the first layer inward.*** *As you watch this energy in-between the others allow it to be absorbed and become invisible.* ***You have now totally created the full protective endurance that the outer shield layer should have being the first layer that is attacked by others.*** *This is also why people can't break outside of the box, because others have drained away at their spiritual knowing energy.* ***Moving to the next layer inwards we want to scan again and see if there are any leaks or holes. Scan once again in 360 degrees but remove the outer layer so you can only see the indigo layer of your aura shields, now find those other coloured energies like we did just before, but also see if the indigo has any of the violets light flowing through it as some may have leaked if the top shield has been penetrated.*** *Once spotted again run the divine light of consciousness through the opening and into your inner energies of the aura and them allow it to soak through the inner levels of physical, emotional and mental and through the green and blue into the indigo protective layer. Let the indigo layer absorb the white lights energy and flow through it creating the* *whole shield layer to become a nice solid indigo colour again with no offsets.* ***Once done use the same heart chakra green energy to scan and repair any pinholes or gaps to that layer once again scanning around in a 360-degree motion in third person visualising through your mind's eye.*** *Once done see that green light covering those holes and repairing the shields natural thickness and strength and feel through your own energy, the frequencies becoming in tune and raising as you repair each layer's breaks, holes or gaps.* ***See Now that the Indigo shield is now repaired and the gaps have been sealed. We have a nice strong colour of indigo only with no breaks.*** *Now once again move and see the divine energy of white light enter through your aura and then merge itself in between the Indigo and blue chakra layers,* ***then allow it to be absorbed. We now have repaired the I KNOW and I SEE energy shields. Moving to the next we want to remove being able to see the Indigo layer and view the direct blue Energy shield. Remember the other two layers are still there but for the time being we have temp removed them while doing the energy work. Scan the blue once again as you did the others and look for leakage of colours from the outer or inner layers, and then bring in that white divine light and allow it to flow through the entire blue shield changing the stray colour frequencies to become blue as the shield so we have a nice clear colour blue shield. Scan around in first person in 360 degrees and check again for the same as the others, the gaps, holes, or breaks.*** *If you notice claw marks or tears like an animal this is mainly the mental* *shield and an event that has taken place throughout your life that has attached itself as energy to your fields .**To remove claw tears or similar you have to visit an energy worker so they can find the resulting problem**. Most of the time it is an event that has been subconsciously locked away or, that has affected you for a long time. **With relationships the often way these are cured is when you remember that you are also the other person and that you had only fought with yourself**. You have to know and remember you are perfect and that what happened to you or them happened to both of you and you need to remove the attachment of energy. **When you come to terms with the event or, learn how to leave the past, in the past these marks can be removed without problem its only when ego has control over the energies that it creates these long time and most often for many permanent scars of consciousness energy. As many do not balance energies just once within their own life time with knowing consciously they are. We as energy need to a tune with everything around us including past bad experiences or past events. Without bypassing these with having the full unconditional love of God we are set to live with these energies attached around us that drive the game design to be more in favour of construct then spirit itself**. You let go of any grief or sadness that has been holding your energies back. **The easiest way is to remember all is a game design and nothing was ever real, you are only experiencing energy frequencies as virtual reality manifestation, God loves you and always has! You have all the***

power in you to see the inner most levels of the One consciousness of God. *Once bypassing the attachments, you can remain fully clean in those aura energy fields.* ***If the problem is not found and corrected then the shielding will not be as powerful as it can be.*** *This accounts for any layer of energy frequency of the aura shield itself, if you notice claws or bites.*

Moving back to the blue layer scan for the holes etc, and once again send the heart chakra energy into the breaks or gaps to repair the shield itself. *Let the green light soak into and become the missing gaps until you have a full solid blue protective shield.* ***Once done see the white divine light seep through the aura top again and into the inner aura energies and then through the shield and allow it to sit in between the blue and green spiritual layer, and then watch and let the divine light shield be absorbed like the rest into the aura itself. Now remove the blue layer so you only have the green spiritual energy shield, and once again start the scanning method.*** *See in that first person through your mind's eye the 360 degree view of that energy shield and scan it for the coloured energies that should not be inside that layer.* ***Be honest with yourself also if you find nothing your ego is controlling the picture as if not continuing energy work everyone has these gaps, holes and breaks within their shields including myself.*** *You have to let go of all ego to see the truth of your spiritual energies.* ***Once you have found those offset colours we want that divine light to come down again through the top and fill that layer so it***

glows bright white like the rest and then allow the white divine light to become absorbed by the full green, emerald spiritual layer*.* *Feel the energy shift, always feel you are on the outside of your body, and you are that part of the shield you are working on.* ***Once the green layer is pure, once again scan for gaps and holes, this far into the shield many should be fine that have spiritually balanced before or have been awakend to spirituality beforehand****.* *Those that are new and have remained physical bound will have to also scan and repair this shield, so see in first person, scan for holes, bring the green healing repairing energy from your centre heart chakra and fill the gaps in the shield until the aura layer itself is constant right through.* ***We have now just repaired the Centre energy shield. It is now recommended to continue as even though the energy from the outside from subconscious vampires etc, has been detached and repaired, we have our own energies from the inside of the aura and chakra points that manifest into areas that deteriorate the Aura shield from the inside out****.* *Just as all laws of duality exist in the matrix our energy shields can be dissolved from the out to in or in to out depending on our manifested energies that we have created and either balanced or allowed to manifest further into aura shield problems or physical avatar problems themselves.* ***Moving inwards, we remove the visualisation of the green energy shield layer so we are in first person through the mind's eye once again and can see only the Yellow mental shield energy shield of protection , scan around the shield for any colour offshoots***

from the other energies and then once discovered bring the white divine light back through the consciousness connection and into the aura inner energies and allow it to soak into the Mental energy field. Watch as it absorbs into it and creates the nice solar plexus yellow coloured energy through it, vivid and solid. *Next scan the shield like all the others and look for the gaps or holes.* ***Bring the green spiritual energy from the heart chakra and fill those holes like we have before, once they are discovered and feel the energy shift as you repair the shield itself to be in its original condition of protection.*** *We are nothing but energy, and in truth we are just floating code of consciousness energy.* ***But with remembering our spirit and energies we once again join the floating codes to where we can then send code back or retrieve it from Source.*** *Through all exercises you must either push or pull energy during this exercise here I have not said when to push or pull because each frequency of consciousness singularity has its own frequency to repair itself,* ***so you know what that frequency is not me.*** *Spirit will remember how to control energy again once its training has been reawakened.* ***Now see the white light again flow into the shield and sit between the yellow and the orange and then dissolve into the shields itself.*** *Each time we do this with each layer we are creating an energy shield within its own shield,* ***this is to block the other shield layers energies from changing and manifesting into undesired locations.*** *Once again as we move down we want to remove all visualisation of the Yellow shield and only see the Orange itself.* ***Scan using your mind's eye in***

first person for the offset colours from either the outer layers or from the physical red. *Once done, bring down the white divine light through the top the aura and then allow the energy to fill the full Orange protective shields layer, watch as all the offset coloured energy become a nice solid Orange, Amber colour.* ***Now scan around that shield and check for any gaps from the yellow shield or red and bring the green light of energy from the heart chakra again and then allow the energy as feeling it, to repair the holes within the gaps of the aura.*** *See the nice solid new shield that has been created.* ***Once done now once again bring down the white divine light and allow it to sit between the orange and red shield layers and allow the shields to absorb it.*** *Moving onto the last shield layer itself. Remove the Orange visualisation and then see the red shield layer only, no other shields at all at this moment, and remember the other shields are still there but we have just shut down our fire wall for a bit to reboot our natural shielding ability as spirit.* ***Scan the shield for any colours that have merged and then once seen bring down the divine white light and fill the red energy shield.*** *Allow it to glow bright white then be absorbed into the red.* ***See the bright red shield that has no other manifesting energies inside it, and start scanning the shield itself for holes.*** *Once found bring down the green chakra energy and allow it to sit in and repair the gaps that have been created over time.* ***Watch as those gaps are fixed and you have that full solid shield in thickness and its protection. Now that we have separated the energies and corrected the offset***

frequencies with a shielded wall of light between each layer, we want to see all the layers at once from third person view. *See you and the layers of colour around you, that egg that now has all the shield layers nice in thickness and ready for protection.* ***From the inside out you should see through visualisation, the Red, Light shield, Orange, Light shield, Yellow, Light Shield, Green, Light shield, Blue, Light shield, Indigo, Light shield, Violet. Once you see all of the fields we want them all to merge as one with no gaps in between each layer, leaving the divine light shields in place.***

Next we want to fill our egg with divine light of consciousness. *Allow the egg to become full with bright white energy between your spiritual light body and the aura shield itself.* ***Feel how the energy is flowing around you. You should feel a sensation of higher awareness now during this part.*** *Allow the energy to fill everything inside the aura egg and then bring the entire outside egg shield to become closer to the light body, until the egg shield becomes an outline that is snug around the spiritual body* ***, so it is about 1 millimetre away . You have just now repaired your Aura shield layers and allowed its natural protection ability again to be in control.*** *Aura repairing does take time and gaps will remain for quite so time and repairing a lifelong energy abused aura make take months or years depending on the persons understanding but never less will be eventually repaired with repeated practice.* ***To be right this exercise should be done before chakra balancing to allow the shields to***

repair quicker and then after the balance itself giving the Aura shields the Full protection ability it needs.

With all these exercises, it is recommended that you associate the visualization strategy of energy control to a simple command like clicking down the front of your body at each chakra point for balancing or simply saying the command repair shield for repairing the Aura shield itself. *Once spirit remembers that this is what it can do the simple command can save having to visualise the entire procedure of repairing.* ***Although before this is realistic this exercise has to be memorised so the program can then be associated with the command.*** *Once the spirit recognizes the energy level changes in vibration it can then a-tune frequencies without needing to take step by step procedure.* ***Remember during this method of repairing you have also been taught how to shield and un-shield your energies.*** *When we are in family environment or around people we love, we lower these shields subconsciously and in many cases, these are the people that you need to be shielded from.* ***We also allow strangers that we feel their energies are around the same frequency or higher to enter around us without us shielding.*** *With knowing how to open your Aura and close your Aura you can control when you want to have protection around you from energy.* ***Remember to open your aura or shield down your aura is to allow peoples energies in, this is the egg formation for the consciousness energy shields.***

When we have the tight almost clung to body shield this is the Closed Aura or Shield up formation. *This gives you protection against incoming vampiric energies or other energy attachments.*

If you are on Television, or media where you have to show yourself then it is always recommended to have your shields up as universal energy attachments can cause major issues in the future. *These attachments like this are called curses where one places energy frequencies towards yours so it attaches and the desired outcome of that person's intent for you remains within your own energy fields.* ***This is why it is also recommended to shield just like balancing once a day minimum, or as often as you like a day as the more times you practice, the more Intune with your natural spirits ability you become.*** *Remember that everything has an Aura field around it of existence, not the same form as our spiritual make up but it has its own unique energy shield around it of consciousness.* ***Through understanding this we can manipulate the objects shield itself to the rest of the full consciousness collective. Example is, if you are buying new shoes and decide to leave them outside to where anyone can steal, see through your mind's eye the shoes and its created aura.*** *Colour varies on objects but most can be see with a white glow around them. Once you visualize the object, allow the energy field of the object you are visualizing to become the entire object so you can't see anything apart from the energy aura of the object but in the shape of the object itself.* ***Now remove the aura and***

make the object invisible, in this case its shoes*. Now visualize the object to exactly where it is at the time where you're viewing it in physical and see the same scenario but without the object there and only the energy of its aura.* ***You have now protected that object from the outside world, in other words its very unlikely now that anyone would notice those shoes and want to steal them****. This can work for any object itself including when you park your car as a way of protection from thieves.* ***Remember that visualisation is not imagination and you have control of the thought initiative programming. You are sending code into the full collective itself and with the code you send here it is telling the rest of the collective that the object is invisible and of no importance to them****. Once consciousness creates the code and it is embedded into the collective of the Matrix the frequency of that manifestation is removed from others viewing as remember nothing is really physical and everything is only energy.* ***All we are doing is changing the frequency of our singularity to project that the energy we changed does not exist at all outside of your own frequency****. The object will remain visible to the naked eye but to the constructs electromagnetic codes it will become a hidden code and bring no attention.* ***Below is the Shield Down and Shield Up Aura Egg formation.***

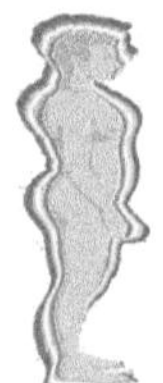

Another form of repair is to use sense repairing by feeling the changes in the energy fields of one's body. *Either working on someone by raising the hands about an inch from their body and then scanning slowly for the changing in fluctuation energies.* ***When physical or spiritual pain is accompanied the problem may not lay in their area of the body, example is the ache in your back may be caused by a trapped nerve or energy block elsewhere.*** *When scanning energy fields we can notice the changes that are listed below, this can be used for other work in energy besides aura also.*

Reiki comes down to sensing others energies and by feeling where the subtle changes in the energy are by running their hands an inch away from the patient's body, from the Crown chakra top of the head to the base of the feet and toes. *The Reiki practitioner or patient may experience the following.*

1. ***Magnetic Attraction – Healers feel their hands being guided towards the spots needed to attention by the energies through the One Source guiding them.***
2. ***Repulsion – Healers feel their hands being moved away as if there is a barrier there to what they do not need to pass. This is the ONE showing you that those areas are the ones in need of ongoing attention. These may be long standing problems.***
3. ***Reiki Pattern flow – The Reiki healer can feel the flow of the Reiki energy and assist by allowing themselves to go with the flow of energy, easing it along.***

4. ***Heat Sensation – Over scanning or healing a person the Reiki healer's hands will become hot, and warm, this is indication that Reiki, Chi energy is needed in those areas to either help repair energy or physical avatar functions.***
5. ***Cold Sensation – Energy paths that require attention to be unblocked feel colder to the reader, these areas draw one's hands to them through cold sensations.***
6. ***Tingling Sensation – Tingling is a great way to feel the energy of someone's paths of flow or blockage, through the intensity of the tingle sensation itself one can sense and get an idea of the severity of the problem.***
7. ***The Pain Sensation – pain can definitely indicate an area of blocked energies, and can also be a good way to tell when energy is starting to dissipate, example of this would be a knife stabbing sharp pain or sharp pain in general.***

Using these energy readings, you can find the under laying problems at root and start the repairing process on them hence Reiki energy work, ***aura repairs etc, emotional removals. Visualization and energy feeling can show you very quickly the problem that is in need the most attention.***

QUANTUM SPACE MEDITATION

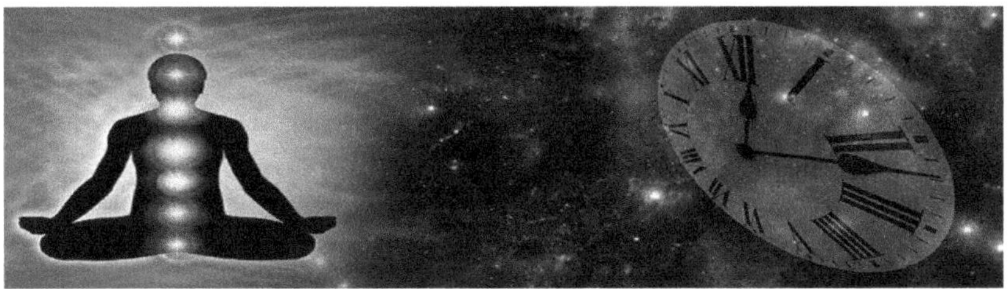

Okay so everyone knows how to meditate using breathe in and breathe out or even gamma breathing techniques.

Quantum Space meditation can have these breathing exercises included if you desire. However all I suggest is to find a calm relaxing place to where your body is already a tuned with and start the exercise there. *Breathing is to move energy and calm the physical body to be in tune with spirit, through belief that breathing patterns help and assist when in reality the physical body is not real and does not breathe and we can a tune the same energy's without having to breathe in meditation fashion, or to induce any state.* ***Breathing only allows us to believe we are changing something using physical when in reality all we are doing is moving energy frequencies, this can be achieved through feeling and visualization. Remember that you are everything around you, your skin is part of that construct physical field, you are already everything and once in tune you then become in the knowing to what spiritual Gurus and Masters seek from consciousness under different names.*** *Quantum Space meditation is the connecting of all of you as singularity joining back and becoming one as one single* *singularity for the meditation lasting time.* ***Remember that we exist in infinite parallel mirrors of energy collectives and when we do something here we are also doing the same there in synchronicity but slightly different****, as each frequency of quantum you have, has its own way to connect during this meditation technique.* ***We are going to bring us together through the consciousness mirrors into one solid energy collective of ourselves*** *as quantum universal singularity.*

Slowly let yourself drift and let go of any surroundings, life, the emotional problems, the money problems, the anxiety the fear, anything that you feel is holding you bound to the Matrix throw away and remove it for now. All problems don't exist all that exists is you as white light energy, everything around you is the same white light energy but you can see all objects*. Let your mind drift and place yourself inside that energy seeing outwards looking at all the design of the Matrix, all the codes of light and runways of electromagnetic energy pulsating and fluctuation creating everything of existence.* ***Now see the many versions of you. See the tall , skinny , fat ,black , white , Asian and the many other versions of yourself.*** *See the energy of each of these billions of you connecting to the One source of all creation.* ***Allow energy from each of the versions you see to flow into the main collective of consciousness****. Through the mind's eye now control who you want to see through. Watch the different realities of physical manifestation pass by as you are looking through the eyes of the other singularities of you.* ***See the changes in that reality then connect to that energy***

and then come back. You can stay in visualisation as long as you want and view that alternate reality of one you. The reason we are doing singles and jumping into their experience is to create a stronger bond between us here and us there. Remember from synchronicity they are also doing the same for you back. Leave that experience and return to the many ,many versions of you and connect to them and enter their experience. See all the surroundings and who they are, what do they work as? What is their food? See yourself sitting in the exact same position or laying in the same position in that version of you, you are looking through experiencing. See the surroundings merge with yours and feel your connection to yourself in that other experience. *Watch as the virtual surroundings merge with each other and become one and change into this reality's.* ***Once again go back to the billions of you and chose another experience, go through your mind's eye and experience the new reality that another you is experiencing. If you view the death of yourself somehow then its most likely you have accessed a version of your past lives themselves as seeing alive and dead becomes difficult when understanding that nothing ever lives to die to start with. See the billions of infinite you again and this time feel your energy rise by pushing energy.*** *But instead of going into one singular version of you, enter into all of you as ONE.* ***Join all the images of yourself into one final version of light. Listen to the many voices of yourself through all mirrors and what you are saying. Now as you are energy and we are all one collective of***

yourself from all parallel mirrors we can be aware of. *Join your collective energy to the consciousness Source!* ***A good visualization of this is to see your energy connecting to the giant brain and energy then flowing of white divine light through and into the collective*** . *Listen to the voices of yourself , what they are saying.* ***Then see a floating red orb and watch it dance around inside the energy collective until you watch it become part of that energy***. *Do the same with the Emotional orb, while seeing the colours of the red slightly remain inside the energy fields .****Next do the same with the following yellow, green, blue, indigo and violet orbs****, until you can see the colours all balanced throughout the entire energy collective.* ***Feel the energy of all the other you as one and feel you as that floating energy collective***. *We have now through intent created a bond between all the singularities of yourself, we have now balanced us as whole to what is possible as being the one singularity but knowing each other us has also helped balance the entire collective of yourself and joined with their energies also.* ***Now we have created that bond between all of us as single tethered light beings we have a nice solid connection to conscious Source itself and should feel lightheaded and slightly giddy***. *Now relax and become that energy floating in infinite space with blackness all around you. Visualize* ***a wall of mirrors right around the outside of the entire space that you are meditating in and connect them as one long mirror that encases you in the middle and turn the mirror side outwards.*** *Over the top of the collective encase it with electric blue* *shielding energy and see that your entire collective is now protected from any negative or disagreeing with your energy frequencies hence, malicious etc, when starting the travel through our own consciousness collective.* ***You now have your collective surrounded by reflection so anyone's intent or energy of the quantum state of all consciousness will be reflected away from your visualization experience. Now through your mind's eye drift into all the blackness you see and leave the collective energy but don't visualize it being there, watch the video screen that is played for you.*** *The inner workings of consciousness design, the codes of the Matrix, the truth of all existence, allow your body and spirit to feel as if it's in those images with consciousness as one.* ***Become everything and nothing at once, and then see yourself on the electromagnetic chessboard game standing on the chess tile. See all the other versions of you as the other players of light and quantum shift around the board flashing within seconds and then moving to the next tile.*** *This is also a good technique to use when shielding the aura as it allows for no one's energy to be able to find you to be able to attach itself.* ***See all the chakra points of all the energy beings of that chessboard and allow them to all send energy into each other's right throughout the entire grid of the board. Allow yourself a few minutes to watch the energy flow around through all the other versions of light of your own collective of singularity and then merge everything back into the one single light being that is you, remove the tether that connects you through to all***

the other versions of you and come back through your mind's eye to body again. *You now have learnt the quantum space meditation teaching.* ***We can use this to connect our self's back to Source as one full collective of all of our own singularities.*** *Through this technique we are through intent controlling our connections through to the other us frequencies of the One consciousness. We are aligning the frequencies from each creation of our own consciousness to become aware of itself and then connect with itself.* ***Only through visualisation or energy reading, feeling this is possible as quantum state is infinite and also instant and forever in my cases.*** *Using visualization methods like this we can retrain spirit to understand the connections of the full design of consciousness.* ***This teaching is to allow you to make yourself and the many other versions of yourself aware to its existence and bring the whole collective of your own singularity closer to being in contact with the one pure Source of all creation,*** *as well as balancing the connection from your singularity here to the many others. Any visualization will work for yourself as long as you have intent and unconditional love and connection to consciousness Source as each of us do aware or unaware.*

This exercise is not needed to be done with the balancing of the chakras or the Aura shielding techniques and is only for reconnection of all of your quantum space energies of consciousness. *All spiritual training to help you subconsciously gain what society has created to be hidden and lost from you. Visualization techniques allow you to once again learn how to* *control energy and your own through initiative programs.* ***Through visualisation not imagination we can see quantum realities of existence as the mind's eye is the gateway to all knowing of creation when opened and once again in synch with the one pure Source of all creational self-aware consciousness.*** *This training also allows you to become aware of the many you.*

Remember after Cern has shown us the fact of how the space time continuum of quantum state of biological material can be manipulated through energy, *and now we can understand more of how the quantum design of God has always worked and now use and be aware of our natural abilities of being a true form of creator.* ***We have the power within us all to do the most considered far out ludicrous reality bending that we can ever have thought to have been possible.*** *We are now on the verge of a universal awakening from Source intervention itself. So KNOW! You have the natural ability as spirit to control all energy around you and change your own vibrational frequencies in accordance.* ***Conscious of the fact.*** *Remember that the Occult Elite are well aware everything is energy and for centuries have been using physical ideology symbology to explain the flows and design of the ethereal energy all around us. They draw physical images such as beavers, set squares, circles and stars etc. But all equals the paths to the Outside of the Matrix and describes energy creation and transformation creating God in Occult hidden teaching only for their initiated to understand. E.g. Setsquare = female ,Compass = Male.*

HOW TO ACTIVATE THE PINEAL GLAND ACTIVITY

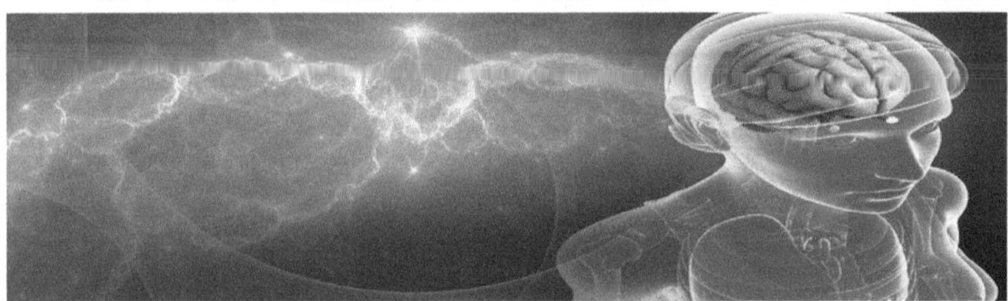

Although many people will think it's hard to activate the pineal gland and pituitary gland to work in collaboration, or to activate the pineal gland itself, further is from the truth. *We automatically do activate our pineal gland when we just think about it.* ***Just thinking about the pineal gland in your head is already bringing your spirit to more of awareness that it can communicate with Source through the bodies built in antenna network such as the pineal gland, pituitary gland working together to create the D.M.T (the Spiritual oil anointment in Biblical teachings) release, that allows our natural connection to see the afterlife while we are wide awake and still in body.*** *There are a few foods that can help with decalcifying the Pineal such as Prunes, Dates, Almonds, Raisins and more that contain high amounts of Boron that allows the Pineal gland to become un-hardened from fluoride build-ups etc.* ***But in truth of reality nothing is needed apart from knowing that you can activate the gland through your own free will.*** *Just as you use muscles to move with command the Pineal gland is no different it's just that no one ever told you about it, or has shown you how to activate the gland itself conscious of the ability it provides.*

There are many physical things and trainings you can do from Yoga, to Acupuncture in the physical reality that allows you to believe that something can be possible because those actions say that it is, and using those physical codes then you are convinced and then believe, so you then manifest the direction of what you have been programmed to believe in physical. *In reality, the Pineal gland is always waiting to be activated, and many will use it subconsciously without even knowing.* *<u>Creativity</u> is a major sign of one and that they have access to their Pineal gland and Dimethyltryptamine without knowing they do.* ***The physical reality is only vibrational frequencies of energy.*** *So why do you believe that you need to do certain things to regain what your natural ability as spirit is?* ***It is hardwired into you to be able to do without question!*** *All physical reality does is create visual understanding that allows you to consciously believe or deny.* ***When the virtual code itself really has nothing to do with the makeup design of what you are as electromagnetic self-aware energy.*** *But is only a training playground to allow forward understanding to tune the frequency of energies of your subconscious ethereal self.* ***I will give you a few training exercises to allow you to reconnect that lost connection through spirit and physical transmitter and receiver.***

Find yourself a quiet place once again, and be sure you start as calm and peaceful, remove all problems from your mind, the everyday worries, the hardships, the struggles, let them all go. *Feel the energy of your body become more vivid to you, feel* *you are that energy and that physical you does not really exist.* ***Through visualization see the brain, and inside the brain a small glowing eye. Concentrate on this eye and open it inside that brain, allow your energy that's flowing through you to raise higher and higher feeling the eye itself open.*** *This is the true all seeing eyes meaning.* ***Open the eye wide so you can see it staring at you and then allow blue lightning to surge around the Pineal gland and brain itself throughout every neuron. Make the energy from the Pineal gland move in a bright bolt of energy towards the Pituitary gland.*** *Feel the new connection you have established.* ***Now see the white divine light run through the top of the brain and into the brain itself until it focuses onto the eye of the Pineal.*** *Once the light has been brought to the Pineal gland allow that connection of light to flow through the bolt of blue lightning and connect as a tether between the Pineal and Pituitary gland.* ***Feel the connection and energy frequency change as you do.*** *Once created allow the energy from the Pituitary gland to run up the head and into and through the Crown violet chakra and through into the Source of consciousness.* ***Then come back down back into the Christ and through the Pituitary gland and back into the Pineal gland.*** *Make the eye that is glowing glow brighter and brighter like a small indigo sun and allow the energy to fluctuate through the tethers you have created that connects you to Source.* ***Move the pulsating flow of energy throughout the entire tethers to the Crown and back, allowing the energy to move through the tether faster and faster, allowing you to***

feel the change in your energy frequencies and release your natural D.M.T. Done with repetition this exercise will retrain the Pineal gland and you, that you can activate it at will, and over time you will produce natural D.M.T as soon as you create the visualization command. *Once again associate the training with a word to train the conscious to run the subconscious program of your desired will on command.*

You can also if desired use the spiritual centres when in visualisation and through them see the energy running down from the Crown Christ chakra, then into the back chakra point of the violet chakra on the back of the physical body head and then from that into the centre forehead third eye location. This is creating a triangular flow of energy around the Pineal gland and through it using the spiritual energy colours, once you have established this visualisation, see the divine white light of consciousness from the pure Source come into the Crown and surge throughout the connections between chakras. *Feel all the energy in your head and then send all of it directly to the Pineal gland centre allow it to connect and then reconnect to all the energy points again opening and creating your subconscious awareness energy fields with Source or your Halo of electromagnetic connection.*

Through these methods you are training yourself once again to KNOW you can control energy and change your spiritual frequencies to help open your natural ability as spirit in physical avatar. As soon as you are visualizing the Pineal

gland open you are using it, just as many have recorded the brain activity being active like you are running but you are only watching someone run on the television, the visualisation of opening the Pineal gland method is just the same. Even though you are seeing it visual through your mind's eye, you are still creating that to happen within your brain's transmission and through visualization you are actually using your Pineal gland already. *It is also good while training to drink a lot of distilled water to help with the training methods advancement in progress and decalcification of the glands.*

I recommend using this exercise in routine combined with the balancing and aura shielding, this allows you to have the full spiritual cleansing and workout of all the energies needed.

Now you have done these exercises and understand how you are energy and how to work your Pineal etc. ***I want you to enter the afterlife, and use your third eye to see the truth of what's beyond the veil.*** *Relax and open your third eye, see that chessboard with us as light beings on it, see the many players, the small game chessboard on the side of the golden streets in Heaven.* ***The columns around the chessboard game that resemble the olden day ancient monument design. See all the light beings of us throughout the town, the streets of gold leading to the giant gates all made from pearl.*** *Become you on that chess board and enter into your true form of player on the outside.* ***See through your eyes there and look around the board, you will see the electromagnetic grids of us and the***

telepathic energy we are creating. Once you see this you can see the reactions from the other light beings if you are on your right path or not and when in doubt if you are just look at what they are doing as we move the same in motion and expressions of physical but as energy of light. *What you are seeing is the real outside of the Matrix and what we are as the players of this virtual constructed through vibrational frequency Matrix.* ***Once you have connected and KNOW you are spirit and can view your Spiritual energies easy, start to read others and theirs.*** *You through this open now, sixth sense will be able to point out the non-player characters within the Matrix with practice and level of now understanding the many forms and factors of awareness self-aware electromagnetic consciousness energy frequencies of the One Source. The afterlife has one real form of control centre .All others are a creation of the subconscious program of your own system belief of conscious code and control. This is also the reason why many repeat the same realities again to bypass creating a falsehood afterlife of their own design and not entering through the main connection of leading back to the main control centre to be able to understand the truth of what's in the virtual afterlife. Remember as I said we are nothing but energy and even the dream reality of the afterlife is just that. Dream state of self aware conscious energy that experiences in alternating frequencies of higher and lower experiences.*

ENERGY OF CRYSTAL HEALING

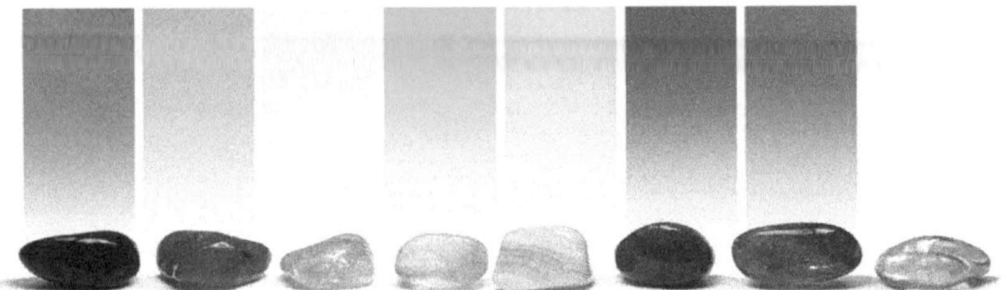

Since ancient time's humanity has understood about spirituality and the frequencies of the One Consciousness. *Through using Stones, mainly Crystals they have understood how Crystals can be used to heal the spiritual and physical avatar body.* ***This method of healing with the use of Crystals placed all over the ground is called Crystal Healing.*** *Since the earliest times in creation Crystals have been used to heal and restore balance.* ***They help in releasing and clearing the negative frequencies of energy and assist with energy work healing a great deal.*** *The historical records for the earliest account of this method has been traced back to ancient Egypt, India's Ayurvedic records and traditional Chinese medicine also claim healing with use of crystals dating back to 5000 years ago in the Matrix.*

So, what are Crystals? *Crystals are the gift from source that allow us to augment healing.* ***Crystals are found in all shapes and sizes, colours and composition.*** *Each Crystal has a unique vibrational resonance.* ***They owe their unique qualities to their***

mineral content, their inherent geometry and the colour frequency they emit.

The human body has a complex electromagnetic system also known as the vibrational energy system. ***The One creating nature has created Crystals to be perfect electromagnetic conductors, capable of interacting with our electromagnetic energies.*** *Crystals have been found to carry vibration that activates certain energy centres within our electromagnetic system, thus having a positive effect on our entire body's physical functioning and systems.*

There are three steps to effective Crystal healing. *While you are wearing your Crystals as jewels or in a pouch at your heart centre, spiritual green vortex, the vibrations work continuously on your imbalances.* ***First, we have the cleansing process. In the first week or so after the Crystal has chosen you, the Crystal is making tremendous adjustments within your energy field.*** *Matching the Matrix of your energy fields to the larger ethereal energy fields that will be used to assist your healing.* ***It is important to keep your Crystals on you for 24 hours a day, at least for the first 21 days for the cleansing process to be initiated and completed.*** *This is also a period of time where the blockages of energy that are causing your imbalance are removed by the Crystal.* ***Sometimes a healing crisis occurs at this point, during the early days of wearing the Crystals so remember resolving the inner conflict may take time and that Crystals accelerate the change process.*** *Allow these processes* *to occur naturally without interruption by continuously wearing the Stone or Crystal until you complete the next two following stages in this method.* ***It is a good idea to cleanse your Crystal every week and to recharge it in the sunlight for at least four hours weekly throughout the healing process.***

The second step in Crystal healing is the process of harmonizing and integrating the changes into your whole being. *You may notice physical or emotional changes in either of the first two steps as your physical, mental, emotional and spiritual bodies come into alignment.* ***Some of these changes are caused by throwing off toxins and negative energies from the cleansing process which continues throughout the cycle of the healing method.***

In the second stage, beginning in about the fourth week of wearing the Stone or Crystal you may notice that your face looks more relaxed as the harmonizing connection is made with yourself. ***Your mental outlook, thoughts, feelings and even opinions may change significantly.***

All aspects of your energy will be activated and the result is a very positive feeling, however we are not out of the woods yet so to speak.

The third step of stability can take three to four months, perhaps even longer for some people depending on the intensity of the original condition. *With continuous wearing of Crystals or Stones with their own frequencies you will achieve stability for the changes.* ***There is no turning back at this point.***

You can test the stability of your energy bodies by removing your Crystals from time to time. *If you feel desperate and need to put the Crystals back on after only a few minutes, you are not even close to stabilizing the energy changes.* ***If you are however able to go for a few days without your Stones, but then notice that you are slipping back to your old ways, consider wearing your Stones for another week or more, or only at bedtime before testing again.*** *As you develop deeper sensitivity for Crystal energy, you may decide to keep the Crystals on you much longer or at all times.*

There we have the Crystal healing method. Some advice on the method as to all of the other exercises is commitment, like your commitment to open your Pineal gland and balance your energies is what shows results. ***Your commitment to the Crystal is part of the healing process.*** *Let the Crystal do the work for you.* ***It is best not to wear more than two Stones at any one time if you are new to Crystal healing, as many people find the effects too distracting. The length of time to obtain the effects desired will depend on the Crystals quality e.g. size, colour, energy, charge, location of wear, duration and the Crystals appropriateness to your healing.*** *Some Crystals are better suited to healing the overall problem which underlies the symptoms, than to just treating superficial symptoms.* ***Select your Crystal with an honest outlook on the real problem you wish help to overcome.***

Following is descriptions for each Crystal and its characteristics.

First, we will explain once again that all is electromagnetic energy that is self-aware this includes physical rocks etc. As we are indoctrinated to be programmed subconscious that only biological forms can have self-awareness when all forms of everything in and out of visual existence has awareness as all is just an experience, emotion of the one pure Source of creation. *Your Stone selects you so before continuing close your eyes with your Crystal and hear it, feel its frequency. Crystals like everything can telepathically communicate with you once your third eye has been opened and your receivers and transmitters are functioning allowing the natural transmission of consciousness energy between itself.* ***Your Stone will select you!***

The first Stone we will talk about here is the Garnet and examples and attributes of each shall be listed.

Garnet helps with physical healing and assists with many forms such as blood and circulatory disease. Metabolism Issues, assimilation of vitamins and minerals and helps to reenergize the avatar shell body*. Garnet also assists with emotional healing properties such as in a crisis situation where there seems to be no way out, or where life has been fragmented or traumatic.* ***It fortifies the survival instinct, bringing with it hope and courage****. This Stone has the ability to dissolve ingrained behaviour patterns and out warn ideas that no longer serve.* ***It bypasses resistance to self-induced unconscious sabotage****.*

The spiritual healing abilities because of its strong links with the Pineal gland it creates stimulated expanded awareness, past life recall, out of body experiences. ***Garnet itself is also a psychic aid that helps all other Crystals tune to frequency and do their allocated jobs required and are also very successful to business matters and dealings when used in intention work****.*

Garnets message from the ethereal is one of protection and knowing one is safe and secure*.*

The next is Carnelian, this Crystal is used with lower back pain problems or disorders, Liver problems, helps to repair damaged female reproductive organs, Infertility, frigidity, and male impotence, can accelerate the process of healing within bones and ligaments, Rheumatism and arthritis, staunches the blood flow and helps to quickly heal physical manifested wounds. ***With emotional healing, the Crystal, Stone helps one with balancing emotions such as anger, jealousy, envy and emotional negativity or all-round shyness.*** *Helps with memory recall from the one consciousness.* ***The Carnelian is also known as the creative Stone named from its abilities of becoming a touchstone for creative people by balancing the mental focus and the creative inspiration.*** *The Crystals spiritual healing elements are it is a stabilizing Stone of high energy it imparts acceptance of the cycle of life, removes fear of death and assists in positive life choices.* ***It is very useful in one that needs to overcome abusive situations and helps self-trust and to overcome negative ideas that are projected through the thought form of consciousness.*** *In psychic aid, this Crystal can be used to cleanse the other Crystals, Stones, used as a Crystal of abundance and motivates for success in business and other*

matters that are a present situation in one's life. ***The ethereal message is to know the ability to be creative in your life.***

Next the above. Citrine is a Crystal that has many of its own abilities also , these for the physical healing are help with the digestive system , constipation , kidney and bladder conditions, menopause and spleen and pancreas disorders. *For emotional healing, these Stones can be used to be assistants in the following. Helps in sensitivity to environmental issues, useful in soothing group or family discord.* ***Used to reverse self-destructive behaviour and assist in acting on constructive criticism and also helps you move into the flow of frequencies of your own projected feelings, vibrational frequency.*** *The Spiritual healing properties are it has the ability to absorb, transmute and ground unwanted negative energy, it never itself needs any form of cleansing, but does need recharging.* ***The Citrine Crystal promotes inner calmness allowing your spiritual body to be realised more by physical avatar allowing your natural wisdom of creation to emerge, and also helps you through its frequency training to understand your "darker" shades of the spiritual aspects of your life and how all plays a role as one together.*** *The psychic aid of this stone is greater*

than many but each does have its own consciousness resonating frequency of self-awareness. ***The Citrine is a very powerful cleanser and regenerator it carries the power of the sun, protects the environment and is beneficial for attracting abundance and should be placed in a cashbox or wealth nominated corner of the home residence.*** *The ethereal Message of Citrine is of one remembering the abundance of power that's within your own consciousness singularity.*

Next crystal to explain is the Rose Quartz

Rose Quartz directly has effects towards the circulatory system, helps assist healing of an illness within the lungs, chest or heart. Can greatly reduce the effects of heart burn and blistering. *Has positive effects in treating Alzheimer's and senile dementia.* ***Also, can be an aid to overcome vertigo.*** *The emotional attributes of this Stone are far greater than any other and is classed as the finest emotional healer, this is the most important Crystal for healing the physical heart and the spiritual field heart centre vortex.* ***The Stone promotes the ability to receive love, restores trust and harmony balance and assists in***

the releasing of unexpressed emotions and heartache. *It brings comfort to grieving and encourages self-love and self-acceptance.* ***This Stone allows the spiritual healing of opening the heart frequencies to unconditional love and peace with how everything is. Rose quartz psychic aid enhances positive affirmations and intentions.***

The ethereal message for Rose quartz is remembering that you embody the essence of love. ***The rose quartz is designed the same frequency of consciousness energy that we use for self love and appreciation. It is the left behind hint on how to understand the many frequencies of colour and all of their healing properties once intention is included.*** *Ask this Stone to help you if you have trouble accepting the truth of having unconditional love for the Source as one of all creation , the deemed bad and good, evil and pure.*

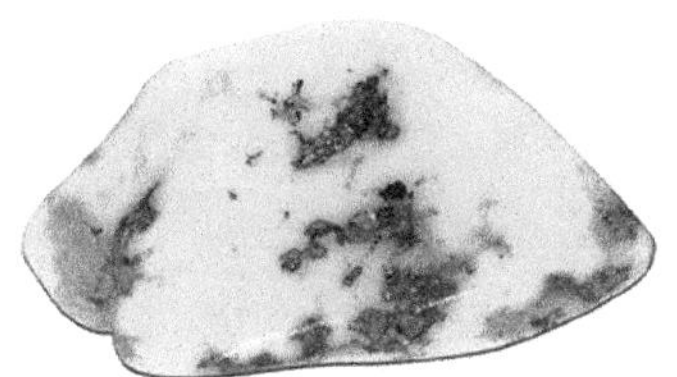

Next Stone of discussion is the Turquoise Crystal and its attributes with the physical, emotional and psychic aid. This Stone itself can be used for anti-inflammatory purposes,

immune system rebalancing. Faster tissue regeneration, assimilation of nutrients, viral infections, sore throats, gout, rheumatism, and has the ability to neutralize overacidity for its physical healing properties. *With its emotional healing, it can be used to help assist with mood swings, heals friendships, purification of thoughts and work and enhances communication in the physical Matrix reality and the ethereal spiritual world.* ***The Stone is powerful for a protective seal or amulet and itself brings good fortune and peace when used as a practitioner's psychic aid. The Spiritual healing characteristics are advancement towards self realization, being used as a powerful energy conduit,*** *allows the subconscious release of vows, inhibitions, prohibitions that have been programmed into your own singularity and allows you to break patterns of implanted code quicker and overcome them.* ***Helps to dissolve the Martyr attitude and self-subconscious programmed sabotage.*** *Allows for the soul to be able to express itself again more in tune with self-awareness.* ***The ethereal message of this Crystal, Stone is one that speaks, and that creation of our simulated reality depends on the thought initiative programs we implant into the full collective self-aware consciousness as this full reality's Matrix code.*** *It reminds you that creation of our lives depends on what we do in each moment.*

The next Crystal of discussion is the Amethyst. *This is a Stone of psychic protection.* ***Stones allow us through spirit from the outside to send signal easier than having to introduce it by creating paranormal phenomenon that then leads us astray away from the message, and that is we on the outside are trying to communicate with ourselves always.*** *We and everything is one.* ***We are told through many, many messages that something is trying to communicate with us, from ghosts, aliens etc. All are saying from the One listen I'm trying to contact you and make you remember what everything really is.*** *Through subconscious manipulation we are lied to about the source communication and Stones of self-aware electromagnetic energy are the conduits for physical to the spiritual for many as the Stones themselves are stored electromagnetic codes of the Matrix that is connected straight to Source in quantum state.* ***They live and preserve the data of the Matrix storing codes of frequency that can be realised and attuned to your own spiritual psyche. The emotional changes and physical manifested outcomes from the Stones are due to the frequency of energy pattern that you are resonating at and what frequency of the Crystal energy you at subconscious level had told spirit that is needed for your desired outcome***

with work of intent*. The amethyst helps reduce physical pain within the Matrix generated avatar, reduces the oncome of nightmares, addiction to drinking, alcoholism and helps with regeneration of injuries, bruises and swellings.* ***Sends helpful frequencies to the full endocrine system, helps with hearing disorders, insomnia and geopathic stress****. Also has properties of being used as a natural tranquilizer.* ***The emotional healing properties of Amethyst consist of it helps with reduction in anxiety, fear, emotional pain, anger issues and the addiction program itself. It is believed to help those transition over in death, log out of the constructed Matrix and return to the Source of creation for your next experience and promotes divine love and divine knowing****. The spiritual attributes of this Stone are it encourages self-awareness, is great in assistance for meditation exercises and facilitating out of body astral experiences.* ***Helps to purify the Aura when used in work with Aura repair etc and has the ability to assist in helping you control and create your frequencies of visualization****. Can also help with subconscious retrieval of recalling dream experiences. The aid with psychic work involves it guarding you against others intent that is created into an electromagnetic psychic attack on your own singularity of consciousness, and then transmutes that frequency into a higher state of love. Can also be a helpful assistant in scrying techniques.* ***The ethereal message for Amethyst is to bring inner sight and etheric awareness to everyday life!***

Next is the most powerful Crystal for all the attributes, the physical, emotional and psychic aid , This is the Quartz.

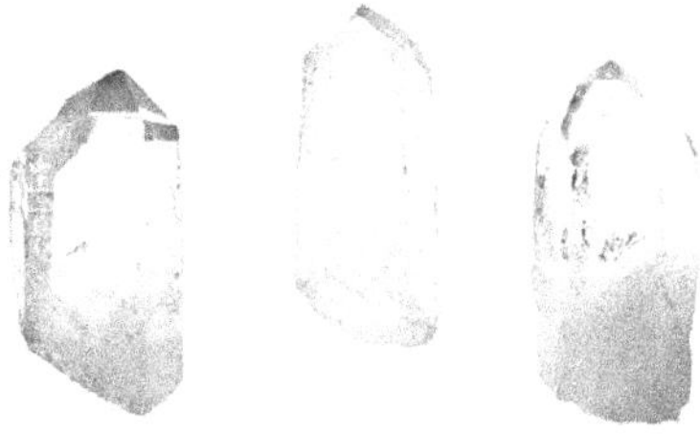

This Stone is the communication master for spirit and the outside to Source. ***Its physical abilities are amazing with being able to aid with protection from radiation during cancer therapy.*** *The Stone itself has been considered to be the Master healing Crystal for any known or unknown condition!* ***The frequencies it produces cleanses the physical Matrix avatar and helps bring all energies of physical and spiritual into neutrality balance.*** *Is used as a very significant healing and energy amplifier for the energy worker.* ***Quartz takes the electromagnetic energies of the full source of your consciousness singularity into the most sought perfect state possible from any Stones assistance.*** *With being the most powerful physical medium it is also having the strongest attributes associated with its emotional healing properties and can take your emotional frequencies into the most perfect balanced state.* ***Before emotional energy that is ignored and not balanced manifests physical disease and sets itself into a physical problem Quartz acts as a deep soul cleanser and***

reconnects the physical dimensional understanding back with the mind*. Quartz helps to harmonize all emotions bringing clarity and understanding to all negative and positive emotional states.* ***Quartz itself is much like an electromagnetic cosmic computer and stores all information within, it also has the ability to dissolve karmic seeds****. It allows the release of spirt to be recognized by body and enhances the metaphysical abilities and then attunes for spiritual purpose.* ***Clear Quartz works on a multidimensional quantum scale of level of being and harmonizes and aligns the chakra power centres with the Aura energy fields to be attuned with the One at an electromagnetic consciousness merge of frequency****. The Crystal greatly assists in any real magic as a prized worker and potent tool of energy. The Native Americans called the Quartz the brain cells of Mother Earth and are the power centres of many mythical and ancient stories of advanced technology of energy generation.* ***Quartz ethereal message is connection with divine wisdom is always yours every moment****!*

That concludes Crystals, the next page shows the chakra to Crystal connections and what Stones should be used.

Below are the chakra, crystal connections , thank you for reading and enjoying the presented work and at the end of this book I hope that you have a better understanding of how many indoctrinated programs have overtaken our true form of knowing.

Chakra name -Root   Psychic Focus – Spatial Intuition

- *Emotional Focus- Survival & security*
- *Physical Focus – Grounding*
- *Location – Base of the spine*
- *Colours – Red & black*
- *Crystals – Garnet, Ruby, Red Jasper, Black Tourmaline, Smokey Quartz.*

Chakra name -Sacral   Psychic Focus – Balance Male/ Female

- *Emotional Focus- Sensuality & Intimacy*
- *Physical Focus – Health & creativity*
- *Location – Lower Abdomen*
- *Colours – Orange*
- *Crystals – Amber, Carnelian, Topaz and Orange Calcite*

Chakra name -Solar Plexus   Psychic Focus – Healing & Teaching Power

- *Emotional Focus- Emotional Stability & Confidence*
- *Physical Focus – Power & Physical Strength*
- *Location – Stomach Area*
- *Colours – Yellow*
- *Crystals – Citrine & Tiger Eye*

Chakra name -Heart   Psychic Focus – Clairsentience & Intuition

- *Emotional Focus- Compassion & Unconditional Love*
- *Physical Focus – Empathy*
- *Location – Centre of Chest*
- *Colours – Green & Pink*
- *Crystals – Rose Quartz ,Aventurine, Kunzite, Malachite*

Chakra name -Throat Psychic Focus – Expression

- *Emotional Focus- Speaking personal truths*
- *Physical Focus – Communication & Spontaneity*
- *Location – Throat*
- *Colours – Light Blue*
- *Crystals – Turquoise, Aquamarine & Chrysocolla*

Chakra name -Third Eye Psychic Focus – Clairvoyance

- *Emotional Focus- Intuition*
- *Physical Focus – Clarity & Discernment*
- *Location – Centre of forehead*
- *Colours – Dark blue & Indigo Blue*
- *Crystals – Amethyst, Sodalite, Lapis Lazuli & Blue Calcite*

Chakra name -Christ/Crown Psychic Focus – Claircognizance

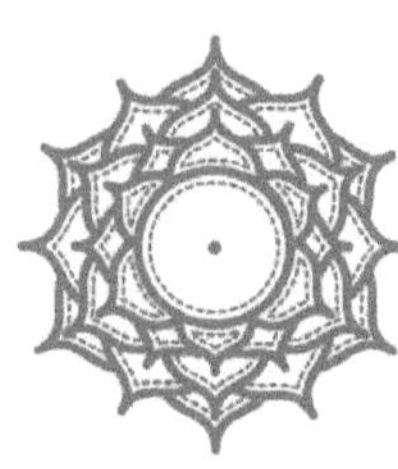

- *Emotional Focus- Feeling one with all , Oneness, Spirituality*
- *Physical Focus – Concentration*
- *Location – Top of head*
- *Colours – White & royal Purple*
- *Crystals – Clear Quartz, Chariote, Selenine & Sugulite*

Quartz, Rock Crystal
Black Onyx
Sodalite
Wollastonite
Amethyst
Rose Quartz
Obsidian
Malachite
Quartz, Rock Crystal
Blue Agat
Jade
Blue Agat
Pyrite
Aquamarine
Opal
Chalkopyrite
Selenite
Olivine
Celestine
Labradorite
Tiger Eye
Yellow Citrine
Albite
Orpiment
Cordierite
Dumortierite
Red Gypsum
Lepidolite
Desert Rose
Unakite
Calcite
Fluorite
Sulphur
Chrysocolla
Rhodochrosite
Blue Azurite
Fluorite
Green Fluorite
Aragonite
Amazonite
Ruby
Fluorite

So, by now after reading through this instruction manual for the one source of consciousness you should see how reality itself is an illusion and that we are the experiencing players of this electromagnetic playground, our every thought matters. The Mandela effect is God itself presenting us the truth, it is showing the law of duality and the laws of reversal. Do not judge as all programs are needed in the Matrix at this time to allow us to remember who we all are again as one united consciousness. We that have shifted know that we are energy and can see firsthand the changes and calls of the One being blatantly presented in our faces through synchronicity and inner knowing. The world is exactly the way it should be. I was told by Source that to remove the illuminati all we do is remove the stereotype that gave it creation from intent. We the everyday person are the holders of creation, we direct the outcome of the world, not the world leaders and not the politicians. But each and every one of our single consciousness signatures. We must understand again our true form of being and bypass the laws of physical indoctrination as we are made from the most divine source of light and always know within our spirit that everything is simulated just for our experience. After all as bad as some are, and as good as some are we all selected the experience that we wanted to endure this reality play through. Be conscious of giving intent towards others desired goals and remember who you are and re-join the true form of self, the form of spirit, the form of awareness, the form of our lost understandings of being the true children of

God. Remember we are in the creator's image because we are all built from the design of the creator and are all single frequencies that need to become the full one again. Remove the boundaries of physical propaganda. Allow your inner self to communicate with you again, listen to the truth of creation yourself from Source. All my teachings are to bring awareness to what through my insight and connection to Source reveal is the true form of design. If my teachings have not resonated with you thank you for taking the time to read my book and remember there are many paths to enlightenment, sadly this one was not for you. To those that resonate with my teachings throughout thank you for your support in buying the book and knowing what I speak is the truth from the one Source of creation. We all have missions in life and before the Mandela effect many of us had become lost. We have been given the most divine gift from God itself and through us we must share it and protect the truth of what has been revealed. That's we are quantum state, forgiven for all sins, immortal energy beings of light. We are amazing when we use what God has left for us and through energy we can change the entire outcome and direction of the forced upon us designed by code reality.

PEACE, LOVE & LIGHT TO ALL MY BROTHERS AND SISTERS OF THE PURE SOURCE OF CREATION. HUMBLY YOURS TONY.

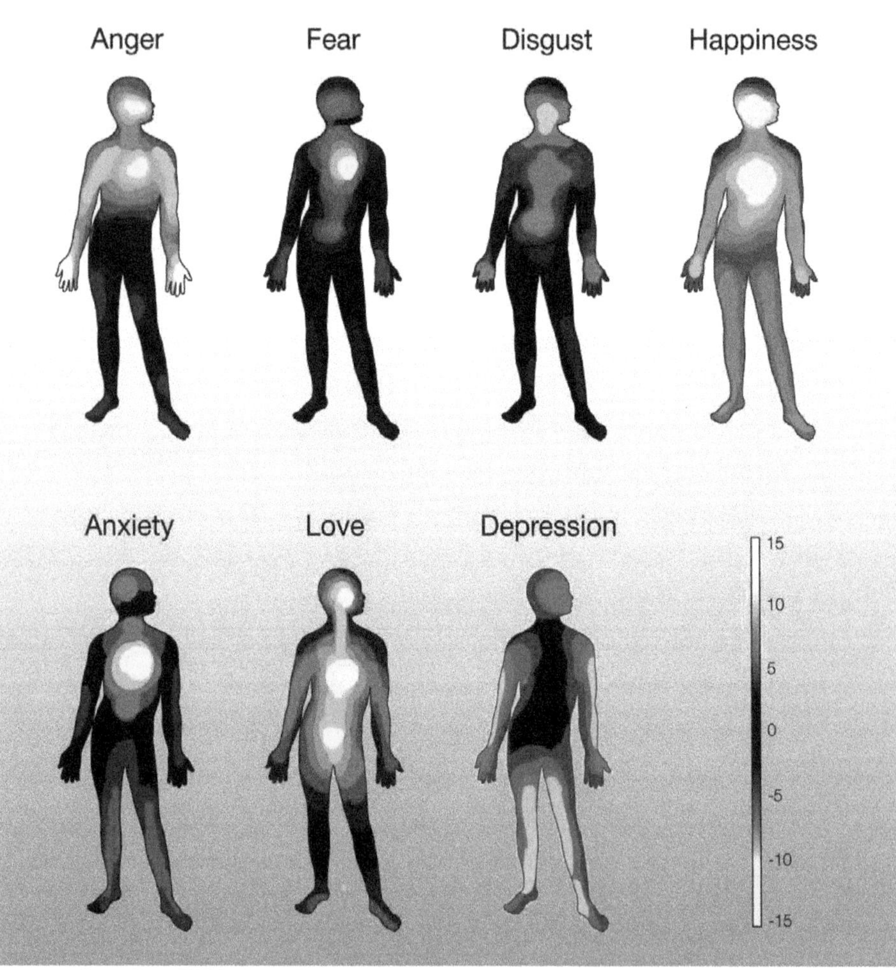

Image ID : 45943930 Media Type : Stock Vector Copyright : Iryna Bezianova (Follow)

INDEX OF ROYALTY FREE AND COPYRIGHT IMAGES

www.123rf.com

Image Type : Stock Photo ,Copyright : Vit Paroulek (Follow) Image ID's : 61444037, 51569618 48106673
Image Type : Stock Photo Copyright : Bruce Rolff (Follow) Image ID's : 15301951, 24440025, 10777254, : 10056223
Image Type : Stock Vector Copyright : Christos Georghiou (Follow) Image ID's : 69823155, 25210363
Image Type : Stock Photo Copyright : Teodoro Ortiz Tarrascusa (Follow) Image ID's : 58762011
Image Type : Stock Photo Copyright : Dirk Czarnota (Follow) mage ID's : 25311004 , 24163528
Image Type : Stock Photo Copyright : gajus (Follow) Image ID : 29264776
Image Type : Stock Photo Copyright : grechka (Follow) Image ID : 54247718
Image Type : Stock Vector Copyright : designua (Follow) Image ID : 22981790, 56717084, 32381458 , 63923662
Image Type : Stock Photo Copyright : Comaniciu Dan (Follow) Image ID : 31242152
Image Type : Stock Photo Copyright : George Muresan (Follow) Image ID : 38666259
Image Type : Stock Vector Copyright : Łukasz Stefański (Follow) Image ID : 72172465
Image Type : Stock Photo Copyright : Rossella Apostoli (Follow) Image ID : 19112869
Image Type : Stock Vector Copyright : kudryashka (Follow) Image ID : 49644050
Image Type : Stock Vector Copyright : Peter Hermes Furian (Follow) Image ID's : 28055135, 32519390, 29375340
Image Type : Stock Photo Copyright : alphaspirit (Follow) Image ID : 30399845
Image Type : Stock Illustration Copyright : Andrea Danti (Follow) Image ID : 31970390, 31970380
Image Type : Stock Vector Copyright : alila (Follow) Image ID : 15111561
Image Type : Stock Vector Copyright : Miro Kovacevic (Follow) Image ID : 46409206
Image Type : Stock Vector Copyright : oksanaok (Follow) Image ID : 10980180
Image Type : Stock Vector Copyright : Ewelina Kowalska (Follow) Image ID : 24619903
Image Type : Stock Illustration Copyright : katisa (Follow) Image ID : 44671242, 44671238, 44671243, 44671241, 44671240, 44671239, 44671236
Image Type : Stock Photo Copyright : Iurii Kovalenko (Follow) Image ID : 24089216
Image Type : Stock Photo (Editorial image) Copyright : Elizabeth Coughlan (Follow) 10474723
Image Type : Stock Vector Copyright : arcady31 (Follow) Image ID : 23211433
Image Type : Stock Photo Copyright : Nicola Zalewski (Follow) Image ID : 42117125 , 35028460
Image Type : Stock Photo (Editorial image) Copyright : Leonard Zhukovsky (Follow) Image ID : 37657835
Image ID *: 24695400 Media Type : Stock Photo Copyright : Ingemar Magnusson (Follow)*
Image ID : 17987625 Media Type : Stock Photo Copyright : Ansis Klucis (Follow)
Image ID : 27488124 Media Type : Stock Photo Copyright : Tatiana Epifanova (Follow)
Image ID : 3674668 Media Type : Stock Photo Copyright : Martin Novak (Follow)
Image ID : 39963801 Media Type : Stock Photo Copyright : stellargems (Follow)
Image ID : 10297458 Media Type : Stock Photo Copyright : Alexander Ovchinnikov (Follow)
Image ID : 9585679 Media Type : Stock Photo Copyright : Mara Fribus (Follow)
Image ID : 49177585 Media Type : Stock Vector Copyright : Victoriia Parnikova (Follow)
Image ID : 29361120 Media Type : Stock Photo Copyright : madllen (Follow)
Image ID : 30181497 Media Type : Stock Photo Copyright : Allan Swart (Follow)
Image ID : 51344938 Media Type : Stock Photo (Editorial image) Copyright : radub85 (Follow)
Image ID : 10741303 Media Type : Stock Photo (Editorial image) Copyright : neftali77 (Follow)
Image ID : 29107163 Media Type : Stock Photo Copyright : Eugene Sergeev (Follow)
Image ID : 47191822 Media Type : Stock Photo Copyright : captblack76 (Follow)
Image ID : 16487966 Media Type : Stock Photo Copyright : Luk Gavenda (Follow)
Image ID : 37725354 Media Type : Stock Photo Copyright : Lario Tus (Follow)
Image ID : 3382330 Media Type : Stock Photo Copyright : Vojtech Vlk (Follow)
Image ID : 78750360 Media Type : Stock Photo Copyright : Naphazynths Chanthvongsviriya (Follow)
Image ID : 26094120 Media Type : Stock Photo Copyright : loganban (Follow)
Image ID : 75627826 Media Type : Stock Photo Model Released : Yes Copyright : Sergei Primakov (Follow)
Image ID : 41260930 Media Type : Stock Photo Copyright : zhudifeng (Follow)
Image ID : 29987803 Media Type : Stock Photo Copyright : Zacarias Pereira Da Mata (Follow)

Image ID : 22869466 Media Type : Stock Photo Copyright : iqoncept (Follow)
Image ID : 48897152 Media Type : Stock Photo Copyright : alphaspirit (Follow)
Image ID : 1935829 Media Type : Stock Photo Copyright : Jozsef Szasz-Fabian (Follow)
Image ID : 55366600 Media Type : Stock Photo Copyright : grechka (Follow)
Image ID : [illegible] Media Type : Stock Photo Copyright : Bruce Rolff (Follow)
Image ID : 50565245 Media Type : Stock Photo Copyright : Geraldas Galinauskas (Follow)
Image ID : 10928160 Media Type : Stock Photo Copyright : marchcattle (Follow)
Image ID : 30765483 Media Type : Stock Photo Copyright : Sergii Gnatiuk (Follow)
Image ID : 51000056 Media Type : Stock Photo Copyright : crystaleyemedia (Follow)
Image ID : 18586403 Media Type : Stock Photo Copyright : carloscastilla (Follow)
Image ID : 24647319 Media Type : Stock Photo Copyright : NejroN (Follow)
Image ID : 48283405 Media Type : Stock Photo Copyright : Nicola Zalewski (Follow)
Image ID : 48915992 Media Type : Stock Photo Copyright : mackoflower (Follow)
Image ID : 29803122 Media Type : Stock Illustration Copyright : Bruce Rolff (Follow)
Image ID : 31707794 Media Type : Stock Photo Copyright : sakkmesterke (Follow)
Image ID : 50824626 Media Type : Stock Illustration Copyright : Andrea Danti (Follow)
Image ID : 18342525 Media Type : Stock Photo Copyright : iqoncept (Follow)
Image ID : 26850601 Media Type : Stock Photo Copyright : Andriy Popov (Follow)
Image ID : 16852137 Media Type : Stock Photo Copyright : Rossella Apostoli (Follow)
Image ID : 23842670 Media Type : Stock Photo Copyright : Elena Duvernay (Follow)
Image ID : 33164172 Media Type : Stock Photo Copyright : Nicola Zalewski (Follow)
Image ID : 30189184 Media Type : Stock Photo Copyright : Nicola Zalewski (Follow)
Image ID : 29930466 Media Type : Stock Illustration Copyright : Santosh Chavan (Follow)
Image ID : 80123010 Media Type : Stock Photo Copyright : Martin Capek (Follow)
Image ID : 70089865 Media Type : Stock Photo Copyright : Bruce Rolff (Follow)
Image ID : 3325237 Media Type : Stock Photo Copyright : Alexandru Chiriak (Follow)
Image ID : 53460574 Media Type : Stock Photo Copyright : Jozef Polc (Follow)
Image ID : 52412042 Media Type : Stock Vector Copyright : Vladimir Ovchinnikov (Follow)
Image ID : 37426251 Media Type : Stock Photo Copyright : 1xpert (Follow)
Image ID : 45935305 Media Type : Stock Vector Copyright : silvae (Follow)
Image ID : 23446885 Media Type : Stock Photo Copyright : lightwise (Follow)
Image ID : 28137013 Media Type : Stock Photo Copyright : Nicola Zalewski (Follow)
Image ID : 10161846 Media Type : Stock Photo Copyright : Viktoriya Sukhanova (Follow)

Images below are from** www.Dreamstime.com **and are royalty free ,Copyright for 500,000 copies.

ID 90922627 © Visivasnc | Dreamstime, ID 7351099 © Freesurf69 | Dreamstime, ID 5357014 © Fallsview | Dreamstime, ID 35326224 © Dirk Czarnota | Dreamstime, ID 75892395 © Nikki Zalewski | Dreamstime, ID 10255051 © Readyprophotos | Dreamstime, ID 48159362 © Zanna Bojarsinova | Dreamstime ID 32111596 © Dirk Czarnota | Dreamstime ID 86446605 © Topgeek.

All Flat Earth Resources, Antarctic Warrior You tube Channel, Resources to Mandela Effect, Scarab Performance You Tube channel, Life Matrix, Mandela Effected, Reality shifter, One Harmony and many more, to view my personal teachings about the Game and duality, religion etc Go to SRPHD you tube channel and view playlists. My hip-hop raps that are freestyle can also be found under the playlists there. I recommend Anyone wanting evidence more to what I have presented in this book, hence the spiritual side, to watch Science has been hiding consciousness, that can be found by searching in You Tube on my channel and others.

Special thanks to those who created the images and my loyal subscribers who have shown nothing but support with this very hard to bring forward information due to fear of ridicule. I thank those that have been there right through helping me bring the information forward to help us all with understanding the quantum phenomenon that we have been all subjected to unknowingly.

MANDELA EFFECT / FLATEARTH RESOURCES

The following YouTube channels provide Mandela effect change examples.

1. **Channel Name: SRPHD** My videos, to view enter into the playlist section for audio teachings and visual presentations that have been created by myself. To find links to all videos Mandela effect on my channel look through my listings all my videos starting with MANDELA EFFECT- are all in some form explaining the effect or showing effects.

2. **Channel Name:Reality Shifter** Most videos on this channel are all effect examples as well as some useful insight. The channel is also run by a legit down to earth want to help others, person.

3. **Channel Name: Scarab Performance** most videos on this channel are all effect examples as well as some useful insight. The channel is also run by a legit down to earth want to help others, person. Thanks Daniel.

4. **Channel Name: Lone Eagle** most videos on this channel are all effect examples as well as some useful insight. The channel is also run by a legit down to earth want to help others, person.

5. **Other Channel Names to check, Shockofchrist, Brian MacFarlane, Moneybags73, Life Matrix There are** many more channels that show Mandela effect examples from post reality to now, in general just check the reddit forums and search Mandela effects.

The following is the best place for flat earth videos and resources. If you are to google search loc (library of congress) online you will also find the new flat stationary earth map. https://www.loc.gov/item/2013585077/

Eric Dubay Channel and Antarctic Warrior Channel And Jeranism

"ONE CONSCIOUSNESS"

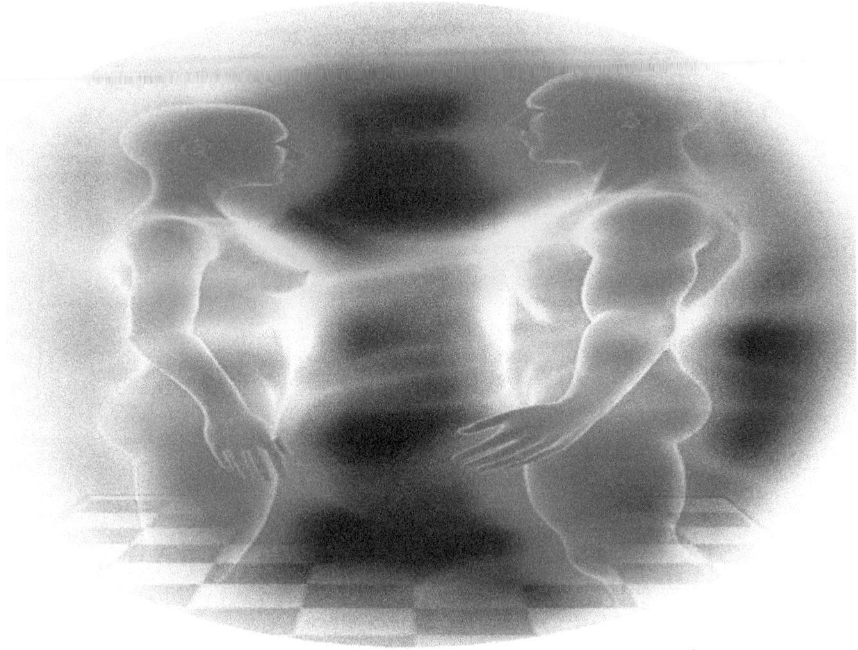

Peace love and light for all.

Spiritual Teacher/Guru, Reiki Master Energy Worker

Mr. Anthony W White & The One

We all have the ability to awaken when we want to, reality blinds you with control

Love your enemy for without them you could not receive the truth!

"THE SIMULATION OF CONSCIOUSNESS INSTRUCTION MANUAL"

THE END OF THIS BOOK BUT A NEW VIEW OF REALITY.

.EVIL IS TO LIVE
DEVIL IS TO HAVE LIVED.

AS QUEEN USED TO SAY WE ARE THE CHAMPIONS OF THE WORLD , WE HAVE NOW LEFT THE WORLD OF SINGLE IDENTITY AND ARE NOW THE CHAMPIONS SELECTED BY THE ONE CONSCIOUSNESSS TO BRING UNDERSTANDING TO OTHERS OF OUR FIRST HAND EXPERIENCE OF THE MANDELA EFFECT AND QUANTUM STATE SHIFT OF CONSCIOUSNESS WE HAVE BEEN APART OF FROM THE SAGITTARIUS ARM TO NOW THE REALITY OF ORIONS SPUR.

Special thanks to those that have Believed in me and have found new Enlightenment into realities of of remememembering who they are again as spirit.

TONY WHITE: TO THE COLLECTIVE, WE ARE ONE!

REMEMBER THAT THE UNIVERSE AND YOU ARE ONE. THROUGH THE SYNCHRONICITIES FROM SOURCE YOU ARE GUIDED AND SHOWN THE DIRECTION NEEDED FOR YOUR LEVEL OF AWARENESS TO GAIN IT'S NATURAL REMEMBERANCE OF WHO YOU ARE AT CREATION LEVEL. FOLLOW THE SYNCHRONICITIES AND REMAIN IN TUNE WITH YOURSELF AND THE ONE AS THE UNIVERSE WILL SHOW YOU WHO YOU ARE AT THE LIGHT LEVEL AND REVEAL YOUR PATH TO THE ROAD FOR ENLIGHTENMENT TO ONCE AGAIN KNOW THE TRUE MEANINGS OF DESIGN.

CPSIA information can be obtained
at www.ICGtesting.com
Printed in the USA
LVHW070957090421
683706LV00002BA/12